Using Stories, Art, and Play in Trauma-Informed Treatment

This book shows new and experienced therapists how to use meaningful therapeutic material in art, stories and play to facilitate shifts in outlook and behavior. Using a wide variety of case studies, Dr. Pernicano lays out a framework for problem clarification, conceptualization, trauma-informed intervention and positive therapeutic outcome with clients across the lifespan. Case examples include working with clients suffering from dissociation, depression, anxiety, mood dysregulation, adjustment to life change, grief and loss, and/or panic attacks. Replete with client-generated illustrations as well as practical tips and strategies, *Using Stories, Art, and Play in Trauma-Informed Treatment* teaches therapists how to think conceptually, plan systemically and intervene flexibly to improve treatment outcomes for diverse clients.

Pat Pernicano, PsyD, has provided supervision, training and trauma-informed treatment in outpatient, residential, geriatric, substance abuse, school, VA and private practice settings. In 2017, she and her husband were jointly honored by the Kentucky Psychological Association as Lifetime Career Psychologists of the year. More information about her work can be found at www.pernicanoplaycreations.com.

Using Stories, Art, and Play in Trauma-Informed Treatment

Case Examples and Applications Across the Lifespan

Pat Pernicano

Routledge
Taylor & Francis Group
NEW YORK AND LONDON

First published 2019
by Routledge
52 Vanderbilt Avenue, New York, NY 10017

and by Routledge
2 Park Square, Milton Park, Abingdon, Oxon, OX14 4RN

Routledge is an imprint of the Taylor & Francis Group, an informa business

© 2019 Pat Pernicano

The right of Pat Pernicano to be identified as author of this work has been asserted by her in accordance with sections 77 and 78 of the Copyright, Designs and Patents Act 1988.

All rights reserved. No part of this book may be reprinted or reproduced or utilised in any form or by any electronic, mechanical, or other means, now known or hereafter invented, including photocopying and recording, or in any information storage or retrieval system, without permission in writing from the publishers.

Trademark notice: Product or corporate names may be trademarks or registered trademarks, and are used only for identification and explanation without intent to infringe.

Library of Congress Cataloging-in-Publication Data
A catalog record for this book has been requested

ISBN: 978-1-138-48468-9 (hbk)
ISBN: 978-1-138-48472-6 (pbk)
ISBN: 978-1-351-00530-2 (ebk)

Typeset in Garamond MT & Futura BT
by Apex CoVantage, LLC

CONTENTS

	Foreword: Using Stories, Art and Play in Trauma-Focused Therapy	x
	HELEN BENEDICT	
	Acknowledgments	xi
Introduction	A Picture Is More Than a Picture	1
Part I	**The Tools of the Trade**	7
Chapter 1	The Building Blocks of Communication	9
	The Salience of Language 9	
	Non-Verbal Communication 10	
	Meaning-Making: Integrating Verbal and Non-Verbal Communication 11	
Chapter 2	Mining for Gold With Milton Erickson	13
Chapter 3	Constructing With Metaphor and Stories	16
	The Nature of Metaphor 16	
	Symbols in Stories, Art and Play 17	
	The Nature of Stories 29	
Chapter 4	The Blueprint of Trauma-Informed Treatment	31
	What It Means to Be "Trauma-Informed" 31	
	Trauma-Informed Knowledge 32	
	Grounded in Neurobiology 33	
	Identifying Blind Spots and Risk Factors 33	
	Working Within a Developmental Context 34	
	Using a Systemic Approach 35	
	A Matter of Good Fit 36	
Chapter 5	The Integrative Tool Bag	39
	Integrative Psychotherapy 39	
	The Therapeutic Stance 40	
	The Tools Themselves 41	

Part II	Case Examples and Applications	55

Chapter 6	Overview of Case Development	57

Case Organization   58
Case Examples in Trauma-Informed Care   58

	Child Cases Using Stories, Art and Play	**61**

Chapter 7	The Bloodthirsty Bats: A Case of Child Sexual Abuse	63

Case Information and Background   63
The Problems (and Reactions to the Problems)   63
The Conceptualization   65
Interventions and the Trauma Narrative   66
The Shift   67
The Progress and Outcomes   67
Termination Progress and Outcome   70
Questions for Case Discussion   72

Chapter 8	The Alligator Eyes: A Case of Complicated Grief	73

Case Information and Background   73
The Problems (and Reactions to the Problems)   73
Initial Interventions and New Problems   74
The Conceptualization   74
Intervention With a Shift   74
The Trauma Narrative and New Shift   75
Progress and Outcomes   76
Questions for Case Discussion   76

Chapter 9	The Boy Whose Sister Said "Fuck": A Case of Parental Drug Overdose	77

Case Information and Background   77
The Problems (and Reactions to the Problems)   77
The Conceptualization   78
Interventions and the Trauma Narrative   79
Shift   83
Shift and Trauma Narrative   86
The Progress and Outcomes   89
Questions for Discussion   91

Chapter 10	Feed the Alligator: A Case of Sibling Trauma Intervention	92

Case Information and Background   92
The Problems (and Reactions to the Problems)   92
The Conceptualization   93
Interventions and the Trauma Narrative   93
The Progress and Outcomes   94
The Shift   95
Progress and Outcomes   96
Questions for Discussion   96

Chapter 11	The House With Many Rooms: A Case of Child Dissociation	97

Case Information and Background   97
The Problems (and Reactions to the Problems)   97

The Conceptualization   97
Interventions: Psychoeducation About Trauma   98
Interventions   99
Beginning Trauma Narrative   99
Shift: Sharing the Inner World   100
New Shift and Continued Trauma Intervention   102
Major Shift   103
Continued Trauma Intervention   105
The Progress and Outcomes   108
Questions for Discussion   110

Chapter 12   The Mom of Many Colors: A Case of the Impact of Parental Substance Abuse   **111**

Case Information and Background   111
The Problems (and Reactions to the Problems)   111
The Conceptualization   112
Interventions   112
Shift and Beginning Trauma Narrative   113
New Shifts   114
Interventions About Parent-Child Issues   115
Interventions: Perceptions of Mom   117
Shift   120
Further Conceptualization   122
The Progress and Outcomes   122
New Shift   124
    Stuck on the River   124
Progress and Outcomes   125
Questions for Discussion   125

Chapter 13   The Boy With a Hungry Heart: A Case of Maternal Neglect and Abandonment   **126**

Case Information and Background   126
The Problems (and Reactions to the Problems)   126
The Conceptualization   127
Interventions and Trauma Narrative   127
The Shift   128
    The Hungry Heart   129
The Progress and Outcomes   131
Questions for Discussion   131

Chapter 14   The Wounded Elephant: A Case of Emotional Wounding   **132**

Case Information and Background   132
Problems (and Response to the Problems)   132
Conceptualization   133
Interventions   133
Shift   135
Progress and Outcomes   136
Questions for Discussion   137

Adolescent Cases Using Stories, Art and Play   **139**

Chapter 15   "Tell Me Who I Am": A Case of Grief and Identity   **141**

Case Information and Background   141
The Problems (and Reactions to the Problems)   141

The Conceptualization   142
Interventions and Trauma Narrative   142
The Shift   143
Progress and Outcomes   147
Questions for Case Discussion   148

Chapter 16   The Zodiac Queen: A Case of Adolescent Dissociation   **149**

Case Information and Background   149
Problems (and Response to the Problems)   149
Conceptualization   150
More Background   150
Interventions   150
Shifts   151
Intervention: The Zodiac Queen   152
Progress and Outcomes   159
Questions for Discussion   160

Adult Cases Using Stories, Art and Play   **161**

Chapter 17   The Girl Behind the Brick Wall: A Case of
Anxious Avoidant Attachment   **163**

Case Information and Background   163
Conceptualization   163
Problems   164
Intervention and Further Conceptualization   164
Shift   168
Trauma Narrative   169
Progress and Outcomes   171
Questions for Case Discussion   171

Chapter 18   The Girl Who Lost Her Voice: A Case of Sexual Trauma   **173**

Case Information and Background   173
Conceptualization   173
Problems (and Reactions to Problems)   173
Interventions   174
Shift to Employment   174
Progress and Outcomes   177
Questions for Discussion   177

Chapter 19   Grief and the Four Stones: A Case of the Woman
Who Chose To NOT Move on   **178**

Case Information and Background   178
Problems   178
Conceptualization   179
Intervention   179
Shift (Four Stones)   181
Progress and Outcomes   181
Questions for Discussion   182

Chapter 20   The Mermaid Who Forgot: A Case of Pending Loss   **183**

Case Information and Background   183
Problems (and Reactions to Problems)   184

viii

Conceptualization   184
Initial Interventions   185
New Interventions and Shift   185
     Dive Deep   186
Shift   187
Progress and Outcomes   189
Questions for Discussion   190

Chapter 21   The Woman Who Got Rid of a Leech: A Case of
Relationship Choices   **191**

Case Information and Background   191
Problems (and Reactions to Problems)   191
Conceptualization   191
Interventions   192
Progress and Outcomes   194
Questions for Discussion   194

Appendix: Resources for Trauma-Informed Care   **195**

The Unleashed Pain *(Pernicano, unpublished manuscript)   195*
Pernicano Trauma-Informed Publications   197
Pernicano Techniques   197
Other Resources   200

The *Meaning* of Color in Client Art   **202**

References   **210**

Index   **213**

FOREWORD

Using Stories, Art and Play in Trauma-Focused Therapy

First and foremost, this book is about trauma-informed treatment using techniques that are effectively grounded in a research and evidence-based practice of play and integrative therapy. The approach taken in this book is based on the writings of Milton Erickson lavishly augmented by both cognitive behavioral and systemic formulations. The author makes a compelling case for using Erickson's "transtheoretical" emphasis on "recognizing meaning in client material, and then utilizing what is offered." This framework is extremely flexible, allowing the therapist to incorporate the illustrated techniques into a wide variety of theoretical approaches. Dr. Perncano exemplifies this in her case presentations, leaving the reader with a clear idea of how to use the ideas presented within his or her own theoretical framework.

The field of play therapy has undergone great change over the past 20 years. This change has been to be increasingly concerned about the importance of the research and evidence-base for play therapy. While the first few chapters lay out the rationale for a research/evidential base for therapy, both play and integrative, the heart of the book is case presentations. A key premise is that case examples are both valuable and necessary for practitioners at every stage of professional development. I wholeheartedly agree. I personally learned a great deal from various cases presented at conferences and in papers and from the cases presented here.

What is unusual about this book is the juxtaposition of metaphor/storytelling and a wide range of trauma cases. It is also unique in presenting child, adolescent and adult cases. This book describes a wealth of case material within clearly articulated case conceptualizations. In addition, there is sufficient detail of the techniques (pictures, metaphors and stories) used that the reader can easily apply the technique in their own practice. In sum, this book is a worthwhile read for beginning and seasoned therapists alike.

Helen Benedict, PhD

ACKNOWLEDGMENTS

The cover art, and artwork in Chapter 17, is provided with permission of Miranda Morris, a gifted young artist. I appreciate her willingness to share her talent.

Thanks to Wiley for permission to reprint two of my client drawings (see Figures 5.2 and 5.3). The drawings were published on pp. 266–267 in Pernicano, P. (2015). *Metaphors and stories in play therapy*. In K. J. O'Connor, C. E. Schaefer & L. Braverman (Eds.) (pp. 259–275). *Handbook of Play Therapy*, NY: Wiley.

A special word of thanks to psychologist Ashley Casto, PsyD, for editing assistance.

Kevin Pernicano, PhD served as my photo editor. Kevin, my husband and a fellow psychologist, encourages me, believes in me and champions my work. I am fortunate to have a spouse who still understands my passion for treatment, teaching and writing after 36 years of marriage. He predicts that our retirement years will be spent in our RV presenting workshops on stories and trauma and him selling my books!

Thanks to Athena Drewes, Charles Schaefer and Cathy Malchiodi for their cover endorsements. Each has contributed to my understanding of play therapy and the many ways art and play may be used for trauma-informed care. I am grateful to George Burns, PhD for his kind endorsement; through him and the Evolution of Psychotherapy, I began to learn about Milton Erickson and the power of therapeutic metaphor. When I was first seeking to publish my work, Athena Drewes, PhD encouraged and guided me in the right direction, even though I was an unknown entity residing in Louisville, Kentucky. At her recommendation, I authored a chapter in O'Connor, Schaefer and Braverman's 2015 2nd edition of Play Therapy Techniques.

At the 2017 Kentucky Psychological Association Annual Convention Awards Ceremony luncheon, my psychologist husband Kevin and I were co-honored with the Distinguished Career in Psychology Award. They had never given a husband-wife award, but we both had extensive Kentucky careers spanning from 1988 to 2017. As I looked out, I saw many former graduate students, supervisees and work colleagues in the audience.

My comments were something to the effect of:

"Many of you will not be surprised that I decided to use a metaphor in accepting this award. I once wrote a story about a girl who had a self-weaving tapestry hanging on her bedroom wall. The tapestry was like something out of Harry Potter, with a life of its own, and from the day she was born it wove in new threads. When something "good" happened in her life, the tapestry wove in a bright, colorful thread, and when something "bad" happened, a dark, "ugly" thread appeared. The good with the bad, it was a beautiful creation.

The girl reached an age where she decided she did not like the dark threads and wanted them gone. They reminded her of "darker" times, and she did not want to look at them or think about them. One day, she took the tapestry down and painstakingly removed each dark thread. She hung the tapestry back up on the wall, but what remained was uneven and sagging. Without the darker threads, there was nothing to hold it together.

A good friend came over later that day and said, "I loved your tapestry before, just the way it was. Your tapestry needs the dark threads with the light; now there is no contrast. The whole is richer and more beautiful; it is who you are today. I hope you will weave those threads back in and restore its beauty."

The girl could see that her tapestry had lost something when she removed the darker threads, and she decided to restore them. The girl wove the threads back into the tapestry, but she changed the pattern and put each thread in a place of her own

xi

Acknowledgments

choosing. It was satisfying to re-weave her history, and she was pleased with the result. She noticed for the first time that there were many more bright than dark threads.

I asked attendees to stand if they had worked with me, taught with me, trained with me, taken class with me or received supervision from me. With many people on their feet, I captured a poignant visual memory of my career.

I would like to recognize you now, because you are the threads of my professional tapestry. Like the girl, my tapestry has many more bright than dark threads, and you are some of my brightest threads. We are woven together, our lives entwined, and together we are richer and better than we are separately. . . . Thank you for being part of my life's tapestry.

I am grateful for each thread in my life's tapestry.

I have thought about writing this book for several years and remained in *contemplation* until I talked with a psychologist mentor, Dr. Helen Benedict, over dinner some months back. Helen was my Baylor University graduate professor in child development, child clinical treatment and assessment in the early 1980s. I experienced both awe and fear in her classes, as she was an astute scholar and brilliant teacher. I also remember her open heart, as she and her husband invited our class over for ethnic meals and music. She helped "root" my interests in all things child and family, but something I most appreciated as a graduate student was her sharing her work with us. As graduate students, we were good "learners," but as a group, we had little clinical experience. Helen described her cases, shared challenging situations, showed videos, offered copies of handbooks she had written (play, assessment, development) and answered our questions. It seemed to us that she knew something about everything.

Many years later, Helen and I reconnected at a play therapy conference where she was presenting; we discussed our mutual interest in attachment, neurobiology of trauma, evidence-based play therapy and trauma-informed care. She has published and presented widely on child attachment. She described her research and clinical involvement with the Talitha Koum Institute, an early intervention therapeutic day care and preschool program for at-risk infants and children in Waco TX. This program allows children to experience consistency, healthy relationships and therapeutic play, which contribute to secure attachment and healthy development.

When I moved in 2017, Helen and I had a phone conversation; I told her I wanted to do what she had done for us in graduate school, i.e., share my work and provide some case examples where stories, art and play were life-changing. She encouraged me to submit a proposal and agreed to come out of retirement to write the Forward if the book was accepted. It was accepted, and I am grateful to Helen for her contribution to this book. I also thank Anna Moore, Routledge acquisitions editor, who worked with me on my 2014 book and on this publication. She and the Routledge team have been invaluable with their advice and encouragement.

We are interwoven with clients and colleagues as we go through our lives and careers. I have become a better human being, clinician and teacher through my work and interactions. Writing a book is a labor of love. It forces me to be more organized and detailed than I am by nature; the *love* part is the opportunity to revisit memories of my former clients and our work together. How fortunate I am to have had clients willing to share their stories, art and play; we learn more from our clients than we do from books and articles alone. I contacted former clients (or parents/guardians) to obtain informed consent to use artwork and case information, and they shared updates, providing news of progress and mostly better lives. I also sent former clients drafts of their chapters, to ensure that the details are sensitive and accurate. This has been somewhat like the process of Collaborative Therapeutic Assessment; many clients sent their reflections after reading the chapters, and I incorporated some into the book. This "follow-up interaction" has been a special gift; therapists so often wonder about therapeutic outcomes and whether treatment made a difference. Writing about each case and reviewing artwork has brought back vivid memories; I realize that the relationships I had with the clients and their families changed me and contributed to my growth. When I wonder occasionally if what I offered was "enough," I realize it is a little like Thomas Merton's great prayer. I walked the road of trauma-informed care, sometimes not knowing where I was heading, but I had a desire to help and contribute to healing. Per Merton, perhaps the desire to help and heal was indeed "enough."

One mother, whose son "survived" a hurricane and the death of his father, wrote, "We would LOVE that. I just read him the email and he smiled so very big. He tells me from time to time that he 'misses puppy' . . . I have learned when he wants to talk about something painful; and with a little support he openly discusses. You were a miracle worker and I am so very thankful! You are welcome to include the name (*he wrote his father's first name on one of his drawings, and I offered to photoshop it out*)- he would prefer it. We love the new house and it has really helped with our healing process. My son is doing well in 4th grade and his sister is finishing her senior year of high school—she has accepted an invitation to *college* and will be majoring in cellular biology and will then go to dental school." "Puppy" is a puppet he cuddled in sessions when distressed, and this girl is the sister who said "fuck." They have come a long way since their shared family trauma several years back.

Another mother wrote, "It is great to hear from you. We loved you and I feel you truly helped *my daughter*, who is very closed about her feelings, to open up. Her anxiety is better for now. At one point I had her on meds but they made her a different kid. I didn't want her different and neither did she. We moved to another house last year. I couldn't live in that same house anymore. We manage. We haven't talked about it. Thanks for reaching out. I'm thankful you were there in my darkest days and helped *my daughter* and me and I will never forget you."

A former adult client recently stated, "First, I love it (the case material in the book). From my perspective, I think you have captured our relationship well and am amazed by the details you remember. Second, it's unsettling to go back and read this, to see how sad I was and lost in the trauma of this. Ultimately, though, it makes me proud of the progress I made and what I learned—and what I keep learning."

Another former adult client asked if she might send me some comments: "There are some things you said to me that really stayed with me. You know I took notes in every session and I still have those notes." She indicated, "Wow, it is amazing how much therapy work you can do in 24 hours! It is so different, now; instead of living it and being in the middle of it, I can look back and see it from where I am now. I can see things more clearly."

Milton Erickson pointed out that clients' problems block them from change but the potential for change is within. The clients whose cases I included in this book are clear examples of the ways in which persons became "unblocked" by discovering and utilizing the resources and strengths within. My son would suggest that we take a plunger and remove the clog! Once things are unclogged (and unblocked), things move right along.

Therapists are not miracle workers, i.e., we offer the possibility of change through new perspective; we reveal the optical illusion and clients see things in new ways. We are catalysts that set off a chemical chain reaction. We are skilled potters, and they are the clay. They see the rocky external geode, and we see the crystals within.

I am grateful to these clients who invited me to be a catalyst of change.

INTRODUCTION

A Picture Is More Than a Picture

A young client, age 6, arrived ten minutes early for her Saturday morning session. She and her grandmother (her custodial guardian, to whom I will refer to as "M") waited in the foyer. It was their 3rd or 4th session, and in previous sessions we had completed an intake and started talking about the child's feelings about her mother recently getting out of jail and moving back home, about being raised by "M," about her mother's substance abuse (which made the girl "sad and mad") and about her difficulty sleeping alone at night because she was "afraid of the dark" and "afraid of monsters." She had experienced anxiety and bad dreams since witnessing the domestic violence of her mother by the mother's previous boyfriend. She was a highly verbal and artistic child who openly shared her thoughts, opinions and feelings, and she responded well to hands-on activities with drawing and storytelling.

It was clear that she was very attached to "M," who was responsive to her needs, and the two of them freely shared affection and conversation. Her mother, who was mostly off in her own world, attended one of the early sessions, and the girl's verbal and non-verbal behavior toward her mother showed ambivalence. She "spit out" irritability (with her words and facial expressions) like one of those mall fountains that suddenly spurts water; then she would move closer to her mom and lean against her like a needy dog wanting to be petted. Her mom was not very responsive; and she *missed* most of her daughter's bids for attention.

While waiting that day, my young client colored a picture, a "gift" for me. She handed the picture to me as she entered my office, a colorful picture of three flowers, in various stages of flowering (see Appendix for full-color picture). I thanked her, then turned to put it on my filing cabinet with a magnet. Clients often bring pictures in with them from the waiting area.

"Aren't you going to ask me about it?" she questioned in a petulant voice. Ah . . . I had not treated it as the "gift" it was . . . I took the picture off the cabinet and invited her to sit down and tell me about her picture.

She asked me, "Which flower do you like best?" Loaded question . . .

The differences in the flowers were obvious, but I didn't know what that meant *to her*. I said, "I like all three, but for different reasons."

In good therapeutic form, I deferred to her and asked, "Which one do *you* like best?"

She said, "The one in the middle, because it has a big sun, it has all its petals, and the leaves aren't torn up."

By "sun" she was not referring to the typical child sun in the upper corner of the paper. She was referring to the center of the blossom, the "heart" of the flower.

"I like that one, too," I said, and then I asked, "Which flower is most *like you*?"

Introduction

FIGURE 0.1

She smiled at me, as if to say, "silly therapist" and replied, "They are all me. The one in the middle is me *now*. The leaves are full, it has all its petals, it has a big sun, and the leaves aren't scratched up."

I reflected that the flower in the middle looked happy. She nodded and said, "It's because I come to therapy," then leaned into me for a hug. It was an unexpected and emotional moment.

I thought to myself, "*A picture is more than a picture*."

The "gift" of her picture had taken on new meaning. And to think that if she had been less persistent, it might have remained on my filing cabinet, without explanation. I put my previous therapy agenda aside so that we could "unwrap" and explore the rest of the picture.

I invited, "Tell me about the other flowers."

"Well," she said, "*this* one (pointing to one on the left) is me when I was little. It has no petals, it is torn up, and only has a little sunshine."

I asked, "How old is *this* flower?"

She replied, "Hmmm . . . maybe two or three years old."

The flower to the left looked ragged and somewhat pitiful, with its brown color and a pale yellow "sunshine" in the middle.

I recognized that as the time period during which my client, as a toddler, had been removed from her mother's care due to neglect and substance abuse. After the child was removed from her mother's care and placed with "M," her mother continued to visit, unreliably, and moved in and out of the "M's" home. My client's mother also had an abusive boyfriend at that time and she paid very little attention to the child when in his presence.

"*This* one (pointing to the right), see, the sunshine grew, it is scratched up a little, and some of its petals fell off." She added, "That's me when I was a little older."

I asked about the age, and she said, "Hmmm . . . probably 4 or 5."

The flower to the right did look more cheerful, but not nearly as solid or *whole* as the one in the middle of the page. It was fragile-looking and the colors were sketchy. Her mother had been

Introduction

FIGURE 0.2

in and out of recovery at that point in time and had been incarcerated at least once. Men were in and out of her life, and that was a sore spot for the client. The "M's" home provided good structure and nurture that offset the mother's inconsistency, but the little girl yearned for a nurturing, consistent relationship with her mother.

She looked at me expectantly and said, "Aren't you going to ask me about the picture on the back?" I hadn't realized that there was a picture on the back, and I turned the paper over. Sure enough. There was one more drawing, a single flower.

"Yes, I said, please tell me about the picture on the back."

She stated, "Dr. Pat, that's me as a baby. No sun. No petals. Two leaves, all torn up."

The picture was simple and a good depiction of a "baby flower" without much color or detail, and it was all alone on the page. I could feel her sadness and her awareness of the needs that had not been met when she was a baby; the picture and description conveyed how neglected she had been. As an infant she had been left alone too much, and both parents had abused substances, resulting in unreliable and inconsistent care. Her mother's life had been very unstable, and the grandmother had stepped in several times to ensure the child was fed and cared for.

I looked at her and said, "That flower has had a rough life. Would you like to talk more about it?"

Her drawings and descriptions were a clear *invitation* and warranted further discussion; they reflected a "shift" in our therapy work, as she was *telling* me through her artwork that she was ready to talk about the past. With her permission, we shared the flowers with "M" and spent that session and several more talking about her stages of flowering and what sorts of things in her life had torn her leaves and made petals fall off. We talked about what a flower needs to grow well, about what sorts of things had allowed her "sun" to grow, also, what in her life provided water and sunshine, because her flower needed to keep growing. She said how hard it was to get "sunshine and water" from her mother and how her mother's angry words and male partners tore off her petals. She was glad that in more recent years, she had a stable caregiver "that really loves me" and was beginning to recover from the past.

This child's case will be discussed in detail later in the book, as her waiting room picture was an "aha" for me, a reminder to pay closer attention to the "gifts" of clients, to unwrap them carefully, to clarify the meaning of those gifts, and to utilize the information in treatment. This bright, artistic 6-year-old reminded me of the ways we need to listen to our clients, to what they say and don't say, and to *capture* the meaning in what they present. It is a good thing that when we don't *get it*, our clients are often persistent until we do.

Introduction

This child's drawing *seeded* my ideas for this book, and the idea *simmered* for over a year while I considered how and when to move forward. This book is not intended to be just another collection of techniques for intervention; it is intended to emphasize the importance of conceptualization in treatment, and how stories, art and play contribute to clear conceptualization and guide intervention. It is most importantly a collection of case studies, across the lifespan, in which metaphor, stories and drawing or play contributed to conceptual understanding or progress in treatment and provided information not obtained through interview alone.

I used to be very involved in training graduate students and providing practicum supervision; I also supervised teams of child and family therapists. Together we would review client history and background, conceptualize and set goals. The most common question trainees asked was, "What can I *do* with this person to help him or her reach the goals? Can you suggest something for my tool bag?" Together we would brainstorm and identify tools that might best propel change and help the client resolve the presenting issues or problems. When we were *spot on with the conceptualization the interventions arose from those conceptualizations and were nearly always successful*. Perhaps the *best* intervention is one that helps the client move forward in the Stages of Change (Norcross, 2011). Many clients come to treatment in Pre-Contemplation or Contemplation, and stories, art and play can help them weigh risks and benefits, consider options and change thinking in ways that they become *ready* to take action. This book is a *"what can I do?"* resource, with conceptual justification. Each story mentioned in the book was written for a client based on client-generated material, then was presented to the client and used in treatment.

The cases I selected for the book provide examples of ways I used stories, art and play with clients who had some sort of trauma-related experience. This book celebrates client success and recognizes those that did the sometimes painful, difficult work to find a life worth living. The materials shared by these clients in conjunction with observed behavior and mood change provide *evidence* of significant change. I have selected cases in which the client's own material contributed greatly to clinical conceptualization and treatment progress. With some clients, a story or metaphor propelled a significant "shift" or "breakthrough" in the treatment. Of course, there is no one *right* or *correct* interpretation regarding case understanding and intervention. The "right" response is the one that proves personally meaningful for the client. Certainly, other therapists may have interpreted or intervened with these clients differently. Our clients are not *one size fits all*, so when using stories, art and play, it is a matter of knowing your clients well enough that what you offer is a really good fit.

Early in the book, I will touch on concepts from Milton Erickson's work, as these promote an attitude of therapeutic curiosity, recognizing meaning in client material, and then utilizing what is offered. Erickson encouraged practitioners to find their own ways of engaging and working with clients, while relying on some core principles. Revisiting these somewhat transtheoretical ideas will remind therapists to listen (to what is said and unsaid) and to attend to, explore and unpackage meaningful client material. The means of *unwrapping* client material may vary by theoretical orientation, since each school of therapy dictates how one is to assess problems and engage in treatment, but the guiding assumptions of therapeutic alliance and collaborative treatment are not theory specific. Stories and metaphors, key to Erickson's school of thought, may be used within most evidence-based practices, and once concerns or problems are *unwrapped*, evidence-based psychotherapy may be carried out that is consistent with that school of thought.

Later in the book, I will briefly describe what I mean by trauma-informed treatment and discuss the importance of working within a developmental context. I will highlight some of the transtheoretical and universal therapeutic tools that I frequently use in my case work. In later chapters, I will address, case by case, how client material contributed to case conceptualization (the why and how problems develop), also, how case conceptualization guided trauma-informed treatment using stories, art and play.

In the case section of this book, client case material (child, adolescent and adult) is provided and organized by the ways in which the material was useful in problem identification (and client/family perception and reactions), conceptualization, selecting interventions/engaging in trauma narrative, identifying the "shift" (a shift in meaning, perception, intensity, emotional response, coping, communication, relationships, behavior, etc.), and identifying progress and outcomes.

Introduction

All therapists, especially trainees or new practitioners, benefit from seeing the work of other therapists. None of us are so experienced or wise that we no longer have blind spots, and we all learn and grow from our clients and what they offer us. It is also important that seasoned practitioners share our work so that graduate students and early career professionals learn to recognize meaning in what clients present and how they may utilize this material in individualized trauma-informed therapy across the lifespan. Ultimately, by listening, attending to and utilizing client material, we develop a stronger therapeutic alliance; the therapeutic alliance has long been the largest piece of variance when accounting for therapeutic change (Norcross, 2011). Through the alliance, the treatment process becomes optimally collaborative, and sometimes, as a result, our clients change in dramatic and memorable ways.

Sometimes a cigar is just a cigar (supposedly coined by Freud), and other times a "flower" has meaningful information to be used in intervention. I hope that the cases and stories in this book provide ideas that spark the creative process and provide tools for therapist tool bags.

PART I

THE TOOLS OF THE TRADE

1

THE BUILDING BLOCKS OF COMMUNICATION

THE SALIENCE OF LANGUAGE

Language is a primary tool of the trade in psychotherapy, a tool with which we communicate and from which we infer meaning. Language misunderstandings can also prove to be barriers in treatment. My husband and I still laugh about a text he sent by voice dictation (see Figure 1.1). He did not review it before it was sent, and there was a significant error. When I got his message, I laughed and playfully responded to the *literal* message, knowing quite well that he meant something else. He clarified his communication, and later sent a picture with a message, "Here I am, caulk in my hand" that left no confusion.

All humor aside, what comes to mind from this are the many ways in which our clients communicate, sometimes *saying things they do not mean*, sometimes *sharing things they don't yet understand* and often sending mixed or confused messages that require clarification. We know better than to accept all client communication at face value, and we remain open and prepared for *the rest of the story*.

We discover the *meaning* that our clients attribute to their experiences as we listen sensitively, for the goal of listening is to understand who *this client is* as a unique individual, not just someone with a DSM-V diagnosis. Therapists sometimes communicate in ways that clients do not understand, and clients may take non-intended meaning from our communication. Our clients want to understand us and to be understood, and we must be cognizant of the fact that they will nod and smile even at things that confuse and baffle them. What is "clear" to the therapist does not always reach the client's mind, and we forget that therapy communication is not a photocopy machine where an exact likeness emerges. Like the old "gossip" game, our sometimes lengthy, abstract or vague messages get *lost in translation* even during the short time lapse between our mouths and the client's brain.

So how do we best understand what our clients are saying and communicate in ways so that we are accurately heard? First, we match and mirror the client's language, and clarify the client's intent, while being culturally informed and sensitive. Client Centered Therapy intentionally incorporates clarification in the universal, "What I hear you saying is . . ." When we offer clients an opportunity to "correct" us and clarify their intent, we settle into the comfortable back-and-forth rhythm of transparent communication, and we come to understand the meaning behind their words. The language of therapy is about meaning-making, and by matching and mirroring our clients, we demonstrate attunement and empathy, and they feel heard and understood.

The Tools of the Trade

FIGURE 1.1

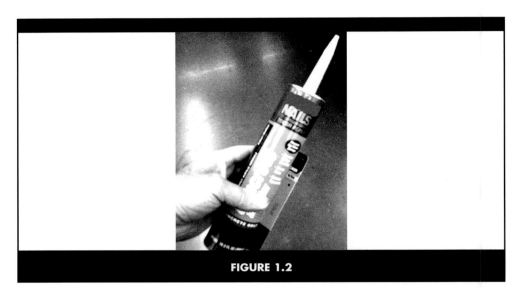

FIGURE 1.2

NON-VERBAL COMMUNICATION

When we pay close attention to non-verbal communication, we intentionally capture nuances such as a head turning away, eyes shifting or a change in mood. Therapeutic communication goes beyond words and language, and some clients communicate more clearly in art and play than they do in words; they *share* things they are not *ready to say aloud or things that they do not yet understand*. When we are attuned, receptive and curious about non-verbal behavior, we begin to infer what the client is not yet saying.

Clients communicate through free form and/or directed art, and a therapist notices what the client chooses to draw, the control or lack of control, the color scheme, visual-motor coordination (indicative of developmental capacities) and emotional tone. In addition to observing client non-verbal cues, a therapist pays attention to his/her non-verbal behavior and own comfort level with clients. Sometimes "threat" or disinterest is conveyed without a word spoken, and a therapist will find his or her mood and behavior changing, with or without full awareness of the trigger.

10

MEANING-MAKING: INTEGRATING VERBAL AND NON-VERBAL COMMUNICATION

Non-verbal communication, in conjunction with language, offers material from which we hypothesize and infer meaning. Clients of all ages use metaphor in language, stories, art and play, regardless of age; clients also have preferred communication styles or modalities, such as writing or drawing, stories, puppets, games, soldiers, knights or sand tray. When we know and understand our clients and their preferred modes of communication, the therapeutic connection is stronger, as the client *feels felt* and understood (Siegel, 2010, 2012).

Peterson and Fontana (2007) compare a client's verbal and non-verbal communication to a *foreign language*. When we learn that language, there is less loss in the translation. *Speaking the same language* enriches communication, deepens trust and enhances the building of relationships. When we neglect to speak the client's language or fail to understand what is presented, the client will usually try again, but in the face of therapist inflexibility or being misunderstood, the client may subsequently drop out, lose interest or humor us by joining our world views or our therapist-centric mis-interpretations of the client's reality. The client's interactions, subtle or direct, verbal or non-verbal, hold meaning; further meaning is communicated through stated themes, action and resolution. We combine verbal and non-verbal information as best we can in order to understand what a client is experiencing and the meaning behind it.

I worked with a 1st grade boy many years ago who was referred for psychological assessment. I struggled at first to *speak his language*, as did most of the people who worked with him. He had unusual social skills (no friends, avoided eye contact, stayed to himself in the classroom), flat affect, hostile/angry interaction if challenged and did not follow directions. His teacher said he was mostly *non-responsive and disengaged*, meaning he did not answer her questions or respond to her requests and did not interact with other children.

I met with him several times and interviewed his mother. His non-verbal communication suggested a reticence or guardedness and his verbal communication lacked social reciprocity. I wondered if he might be on the autistic spectrum, but he did not speak in the manner of what we then called Asperger's clients, nor did he engage in ritualistic or fixed behaviors. He seemed interpersonally avoidant or schizoid, which is somewhat unusual for a 1st grade child.

His mother was warm and effusive and fairly unconcerned about her son's interpersonal and behavioral difficulties at school. She relayed that the child's father had been depressed due to a job situation and got angry when he was in a bad mood. Her view was that her son was fooling others, especially women, because, "He pulls it over on them." In her mind, he intentionally manipulated others to get them to leave him alone. She could not name any friends he had at home or school, and he was an only child. When asked about his angry responses to his teacher, she replied, "He's not really like that. It's all a game."

I administered a test battery, and responses were atypical for a boy his age. I can picture his Kinetic Family Drawing even though this testing was over 20 years ago. The instructions were: "Please draw me a picture of your whole family, each family member doing something."

He drew an artistically precise, finely detailed spaceship with little porthole windows, out of which arrows and projectiles were being launched. Each porthole was well armed. Explosions were taking place outside the spaceship. It took 30 minutes for him to complete the spaceship, after which he handed it to me and said, "Done."

The drawing suggested paranoia and fear, self-protection, or perhaps a retaliatory "fight" response. I queried, "Thank you. I wonder if you could repeat the instructions for me."

He replied, "You told me to draw my family. Each person doing something."

"I see a spaceship," I said. "Where is your family?"

With a look of disdain he pointed at the spaceship and said, "We're in there! Who else do you think is firing the weapons?!"

OK. Fear and anger confirmed. Also, the drawing suggested that he and his family were isolated together inside the spaceship, protecting themselves from invaders or dangers. He refused to tell a story about the drawing other than to say it was a battle, and they were fighting it alone.

His language in this drawing was one of fear and self-protection. I commented, "Ah, I get it. You and your family are inside the spaceship guarding and protecting each other from the dangers. Space is a very dangerous place?"

"YES!" he said as he made first eye contact of the day.

His TAT stories were full of danger, anger and self-protection; they did not flow logically. He "lost track" of the story line as he described the pictures on the cards. He provided obsessive details about the means of protection and feared violence.

The Rorschach did not deter him, and he saw many things; however, a number of the things did not match reality. For example, "I see an Antler." "Good," I thought, a more typical response. "Show me the antler, where you see it and what makes it look like that."

"Here it is. It is escaping. An Antler is a little like a deer. He shoots poison darts out of his eyes and you don't want to get too close."

That response was guarded and paranoid, and he had made up a new word with his unique meaning, a response more typical of psychotic individuals, and I had not seen a psychotic child before. I examined the rest of his responses, and there were several more neologisms (new words), tangential thinking and circumstantial reasoning provided with a matter-of-fact tone.

Buried in his language and stories (on the TAT and Rorschach) were subtle hints of trauma in the themes of danger, victimization and hypervigilance. I found symbols of coercion and force, and some possible sexual themes. I scheduled a risk assessment, with his mother present. When I asked if anyone had ever touched him on his body in a way that he didn't like or made him do things to their body, he nodded his head. He pointed to his "butt" and "penis" and said he had been asked to do things to an older male. He did not display anxiety and was matter-of-fact in his detailed, accurate description of sexual abuse. I told the mother I believed that his anxiety about the abuse might be responsible for an acute psychotic reaction. His mother blanched and teared up. She agreed to take him for therapy for his trauma and also to go for a child psychiatric exam. The psychiatrist phoned me and thanked me for the interesting referral, saying, "He's a weird kid, psychotic. I want to start medication." With this opinion, the mother saw her son more clearly and started to come to grips with her son's mental illness.

I had recognized that something was wrong after viewing his spaceship drawing, which communicated nonverbally quite a bit about his family, their isolation and need for protection. His dad's angry behavior made him feel vulnerable, and the sexual abuse left him feeling alienated and alone. His "language" communicated fear and victimization through his stories and drawings, and it guided us in a new direction.

The point to be made here is that meaning could not be made until the boy was allowed to *communicate in his own manner*. The case outcome would have been different, for example, if only school-based social skills training had been done. I remain concerned about misdiagnosis due to inadequate information, and I believe that by adding art, play and stories to our protocols, we gain better understanding of our clients' conceptual underpinnings.

2

MINING FOR GOLD WITH MILTON ERICKSON

I am not an Ericksonian play therapist per se, nor formally trained in that modality other than some workshops and extensive reading; however, I am a storyteller, and I recognize Erickson's influence in my work. I am strengths based, use language sensitively and carefully, and metaphor, stories, art and play have turned out to be my most-used tools of the trade.

In the Forward of the 2nd edition of *Therapeutic Metaphors for Children and the Child Within* (Mills & Crowley, 2014), David Crenshaw writes,

> In a world where shadows are inevitable, light can be found in many forms if we know where to look. One of those sources of light, warmth, healing and hope is to be found in the theory and work of Milton Erickson. The language of metaphor and storytelling recognized in the original book as located in the right hemisphere of the brain has been studied extensively the last 25 years by the fields of neurobiology and neuroscience through neuroimaging studies of the brain. The language of play and metaphor are right hemisphere dominant but integrated with the dominant language-based activity of the left hemisphere to create coherence, meaning and well-being. Erickson's methods offer an alternative of approaching the trauma material indirectly through metaphor and at the time activating the internal but often unconscious healing resources to move forward and achieve a psychological separation from a traumatic past.

I have heard Dr. Jeff Zeig speak over the years, and he has talked fondly of spending much time with his mentor and friend Dr. Milton Erickson. He often tells the story of Erickson asking him something to the effect of (not a direct quote), "So Jeff, what is it that you do in therapy?" Jeff, wanting to impress, cited a number of theoretical and clinical influences and started telling Erickson what he had learned from them. Erickson stopped him and said something to the effect of (not a direct quote), "Jeff, I'm not asking what you *do* in therapy; rather, I'm asked what it is *You-Jeff* do in therapy. What is the *Jeff style*?" The emphasis on the *You* and not the *Do* changed the whole meaning and context of the question.

Each of us has to find his or her "way" of *being* a therapist, and Erickson's work points to the impact of metaphor and stories in psychotherapy. He, and others who followed, stressed the importance of listening, curiosity, natural trance states, utilization, stepping out of the box, seeing new possibility, creating "aha" moments and transformation. According to Carlson (1999), Milton Erickson was the first to advocate the use of stories and metaphors in child and adult therapy. He, unlike Freud, believed that the unconscious was a positive energy source, malleable and affected by experience. He posited that a therapist could influence a client's unconscious experience by providing new information, arousing feelings and creating new experiences through stories. Mills and Crowley point out that Erickson remained *atheoretical* regarding how and why his metaphors worked until his collaboration with psychologist Ernest Rossi in the last decade of his life, at which point a neurobiological theory arose.

Stories move the listener to a vulnerable, receptive state of readiness; for children this is a readiness to play, and for adults it is a readiness to be open and shift one's inner state of mind

13

The Tools of the Trade

and emotion. Milton Erickson did not believe there was *a right way* to work with clients, and he sought to help a therapist *discover a way that was right for him or her* (Mills & Crowley, 2014). For Erickson "utilization" meant accepting a client's presenting symptoms and using metaphor to incorporate them into treatment.

Erickson viewed symptoms as *blocked resources*; client symptoms reflect attempts to adapt and cope with difficult circumstances within the bounds of that person's neurobiological development. When we use Erickson's concepts, we *mine for gold* with our clients, and the gold is within them to be found. Some years back I wrote a story, *Gold in the Desert*, a tale about a man sifting for gold in dry sand. He became increasingly frustrated because none was to be found. Someone reminded him that to find gold you have to use the right tools and be in the right place. Therapy frees and builds upon client resources; stories, art and play provide the tools to discover solutions to problems. The *gold is there*; we simply need to use the right tools to mine it and bring it to the surface.

In *Reflections on Milton Erickson* (2011), Wedge describes Erickson as mastering *life's curveballs*. He had polio when he was 17 and was expected to die or to never walk again; he was very active in overcoming his adversity and only used a wheelchair later in life. He believed that solutions to problems were within the person in the "unconscious mind." For Erickson, the unconscious mind was a source of strength and healing, and he relied on this for his own healing. He believed that therapy allows the person to "become aware of the strengths and resources within himself" and to have interpersonal experiences that result in change.

Erickson viewed utilization as a willingness to make use of what the client presents— symptoms, behaviors, attitudes, beliefs, emotional reactions, and so forth. Per Roffman (2008), metaphors establish connections that do not require conscious mediation. Utilization makes contextual shifts possible in relation to problems such that new action and/or meaning arises. Roffman describes a fascinating case where he and a boy with encopresis discussed the use of equipment at a construction site. They talked about dumping dirt; that workers don't just dump dirt wherever or whenever; they do it in the right place at the right time. They never really discussed the boy's encopresis directly, but after that session, the boy rarely had an accident. It seems to have been the metaphor that allowed the boy to bridge from "taking a dump" to construction equipment.

Roger Fritz (www.invisiblecows.com) writes about Erickson's work and techniques that include indirect suggestion, paradox, metaphor, therapeutic double binds, symptom prescription, relabeling, redefining and reframing. Erickson promoted brief therapy, the use of directives, focusing on the problem, family therapy, encouragement rather than confrontation and utilization of resistance. Per Fritz, Erickson engaged in persuasion, joking, cajoling, playfulness, making phone calls and doing whatever was necessary to reach a therapeutic goal. He described Erickson's skill at using multi-level communication (several levels occurring simultaneously).

Erickson used anecdotes, trance phenomena, metaphor, imagery and indirect suggestions as the means of introducing choice. He pointed out that *sick people* do want to try, but usually they don't know how; his work was a precursor to later solution orientated psychotherapy, a model that includes possibility language and flexible, "what if" thinking. Erickson's goals for treatment included such things as improving adaptive functioning, increasing client responsibility, symptom transformation or amelioration, and corrective emotional response. By arranging a situation that requires new behavior, the therapist engenders a new experience and reinforces that change is possible. Erickson viewed change as inevitable, not just possible.

The cases that follow in this book are examples of the ways in which multi-level language, metaphor and symbolic communication contributed to growth, new perspective and change.

In sum, I adhere to a number of Erickson's basic premises, and these tools and techniques remain relevant. Therapy . . .

- Is a collaborative process.
- Is strengths based as opposed to pathology based.
- Reduces learned helplessness and improves self-efficacy.
- Alters perspective and context.

Mining for Gold With Milton Erickson

- Allows previously unrealized connections and solutions to be accessible.
- Uses therapist as a catalyst to allow the as yet unconnected to become connected.
- "Solutions" are within the client and may be seeded by the therapist.
- Helps clients access their own resources.
- Utilizes a genuine, trusting, transparently open relationship for change.
- Remains choice and solution focused.

3

Constructing With Metaphor and Stories

THE NATURE OF METAPHOR

Metaphor is a little like *universal shorthand* or Morse code—it sends a complete message in very few *clicks*. Metaphor provides a *Morse code shortcut* when a client struggles to put trauma experience into words. Consider a client's recent statement, as she summarized her relationship with her mother in a single phrase: "My mother was a snake who gave birth to her children and then slithered away."

Metaphor is helpful to our clients when language fails, because the symbolic meaning is in the metaphor itself. The "aha" of insight sometimes takes place without conscious contemplation. Bessel van der Kolk (2014) addresses the body-mind aspects of trauma and the limitations of language in processing traumatic memories; he points out that many aspects of trauma are nearly impossible to put into words. When engaging in storytelling, art or play, reality is suspended (but remains present within), and the client may experience memories and feelings without the barrier of language.

Families communicate through metaphors ("don't air your dirty laundry," "don't dig up the past," "bury your secrets"). A teenager whose father struggled with alcohol once said his family was like "a football team without a coach," and there was "no one driving the bus." To say, "She is like a feral cat" conjures up an image of someone "spitting mad," whereas saying someone is like a "cold fish" sends an entirely different impression. When a recently widowed mother says she is "sinking in quicksand," the perceived futility of her struggle is clear. We might speak of a family having an "invisible" father, or someone behaving "like an ostrich with his head in the sand," and others "get it" without further explanation.

In *Recognizing and Communicating through Metaphors* (2011), Kottman describes using metaphor in treatment. The therapist recognizes the metaphor when it is spoken, understands the meaning of the metaphor for the client (which is sometimes outside client awareness), then uses the client's metaphor to communicate with that individual. I once commented to a *geeky* teen who balked at trying new things ("I can't change myself") that he might want to think of himself as an *avatar* (he had played many roles while gaming) or a *Transformer* (toy), because he so often played with these at home. He could create a new persona, or with some clever twists and turns, he could change his format and function. These metaphors shifted his thinking, and with that context, he *believed* that change was possible. I once told a couple of feuding brothers (who played baseball on the same team) that they wouldn't win many games if they tripped their own runner as he rounded 3rd base. They grinned at this and began to discuss the ways they set each other up. An adult client said, "Yes I always had a well-developed antenna." I reflected back, "Perhaps the abuse you experienced turned your antenna into *radar* at a very young age." That was the word that grabbed her attention; a single word described her hypervigilance and mistrust.

16

Trauma victims, especially those with visible hyper-arousal or hyper-vigilance, often use metaphor (in art or play) that reflects fear, freeze, flight or fight, and therapy may be driven by what is experienced or sensed (sensory, physiological, emotional) before it is fully understood or cognitively processed. Recently, a local newspaper carried a story about those who lost loved ones in a rural Texas church mass shooting. One man, a survivor whose family members had been killed, said to a newspaper reporter that his grief felt like using a hula hoop with a couple of spikes inside. Randomly, a spike would hit, pierce him with sudden pain, and remind him of his loss. This is a poignant depiction of the pain that pierced him through. Readers interested further in the history and use of therapeutic metaphor may wish to explore the 2nd edition of Mills and Crowley's *Therapeutic Metaphors for Children and the Child Within* (2014).

SYMBOLS IN STORIES, ART AND PLAY

When I think about symbols, Carl Jung, who wrote of archetypes, myths, dreams and symbols (considered to be the meaningful material of the unconscious), comes to mind. Years ago, I was fortunate to obtain a limited edition of *Man and His Symbols* (Jung, 1964). It is a beautiful book of writings, symbols and art; Jung and his contributors write about the concept of *unconscious* (similar to the *subconscious* of Freud), which is as "real and vital part of the life of an individual as the conscious, 'cogitating' world of the ego, and infinitely wider and richer. The language and the 'people' of the unconscious are symbols, and means of communications dreams" (p. 12). What Jung referred to as unconscious might, from this author's perspective, contain both universal symbols/archetypes as well as not-yet-conscious material, i.e., implicit memories with their abundant sensations, feelings and attachment reactions and their associated responses.

Jung speaks to the ways that symbols may be meaningful in understanding client core issues, some of which may have been forgotten, discarded, non-processed or avoided. Jung addresses "forgetting" in the statement, "There are many reasons why we forget things that we have noticed or experienced; and there are just as many ways in which they may be recalled to mind" (p. 37). *Forgotten memories* may be triggered by a cue or trigger such as a sight, smell or sound, and symptoms arise when these memories begin to intrude on and interrupt one's functioning (Jung, p. 36). This process is common in those who experienced trauma, especially complex trauma, where no one event can be identified as the source of distress; our current knowledge points to neurobiological underpinnings.

Clients communicate symbolically in therapy; dreams, poetry, art, stories and play may reflect not-yet-realized client feelings or concerns. John Freeman, in the Introduction to *Man and His Symbols*, points out (pp. 10–11), "The dream is an integral, important and personal expression of the individual unconscious. The dreamer's individual unconscious is communicating with the dreamer alone and is selecting symbols for their purposes that have meaning to the dreamer and to nobody else." Jung stated (p. 51), "The general function of dreams is to try to restore our psychological balance by producing dream material that re-establishes, in a subtle way, the total psychic equilibrium."

In the same manner as dreams, stories, art and play are neurobiologically integrative; they help our clients *restore balance* and connect the implicit to the explicit. Jung described archetypal figures that so often play a role in client stories and play, including mother, father, child, hero, villain, tempter, trickster, hero and rescuer, good and evil, the shadow, life and death. Archetypes are core, universal, age-old symbols; Jung wrote, "One can perceive the specific energy of archetypes when we experience the peculiar fascination that accompanies them . . . they seem to hold a special spell" (p. 79). Similarly, when clients present meaningful, personal symbolic material, they do so with persistence and intensity, and the material carries with it an energy that propels the work of therapy.

Jung points out, "There are, for instance, many representations of the motif of the hostile brethren, but the motif itself remains the same" (p. 67). There is *instant meaning* in artwork that portrays "a tornado tearing apart a house"; the words "tearing apart" convey aggressive power, victimization and helplessness. What you don't know, however, is whether the client is the storm, the house, a bystander or even someone inside, so exploration of meaning in client material is crucial. When a client spontaneously generates symbolism or metaphor, the meaning must be explored. A thunder cloud in the sky may be before, during or after a storm; for some the storm

The Tools of the Trade

is frightening and for others an exhilarating moment to watch the rain and listen to the thunder. A client may assume the role of victim or "monster," depending on the circumstances. A client may *be the tornado* or *fear the tornado*. Metaphor is the *what* of client material, and it is up to the therapist to discover *how, when* and *why*. Symbolic material may represent the client's current situation, a memory of the past, a fear/concern or a hope/wish/yearning. As Jung reminds us, dream (and play) characters and themes are meaningful and symbolic, but not necessarily literal; they may even represent different aspects of the dreaming individual.

Drewes (2010) and Erickson (2011b) point out that themes present in art and play (triumph/conquering, fearlessness/courage, power/control, dependence/independence, abandonment/separation, safety/security/protection, chaos/instability, grief/loss/hopelessness, forgiveness/revenge, and mastery/competence) are coherent metaphors in and of themselves.

We assume that the client holds the meaning in his/her symbolic communication, and that with further interaction and exploration, meaning becomes clearer. When a client *offers* symbolic or metaphorical material, it may interrupt the therapist's planned *agenda*, but this is an opportunity for a *therapeutic detour*.

Following are some client examples of symbolic metaphor in art, organized by theme.

Themes of Power and Control

These themes include depictions of *good* or *bad power*: battles, dragon, wizard, magic wand, storms and volcanos. This theme includes one-up, one-down situations, and it is important to identify where the client identification lies.

A boy with bipolar disorder drew the following "happy helper giant" who had "special powers." The boy was often unintentionally bossy and demanding with his parents and did not

FIGURE 3.1

Constructing With Metaphor and Stories

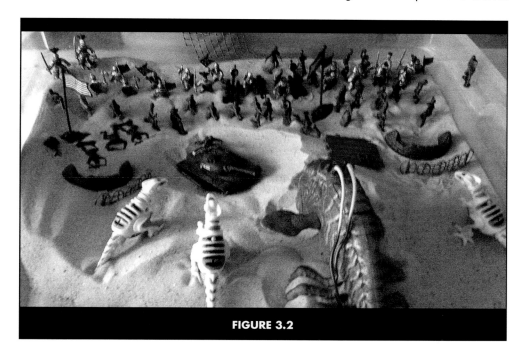

FIGURE 3.2

FIGURE 3.3

understand that his comments were rude or critical due to poor awareness of social cues. He had endless energy and did not think before he spoke. He was easily frustrated when told "no" and quick to anger. His moods ranged from irritable to gleeful. His parents were very critical and judgmental even when he was not bossy. They didn't like him playing so many video games, but they were inconsistent in following through on limits. His younger sister baited him in sneaky ways and was not held accountable. This really tried his patience. I worked with this little boy and his mother for a

19

year, and it became clear that a primary source of her frustration was her spouse who used power/control strategies to get his way, also that when growing up she had been victimized by an angry older male sibling. She was close to her son but vacillated between passive depressive behavior (sleeping late and disengaged) and angry punitive behavior when he did not comply or when he became verbally aggressive. When he was loud and angry, the mother responded to her young son *as if he was her abuser*, and at those times she was quick-triggered into a fight-flight response.

The sand tray battle in Figure 3.2 was created by an abused, angry, oppositional 10-year-old boy. Due to his skewed, filtered view of others, he struggled to take responsibility for his behavior and believed he was justified in his angry outbursts and stubborn non-compliance. He had good reasons to not trust others because of past abuse and feelings of helplessness (not able to protect his siblings), and like an onion, his anger was on the surface, mixed with fear. His fear was triggered easily by misperception, and he seemed to feel less vulnerable when engaging in power-control strategies with his siblings.

A fearful, angry abused client shows the power of angry consumption in Figure 3.3. The client might identify with the angry monster or fear the angry monster, but the power is clear in the manner in which he shoved everything into the monster's mouth.

Themes of Anger

Anger is often depicted in out-of-control situations such as storms, eruption, volcanos, fire, explosions and battle. Anger may be depicted in the energy, action, colors or action. Anger and fear may go hand in hand, with fear or hypervigilance triggering angry reactivity.

The following picture was drawn by an angry 6-year-old female who struggled with a parent's volatile moods. The volcanic explosion suggests impulsive loss of control with resultant fire and destruction. There had been a particular scary situation when the parent had a gun (while under the influence) and shot it in the children's presence. He had locked the door to the house, preventing their escape. After this and several other incidences, the client started "erupting in anger" at home and school.

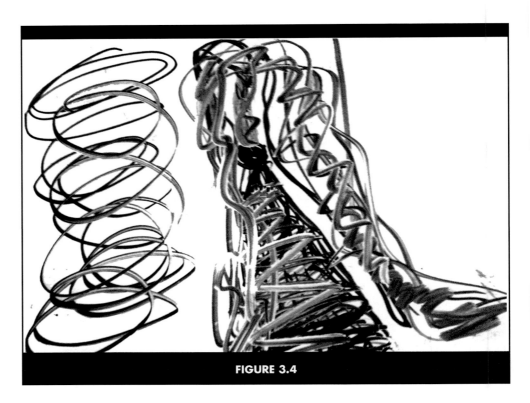

FIGURE 3.4

Constructing With Metaphor and Stories

Themes of Anxiety, Worry or Fear

When clients are anxious or fearful, their drawings depict "freeze, flight or fight," i.e., themes of fear, worry, attack, self-protection or even aggression depicted as self-protection in the face of danger. A "what-if" theme often appears in their therapy interactions. Anxious clients worry, obsess, ruminate and picture negative outcomes.

A young girl with separation anxiety addressed her anxiety in a Dry Erase Squiggle Story. She struggled between wanting "fresh food" (positive things in life, like friendship and going to school) and avoiding it because of the sharks (she had a negative experience at school due to bullying and criticism from a teacher). Figure 3.5 depicts the pros and cons of reducing avoidance and increasing behavioral activation.

The picture in Figure 3.6 was drawn by an anxious girl who reported having "jack in the box feelings" after abuse. She described how her feelings would pop up and startle her, just like the toy. This type of startle reaction is common post-trauma, due to hyperarousal and autonomic activation.

The next picture (see Figure 3.7) was drawn by a hypervigilant girl who displayed her fear in the form of anger following abuse. She seemed to have some awareness that her anger was protective and that she was scaring others off, but "not really mean." When she was fearful, she snapped at people and refused to interact. Others sometimes interpreted her moods as grouchy or "mean" but at the core was fear and anxiety.

This female "ripper" with a bow in her hair (Figure 3.8) was drawn by a traumatized girl with high anxiety (See Appendix for full-color version of this picture). She warned others away when she felt most fearful of harm/in need of self-protection. She has a red bow in her hair, a red belt, a black tunic and a knife with a red handle.

A fearful, angry 10-year-old girl drew Figure 3.9 when she was being bullied at school. The head and hands are bright red, and the hair and hand spikes are dark black. The eyes are veiled, and the message of "get back" or "keep away" is clear.

This next drawing (Figure 3.10) was done by an anxious, compulsive 11-year-old boy who worried about getting hurt, about failing, about disappointing his mother, and about not getting his work done on time at school and missing recess. He was very self-conscious and tended to obsess about most

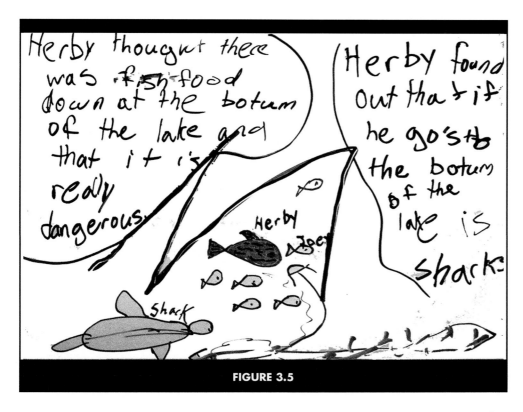

FIGURE 3.5

21

FIGURE 3.6

FIGURE 3.7

FIGURE 3.8

FIGURE 3.9

The Tools of the Trade

FIGURE 3.10

FIGURE 3.11

things, also, he was very uncomfortable with his emerging pre-teen sexual feelings. The reader will see the multiple "opportunities" for harm in the picture below, with bees and wasps everywhere.

A fearful child, who felt overwhelmed by environmental threats, drew the erupting volcano above in Figure 3.11. She is not the volcano; rather, she fears the danger and damage. She said that she was in the town below the volcano and that the fire and lava were coming "to get us." The outside of the volcano is green, suggesting you can't see the anger/lava until it erupts. The volcano is spouting fire, and it is red hot at the core. Her parents had engaged in domestic violence, and when she visited her dad, she feared his temper. Recently she had been at his home when he got drunk, locked the children out of his house, and then proceeded to shoot a gun outside in anger. The child cried and tried to get back in the house, and he ridiculed her.

Constructing With Metaphor and Stories

Themes of Hope and Well-Being

Clients who are starting to feel better often use brighter colors and draw such things as rainbows, the sunshine emerging and flowers blooming. A child nearing termination offered the following spontaneous drawing of a creature celebrating inside a colorful rainbow. What is different is that the rainbow is anchored at both ends, to ensure that it is tied down and won't go away.

The flower arrangement in Figure 3.13 was presented by a 9-year-old girl with dissociation. It represented growing trust in the therapy relationship. See Appendix for full-color version of

FIGURE 3.12

FIGURE 3.13

25

this picture. The client had asked if she could "use" the roses that were in a vase in my office "for something." When I agreed, she handed the roses to me, one at a time, naming each one: "This one is for therapy, this one is for the medicine (SSRI), this one is for playing with me, this one is for stories, and this one is for love . . ." I was touched by her spontaneous offering of trust and affection. She was feeling some relief from depression and morbid suicidal thoughts, finally experiencing hope. Next, she created the arrangement, added the iris, and said, "This is one of a kind." I wasn't sure if she was referring to her dissociative states, feeling unique/different, or being one child in a large sibling group in foster care. I thought about how I might best respond to her and portray "one of a kind" in an accepting context; I presented her with some affirmations of my own: "Thank *you* for being loving, having a big forgiving heart, for your creativity, for art/drawing, for humor and laughter together, for hard work on things that are tough, for telling me stories, for being beautiful and one-of-a kind." She quietly accepted my affirmations, and I took a photo of her iris among the roses.

Themes of Chaos/Confusion

At times, a client's artwork portrays decompensation or poor internal organization. The art may be chaotic and poorly organized, with themes of storms, swirling wind/rain, etc. Artwork changes may occur, with visible decompensation and disorganization, during periods of high stress or in trauma aftermath.

A 10-year-old boy drew the picture below from a Squiggle. There is a "mess" of scribbled colors, with dark purple in the middle, and swirls of green, brown, black, red and blue. He is trapped in this morass, and at the corners of this "web" are portals sucking everything out, including him, and he is crying "Mom" (it is "echoing"). He was being treated for severe separation anxiety (from his mom) that he experienced when visiting his biological dad who had been absent most of his life. During visits with his dad, he cried and stayed in his room, begged to call his mom and worried about something bad happening to her if he wasn't there.

His artwork was chaotic and sometimes confusing. He had difficulty with verbal communication due to expressive language deficits, and his pictures were visually intense and disorganized.

FIGURE 3.14

Constructing With Metaphor and Stories

One of his frequent drawings and stories, self-created, was of getting sucked out of his universe through a portal to an *alien universe*, where he had no protection or means of return. See Appendix for full-color version of the picture that follows.

Themes of Depression/Sadness

Depressed clients present art that is dark and often monochromatic, with themes of loss, darkness, dark clouds, blocked sun, etc. Characters may have low energy and lethargy, or hopelessness may be acknowledged.

This first drawing below is done by a 6-year-old boy who was depressed after the death of his father. The black clouds are directly overhead, and there is rain pouring down, thunder and lightning. The figure appears off balance and about to fall. At this stage of therapy, the child was feeling emotionally unbalanced due to the changes in his family and personal life.

A depressed, irritable pre-teen drew his self-talk inside a volcano in Figure 3.16. He experienced anxiety and depression, and voiced negative views of himself, others and the world. He displayed dysphoric mood and pessimism, and he had poor frustration tolerance. This drawing allowed us to use these thoughts with CBT, and we talked about ways that he might be able to "cool down" the volcano. He suggested he use "ice water" and "pour it inside to douse the black thoughts," then replace them with affirmations, activities and positive relationships.

An artistic, depressed older teen drew the next picture in Figure 3.17 a sad, grieving self-representation. She had been depressed and suicidal, in part related to the loss of her dad but also due to negative views of self.

FIGURE 3.15

FIGURE 3.16

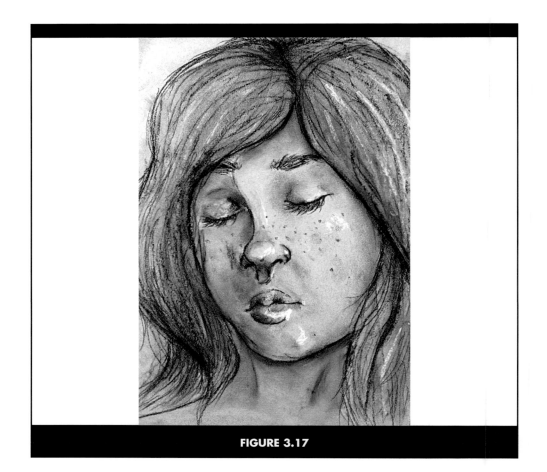

FIGURE 3.17

THE NATURE OF STORIES

Lawrence et al. (2006) indicate that storytelling is at the heart of all therapy, and Siegel (2012) states, "We are storytelling creatures, and stories are the social glue that binds us to one another" (p. 31). Metaphorical stories, as opposed to direct concrete problem-solving stories along the line of, "How Joey copes with fear of the dark," allow the client to process and respond without the interference of imposed mental sets.

When we share stories with clients, we communicate that we understand their issues, empathize with their confusion or pain, and offer new or out of the box possibilities for change. When clients tell us their own stories, they convey much about their feelings, thoughts and perceptions. I was asked recently by a graduate student, "How do I *learn* storytelling?" This question was hard to answer, because you don't really *learn* how to tell stories. There are *canned* metaphors provided in ACT or DBT, but I find these to be less powerful than unique spontaneously generated client-created material. You begin to tell stories by listening to your clients, and when you listen, you hear the client's concerns, values, unique language use and self-representation. Perhaps everyone *is* a storyteller, in his or her most open, vulnerable, flexible moments. Stories emerge while reflecting on childhood, memorable life events and life-changing relationships. It is usually enough to capture a metaphor and use the client's language to depict a client's process *in the moment*.

Most of my stories were originally written for specific clients as *catalysts*, *entranceways*, or *tools for change or acceptance*, and then later shared with other clients with similar problems or concerns. I began to share stories with other therapists, and through our shared work, we discovered the *universal* nature of some of the stories and characters. The stories, characters, metaphors and meaning are mostly intuitive and simple: an eagle who wore tennis shoes to walk to Tennessee because he was afraid to fly, a mermaid who *forgot* she was a mermaid (trying to swim through a storm instead of diving deep below the storm); a girl who flung poop at barnyard animals (like people fling words when angry); a soldier who was looking for landmines, in Disneyland (missing the pleasure in life); a cracked glass bowl (damaged in a storm) that had to *melt and re-form* to heal from the inside out; a man sifting for gold in the sand of the desert rather than moving to where the gold might be; an ostrich who learned that "what you don't see can hurt you"; a lonely squirrel with a "hungry heart"; a dog who grew up "swimming in the swamp" and now wants to get "clean"; a girl who sent her "real heart" on vacation and replaced it with a plastic one; and a pain monster who kept a girl on a leash until she learned to live with and manage the pain.

During a recent intake appointment, an adult female client relayed that she keeps too much inside and that when she lets it out, she loses control, screams and rants. I quickly told her the story of the elephant in *A Little at a Time* (Pernicano, 2012, 2014a). Ella started holding in her feelings and her "shit" (word in book is "poop") when she was young, and now, as an older elephant, it immobilizes her. Her friends advise her to let it out, *a little at a time, both her shit and her feelings*. Telling this story validated all the "shit" this woman had experienced and suggested that it is not helpful to keep it inside. As we prepared to say goodbye, I said, "We can go slow, a little at a time." She grinned and said, "Yes, like the elephant!" At her next appointment over a month later, she was quick to mention the elephant story and began talking about the "past shit" that she still carried around.

Stories, both client and therapist created, help clients of all ages express feelings, process trauma and clarify ambivalence regarding change and relationships; the disarming nature of stories lowers defenses and propels change in ways that verbal discussion alone does not. Cattanach (2006, p. 82) writes, "Clients usually have a story to tell about themselves and what has happened to them"; she notes themes such as fear, loathing, loss, abandonment, heroes and wishes (Cattanach, 1997). Peterson and Fontana indicate that a client often visualizes his or her associations during a story and "may spontaneously access memories from other experiences" (Peterson & Fontana, 2007, p. 2). Stories elicit sensory components of remembered experiences in images, smells, colors and feelings associated with the story.

As we continue to learn more about neurobiological pathways and right brain contributions to trauma and attachment, we better understand the ways in which stories activate sensory memories, trigger strong unresolved emotions and stimulate the "aha" of insight that propels

The Tools of the Trade

treatment toward behavior change (Pernicano, 2014a, p. 19). Gabbard, in the Preface of *The Metaphor of Play* by Meares (2005), writes, "Despite the hard wiring of neural networks, new networks can be formed" in therapy. Stories and art can bypass conscious, logical thought processes and connect with less "verbal" parts of the brain. Gil (2013) notes that the right hemisphere uses symbols, metaphors, fantasy and play to process information, and therapists may deliberately engage in right hemisphere activities so as to amplify the impact of metaphor and symbolic communication.

According to Pernicano (2010a, 2012, 2014a, 2015 a, b), metaphor and stories may be used within most theoretical orientations, including client-centered, cognitive behavioral, Adlerian, narrative, family, Gestalt, Jungian, psychoanalytic, object relations and psychodynamic; the clinician's theoretical underpinnings guide the manner in which the material is utilized. Solution-oriented treatments, hypnotherapy, filial therapy, narrative therapies, ACT, mindfulness approaches, cognitive behavioral therapies and a variety of play therapies all utilize stories or metaphors. Depending on the therapist's theoretical orientation and approach, metaphor and stories are used to discover, change or create meaning, teach or model concepts, see change, alter schemas, change behavior, induce hypnotic trance, strengthen parent-child relationships, change or construct a personal narrative, trigger an "aha" moment, or reduce defensiveness and resistance.

Metaphor and storytelling help a therapist access the *unseen and unspoken* inner world of the client and help the client make sense of that world. "Through metaphorical communication, clients reveal their concerns, demonstrate their desires, express their emotions, gain a clearer understanding of their experience, and create solutions to problems" (Snow et al., 2005, p. 63). In one of the first comprehensive storytelling books, *101 Healing Stories for Kids and Teens*, Burns (2005) describes how stories inform, educate, teach values, build experience, facilitate problem-solving, and propel change or heal; *Healing with Stories* (Burns, 2007) provides a fascinating set of contributed case studies. Greenwald's *A Fairy Tale* (www.childtrauma.com) helps trauma victims *conquer* their dragons using metaphor and medieval story themes. Stories and subsequent interventions help clients of all ages make meaning of life events, reduce arousal, increase self-efficacy, and bolster trust and attachment. The reader is directed to other resources that illustrate many ways in which stories, metaphor, art and creative play may be utilized across treatment modalities to contribute to client change (Blenkiron, 2010; Burns, 2001, 2005, 2007; Cattanach, 1997, 2007, 2009; Drewes, 2009, 2010; Erickson, 2011a, 2011b; Gil, 1994, 2013; Greenwald, 2009, 2014; Kopp, 1995; Kottman, 2011; Kottman & Ashby, 2002; Markell & Markell, 2008; Oldford, 2011; and Pernicano, 2010a, 2010b, 2014a, 2014b, 2015a, 2015b).

4

THE BLUEPRINT OF TRAUMA-INFORMED TREATMENT

WHAT IT MEANS TO BE "TRAUMA-INFORMED"

Marion Woodman, a Jungian analyst, and her co-author therapist Jill Mellick speak to the role of stories and metaphor in growth and healing in *Coming Home to Myself* (1998). Their writing reflects the non-judgmental, light-dark process of trauma-informed care.

> *While we might hold another's pain with a loving heart, we cannot remove it. Our souls must grow and heal in their own time. These stories remind us to receive non-judgmentally both our own and others' non-veiled moments of light and darkness. They remind us of the ways in which we each struggle with demons and dance with angels.*
>
> *(p. 14)*

Being trauma-informed includes a body of knowledge that guides intervention, a well-tuned *radar*, sensitivity and understanding that arises out of client-therapist interactions. I have worked with trauma cases for over 30 years, long before I had *labels* for some of the things I actually *do* in my practice, and long before we had EBP's or today's understanding of the impact of trauma on neurobiology and development. Like most therapists in the late '70s, I learned about trauma *from* my clients by observing their interactions, listening to their communications and developing treatment interventions that were a good fit. I could see the ways in which trauma skewed thinking, altered mood and impacted self-esteem.

PTSD was not a defined disorder until the DSM-III in 1980, and by the time I did my doctoral internship at a VA in 1984, we were able to more consistently identify trauma-based symptoms in Vietnam veterans. Trauma-informed therapy was not yet "packaged," so we challenged irrational beliefs and used psychoeducation, empathy, listening, forgiveness, compassion and encouragement.

Trauma-informed care has expanded its knowledge base, but the *ingredients for change remain much the same*. There are a number of evidence-based models and methods for treating trauma-related mental health symptoms as well as full PTSD. We know that people react differently to traumatic life events: some developing PTSD; some becoming depressed, anxious or angry; some becoming rigid and compulsive; and still others using substances to numb their feelings, find sleep or avoid thinking about the past. We also know that some persons are more resilient than others and that some individuals experience post-traumatic growth.

Trauma recovery seems to be a matter of biology, early experience, coping resources and environmental supports in addition to formal treatment; this is a rich field, with new techniques and resources emerging on a regular basis. I remember hearing Bessel van der Kolk (2014) present at the Evolution of Psychotherapy conference in the early '90s. Harvard scientists were skeptical of his proposed "Body Mind Therapy" for trauma, with an emphasis on alternative therapies that included touch, massage, mindfulness, Yoga and meditation. He was wise before his time in his understanding of neurobiology and intrinsic memory with its sensory and physiological components.

The Tools of the Trade

Let me take a minute to further describe what I mean by "trauma-informed care." Trauma-informed care takes place within evidence-based (but not strictly manualized) treatment models, within which there may be individualization of delivery. Stories, art and play are well-suited to individualized interventions; client-generated material provides unique information about mood intensity, thought patterns, views of self/others/world, and client attributions.

To be "trauma-informed," a therapist is compassionate, aims to "do no harm," is a good listener and process observer, is aware of the many types of life circumstances that can result in trauma-related symptoms, and is knowledgeable of and watchful for the many types of symptoms that can emerge following trauma (immediate or delayed). If and when traumatic or potentially traumatic life events are reported during therapy, the therapist asks appropriate questions to evaluate the client's response, spoken and unspoken. A trauma-informed therapist is flexible and well-paced, able to adjust intervention to minimize re-traumatization and to reduce emotional/physiological dysregulation. Re-traumatization can occur when a therapist is unaware of client triggers or moves too quickly into trauma narrative work before ensuring that the client has the resources to self-regulate mood and anxiety. Clients may drop out of treatment when interventions become personally overwhelming, and therapists may unwittingly label this as "resistance." A trauma-informed therapist develops a relationship with the client (and family members as appropriate), and in the context of that relationship becomes more aware of triggers and opportunities for change.

TRAUMA-INFORMED KNOWLEDGE

Trauma-informed therapists need to understand the basic neurobiology of trauma and the many ways in which symptoms present; it is also necessary to have knowledge of interpersonal neurobiology, attachment, family functioning, child protection, forensic processes, sexual trauma, intimate partner violence and substance abuse. Therapists need to be informed about military stressors, combat conditions and moral injury. Readers are directed to other books and resources for detailed knowledge and information in the above areas.

A good understanding of the developmental impact of trauma is necessary to work effectively with clients; the impact of trauma may be acute, chronic or residual. Child clients may present with trauma-related symptoms of depression, anxiety or agitation/hyperarousal that look like Attention Deficit Hyperactivity Disorder (ADHD). The reader is directed to the 2014 May/June edition of the Psychotherapy Networker for a case illustration of ADHD vs. PTSD (Pernicano 2014b). After trauma, children may be interpersonally challenged, and the attachment style of the child affects how trauma symptoms are displayed. A child's interpersonal response to trauma depends in part on his or her attachment avoidance, anxiety or disorganization. Adult clients may experience trauma-related numbing, tuning out, disengagement and/or heightened autonomic arousal with vigilance to cues/signs of danger (real or imagined), even many years after the initial traumatic event. Furthermore, adult clients may not associate their current mental health symptoms with past trauma. Adult clients with high autonomic arousal may seem overly busy, talkative, intense, hyperactive or restless. They may not sleep well due to the arousal, and they may respond more impulsively due to reduced cognitive control. When the adult is triggered by cues that remind him or her of traumatic events or threaten attachment security, he or she may react with freeze, flight or fight behaviors, depending on his or her adult attachment style and typical style of coping. Numb or disengaged clients may present with flat affect or seem bored or non-responsive in session, and trauma-informed therapists need to be sensitive to this so as to not mislabel this as some sort of "resistance."

There is a psychoeducational component in trauma-informed care, for both the client and family members, and the psychoeducation can be direct/didactic or introduced through story and metaphor. Didactic psychoeducation includes the impact of trauma and the trauma continuum, and examples of trauma reactions are to be found in stories I used with cases in this book, such as *The Cracked Glass Bowl, Lucky the Junkyard Dog* or *Bear of a Different Color* (all to be found in Pernicano, 2014a).

32

GROUNDED IN NEUROBIOLOGY

Bruce Perry's Neurosequential Model of Therapeutics has contributed to our understanding of state-dependent functioning after trauma (Perry, 2006, 2009; Perry & Hambrick, 2008). Perry points out that the response to trauma varies by the individual's developmental functioning at the time of the trauma and is easily activated by fear. His elaborate assessment allows a mapping of functioning, and his trainings provide information about developmentally appropriate intervention, so as to not trigger new fear responses and to respond in ways that enhance self-regulation. Cozolino (2014) describes the neuroscience of psychotherapy, and the ways in which parent-child interactions impact early development. In *Mindsight*, Siegel (2010) speaks to neurobiological integration and the ways in which psychotherapeutic attunement, empathy and resonance contribute to a client's integrated functioning. His concepts of chaos/organization and rigidity/flexibility allow therapists to ensure a good fit between intervention and client states and characteristics. Bremner's work (2002) points out that trauma can be associated with neuroendocrine changes, a decrease in hippocampal size (memory areas), increase in limbic arousal (fight/flight) and decreased left brain cognitive control. Siegel would say that these changes result in a lack of neurobiological integration, i.e., the "bottom" without the "top" and the "right" without the "left."

What used to be understood as the "unconscious" might now be described as a neurobiological state where material is available, but not yet activated. It is a lighthouse with an out-of-order light, or a radar turned to *off*, and memories, sensory triggers and stories have the capacity to flip the switch to *on*. We recognize that after trauma, clients may react and respond without awareness, because their neuronal connectivity is *out of whack*; the capacity to access memories and to use language to describe their experiences has been changed. Memories of traumatic events may be avoided or even forgotten as a result of these neurobiological changes; yet, what we refer to as implicit memories (sensory, physical, cognitive) have the continued power to activate the nervous system, with heightened reactivity to trauma triggers. The client may experience significant distress without knowing why and behave in ways that seem confusing or non-adaptive to self or others.

Siegel (2010) conceptualizes therapy as a "brain-to-brain" relationship that promotes neurobiological integration (lower-to-higher and right-to-left integration). He posits that "integrated" or mindful adults achieve an integrated balance of cognitive and emotional resources. Trauma, however, contributes to poor neurobiological integration, with some clients becoming more emotionally chaotic in their functioning, or under-regulated, and others overly cognitively regulated/controlled. When abuse or neglect happens at very early ages, the capacity for secure attachment, resonance and attunement are often impaired. The nature and activities of trauma-informed therapy move clients toward integration through brain-to-brain relational connections.

In sum, trauma-informed care provides "brain-to-brain" empathic, attuned interactions that activate neurobiological change (Siegel, 2010). With effective trauma-informed treatment, the client becomes able to process what was formerly inaccessible. Readers are referred to other sources for more detailed information regarding the neurobiological impact of trauma on development.

IDENTIFYING BLIND SPOTS AND RISK FACTORS

Therapists need clinical awareness of client blind spots, as without this, conceptualization will be incomplete or inaccurate. Clients may filter or even re-define events, to reduce dissonance, lower anxiety or justify their behavior. Dissonance is resolved by altering the facts, not by altering one's perception of or response to the facts. Stories, art and play *come in through the back door* and circumvent blind spots while illuminating risk factors. Blind spots are common in families involved with child protective services. Years ago, a program manager and I met with a mom to give her feedback about her progress in parenting her children, and we provided her with very detailed examples. We shared that her placement in the program was on shaky ground; in the past month she had subjected her children to abuse, had neglected to supervise them and had been sleeping while her children wandered outside. As we ended the conversation, encouraging her to be more protective and nurturing, she commented with a smile, as if she had not heard a word we said, "Well, good. I guess we're all on the same page." My colleague and I noted after she left that a mother like that could "turn shit into sugar without batting an eye." To help clients avoid blind spots, a trauma-informed therapist picks up on and asks about life events that might be associated with higher risk of trauma; these include multiple moves, frequent adult partner change, poor parental supervision (due to job or lifestyle), drugs/alcohol abuse, history of violence/incarceration or a crowded home environment.

WORKING WITHIN A DEVELOPMENTAL CONTEXT

The impact of trauma is dependent on a person's development at the time of the trauma and his or her capacity to adapt and cope. Responses to trauma vary by age and neurobiological developmental capacity. As Perry and Hambrick (2008) point out, the age of the client when trauma occurred has bearing on the emergence and nature of trauma symptoms. For example, when trauma occurs during infancy, sensory and emotional systems are activated, including the attachment behavioral system. The infant can either launch a protest (cry, fuss) or eventually shut down (dissociate, tune out). At each later stage, clients cope using their available resources, and neurobiology limits the range of response, which explains why trauma in the first years of life can be so devastating in terms of later attachment, mood regulation and behavioral adaptation.

Trauma itself sometimes results in developmental delays because of its neurobiological impact, thus we can't assume that a client's chronological age reflects his or her functioning capacity. Perry and Hambrick (2008) point out that traumatized clients display state-dependent symptoms and functioning that parallel neurobiological adaptation. When doing trauma-focused work, the therapist must first have a rough estimate of that individual's developmental functioning. If we over or under estimate a client's verbal and cognitive ability or his/her capacity for self-regulation, communication is more likely to short-circuit, and what we "send" will not be "received." It is like writing an email, hitting "send" and getting back that annoying message that says "this message cannot be delivered," or "mailbox not available."

Younger children are more literal and concrete in their understanding, as are developmentally delayed adults, and assessment and trauma work with these populations must be more hands-on. Children can be taught how to tell stories and communicate about feelings, but they can't process much beyond their current developmental capacity; their attention span is shorter than that of adult clients, and they need repetition to learn new skills. Children naturally communicate using make-believe and metaphor in their play, and their play reflects feelings and attitudes about self, others and the world. However, their communication can't be taken literally without confirmation of events. Children's play, although not literal, often reveals the "gist" of what may have been experienced, in symbolic form. The 5-to-7-year-old shift in children corresponds with new brain development, opening the door for CBT and play therapies with more verbal interaction. A child younger than about age 7 lacks the ability to do cause-effect thinking or self-other processing.

It is important to remember that young children, and some adolescents or adults (because of mental health symptoms or cognitive limitations), have poor sequencing ability, so accuracy of dates and time frames are less reliable. For children, "yesterday" may be two years in the past, and an adult may be off by a year or two when engaging in free recall without an anchoring time line. The therapist can better pin down time frames and details using anchors like the season of the year, where the client lived at the time, what they were wearing when something happened, what they saw or smelled, what room they were in or what grade they were in. When we provide anchors and structure, clients become able to describe their traumatic experiences.

When working within a developmental context, a therapist remains process oriented and understands that clients are active organisms and subject to change. We pay close attention to context, risk and resilience, understanding that risk and resilience are fluid variables. It is important to note that research suggests that most persons are able to reasonably recover from a one time single episode of abuse or neglect. It is in the face of multiple and repeated threats or stressors that adapation is most challenged. Cummings et al. (2000) provides an excellent

The Blueprint of Trauma-Informed Treatment

description of developmental psychopathology and reminds the reader that multiple causes can lead to a single effect, and a single cause can have many different effects. In other words, there are multiple pathways to the same outcome at any point in time. Different life pathways (experiences, interactions) may result in the same "end" or observed symptoms and behavior. In this respect, "symptoms" of hyperactivity, poor focus, difficulties with concentration and inattention can arise via different pathways, including ADHD, trauma, depression, drug use, caffeine use or anxiety. Clients with the same symptoms do not necessarily develop them in the same ways for the same reasons; nor would these conditions be treated in the same manner. When working in a developmental context, we avoid quick assumptions and attempt to understand risk and resilience factors that impact development.

USING A SYSTEMIC APPROACH

Bronfenbrenner's Ecological Model (1977) and the Ecosystemic Model (O'Connor & Ammen, 2013) are helpful when considering the various systems of influence in clients' lives. A systemic approach points to the importance of understanding the inner, outer, historic and contextual worlds of our clients. Relationships with significant others, life experiences, geography, religious institutions and other cultural influences shape client views of self, others and the world. For example, when working with a client who is involved with child welfare, a systemic therapist understands that this involvement impacts trust and openness in the therapy relationship.

When using a systemic approach with children, family members or caregivers will be involved in the treatment, as well as others such as school personnel, child welfare staff, and/or other agencies or medical providers. It is important to educate the client and family members about the therapy process and ways in which therapy differs from other forms of social interaction, also, that "rules" of communication vary from "social" norms. Following are a few things that may be conveyed to families when engaging in trauma-informed therapy, because therapy *rules* differ from family/home/public rules:

- There are limits to confidentiality when courts order the treatment.
- Therapists model openness and curiosity.
- Therapists stay away from absolutes and seek the "gray" and the dialect.
- Symbolic communication and play are not literal; there may be aggressive, sexual and/or vindictive themes.
- Especially if the child has experienced sex, we remind caregivers that neither "sex talk" nor reactions to sexual feelings can be considered taboo.
- Therapist can ask and coach caregivers to not "correct" or "judge" stories or play content.
- The child has an "equal" and "respected" role in the therapy room.
- The child's ideas and opinions are valid and encouraged.
- We recognize the child as "teacher" and "expert" regarding his or her own experience.
- We don't assume we know the whole story, and we maintain an attitude of curiosity. We remain open to the possibility of new disclosures.

In all therapies, we "do no harm" and keep the client's best interest front and center. When working systemically, the therapist meets the "players" and gets a clear picture of relationships and interactions. Working systemically may involve inviting a caregiver to watch therapist interactions with the child or including the caregiver directly in the therapy. A child may not be ready to fully involve the caregiver in the session for fear of criticism or judgment, but the therapist can mitigate against this by clarifying roles and boundaries with the players. The therapist can position the child to not be able to see the caregiver, to minimize non-verbal control and reduce anxiety. As a *fly on the wall*, the caregiver can observe and learn about the therapy activities in sessions before directly participating. Collateral sessions may be needed to teach a caregiver about therapy and provide feedback, so that the therapist can prepare the caregiver for the therapy work and guide things in a positive direction.

It is helpful to meet an adult client's live-in partner, significant other or spouse, because the client's description of that person may not match the therapist's perception. Like the story of

The Tools of the Trade

the Blind Men and the Elephant, when the "blind" are touching different parts of an elephant, the perception is affected by where that person is standing in relation to the others. Any one individual's "view" is filtered and "skewed" due to limited access to information.

A systemic therapist shows awareness and sensitivity for culture in all its aspects, including religious, rural/urban, socio-economic, and racial, gender, ethnic and sexual diversity. It is important that we affirm differences and also work within our client's world views when possible or refer out if we feel unable to do so. Therapists need to be aware of family beliefs and also point out, without judgment, ways that those beliefs may interfere with trauma recovery and family relationships.

Systemic therapists remain flexible and adjust treatment when new things emerge. When new issues emerge, the therapist's conceptual "map" and treatment goals are likely to change, to incorporate the new issues. When providing therapy within a systemic context, we involve caregivers in the treatment of traumatized children and youth. Family therapy is helpful in assessing family roles and relationships, exploring or resolving family problems, and in teaching caregivers new ways to respond to children.

A MATTER OF GOOD FIT

We sometimes *lose* clients in trauma-focused therapy for a variety of reasons. Some drop out prematurely when *anticipating* what comes next in evidence-based protocols or when our selected interventions are a "poor fit." When we expect people to *color within the lines* (Mills & Crowley, 2014), we lose flexibility and what we offer may be a poor fit to the client. Norcross and a number of contributing writers, in *Psychotherapy Relationships That Work: Evidence-Based Responsiveness* (2011), describe many variables that contribute to positive therapy outcomes, including the alliance (therapist characteristics) and unique client characteristics; they make a strong case for offering treatment that is a "good fit" for the client and adapting treatment where needed based on client characteristics. Providing services that are a good fit to clients within a strong therapeutic alliance ensures optimal therapy outcomes; further research on "good fit" will help us develop better evidence-based practices that take into account client individual differences in trauma intervention.

Norcross (2011) states on page 10, "As every clinician knows, different types of patients respond more effectively to different types of treatments and relationships." Continuing, he indicates that "the goal is for an empathic therapist to arrange for an optimal relationship collaboratively with an active client on the basis of the client's personality, culture and preferences." When a client is not responding, it behooves the therapist to consider whether he/she has preferences with which the therapy is incompatible, whether the client is "not ready" to make those changes (stage of change) or whether the client is uncomfortable with the therapist style ("reactance").

Recently, I have been considering the personality dimensions of sensitizers and repressors with regard to trauma intervention, and to EBP's more specifically. These groups have been shown to differ in their response to medical procedures based on the amount of information provided. Sensitizers overall have better outcomes when they are provided, in advance, explicit information about risks and benefits and details of medical procedures. They tend to ask questions, read extensively about their conditions and have better response during procedures and in post-procedure recovery when receiving such information. Repressors, on the other hand, have higher anxiety when provided information in advance and they tend to have the attitude that the doctor is the expert and the procedure is in the doctor's hands. Repressors avoid talking about the procedure, engage in distraction or avoidance, and do better during and after procedures when provided minimal information. When repressors are given too much information, they evidence high autonomic arousal during and after the procedure. Repressors tend to deny feelings, report being happier and better adjusted and engage in low rates of self-disclosure of feelings, whereas sensitizers are open to feelings and want to know about risks, pain, etc. Research has suggested that some people, i.e., repressors, may either need to deny, avoid or distract themselves by thinking about other things; or need a great deal of advanced warning, information, practice, reassurance and support in preparing for a stressful event.

The Blueprint of Trauma-Informed Treatment

These personality differences point to the need for "good fit" between clients and interventions. I find myself wondering if trauma intervention needs to be more sensitive to these sorts of differences and take them into consideration when planning treatment. Some trauma victims "move on," without treatment, using coping resources and developing relationships that allow them to adapt and function in a healthy manner. Some clients complete EBP such as CPT or PE and report that they "get worse;" their symptoms, when measured, show little improvement. Other clients refuse EBP or drop out of treatment at the point where exposure or trauma narrative work is to begin. On the other hand, some clients benefit from EBP and from writing and/or talking about the details of traumatic events. These possible sensitizers may find EBP's a "good fit." Perhaps we provide "too much information" to repressors and would do better to assign them to anxiety reduction protocols such as positive activities, behavioral activation, relaxation, mindfulness, breathing practice or meditation.

This is only one example of client characteristics that might impact a client's response to EBP's. Norcross (2011) describes the limitations of EBP's (p. 10), stating, "It is a false and, at times, misleading presupposition in randomized clinical trials that the patient sample is homogenous." Clients are excluded from clinical trials for EBP's for diagnoses or functioning level; exclusions include poorly developed cognitive and verbal resources, unstable functioning, substance abuse history or other mental health issues. Norcross notes that manualized EBP's do not place adequate emphasis on the therapeutic alliance and that it is important to consider not only the "what" of therapy (tools, techniques), but also the "how" (variables related to client individual/cultural differences) and "who" (therapist characteristics). I make this point because unless we assess an individual's expectation for treatment and risks/benefits of different interventions, it is difficult to select interventions that are the best "fit."

Child and adolescent evidence-based trauma therapy is a rapidly expanding field with supporting research and literature; available modalities include creative forms of CBT, play therapies and parent-child interventions. TF-CBT (Trauma-Focused Cognitive Behavioral Therapy), an excellent evidence-based program, has consistently endorsed use of play, stories and creative art when working with young children, and evidence-based play therapy is a rapidly growing field.

Evidence-based trauma psychotherapies for adults such as CPT or PE are not sufficient to address trauma symptoms given unremitting symptoms, research exclusion criteria and dropout rates. Lisa Najavits (2015), who has worked within the VA healthcare system, addresses the problem of retention and dropout from "gold standard" PTSD therapies such as Prolonged Exposure (PE) and Cognitive Processing Therapy (CPT).

She states (p. 3), "Most patients with PTSD do not stay in these treatments (PE/CPT) for their intended lengths." Also, many patients refuse to engage in these offered EBT's. In the largest VA study to date of CPT/PE, conducted by Watts et al., the median number of sessions attended was five (CPT requires 12, and PE requires 8–15). Only 2% of the sample attended an "adequate dose." In another VA study by Mott, Mondragon, Hundt, Beason-Smith, Grady and Teng (2014), CPT dropouts most commonly occurred after the 3rd session and in PE after the 2nd. Most PE dropouts were before the imaginal exposure component; 68% of Iraq/Afghanistan veterans being treated in a VA PTSD clinic dropped out prematurely. Clients who dropped out of PE or CPT treatment reported "more PTSD avoidance, greater arousal, higher overall PTSD severity, more severe depression, and more impaired social functioning at intake." Clients with a diagnosis of borderline personality disorder had double the dropout rate of those without that co-morbid diagnosis. According to Watts et. al. (2014), only 6% of VA patients received any evidence-based psychotherapy sessions for PTSD, in part due to client unwillingness to undergo the protocols.

I would like to propose that incorporating the use of stories, art and play (as well as other *holistic* modalities) into adult trauma intervention might well help us *ease* veterans into PTSD treatment, achieve the desired outcomes and reduce dropout. Adult trauma interventions are generally verbally laden, not allowing good connections between implicit and explicit processes.

Preliminary research on creative modalities has reportedly demonstrated some effectiveness at reducing PTSD symptoms, reducing severity of depression and improving quality of life. Malchiodi (2014) describes a variety of trauma-informed expressive arts interventions that may be matched developmentally to the client's current functioning; her work has included adults, combat veterans and children. Malchiodi points out that after trauma, implicit (sensory) memories

The Tools of the Trade

may activate and drive behavior without conscious awareness; symptoms represent adaptive coping strategies. When words are not available to speak of the past, creative interventions provide a means of communication and connect the implicit to the explicit. The sensory-based qualities of art, music and movement help individuals access, communicate and repair traumatic memories.

Stuckey and Nobel (2010) explore the relationship between engagement with the creative arts and health outcomes, specifically the health effects of music engagement, visual arts therapy, movement-based creative expression and expressive writing. Smyth and Nobel (2015), in an online white paper published by the Foundation for Art and Healing, point out that successful treatment of PTSD is complex and difficult, due to re-experiencing and other symptoms; they specifically address the use of creative and expressive modalities in treating PTSD. Clients may avoid PTSD treatment because of the strong negative reminders of trauma that occur during conventional treatment. Stories, art and play are well-suited for psychoeducation, indirect exposure and trauma narrative work when treating PTSD and trauma-related symptoms, without sacrificing the inherent models trauma intervention. Such interventions allow the client to more gradually confront the anxiety associated with the trauma.

I recently used *The Cracked Glass Bowl* intervention with a former non-commissioned officer veteran who had been treated with EBT's for PTSD in military service but who experienced significant residual symptoms. I explained that I chose this non-verbal intervention to bypass verbal processes and stay more in his "right brain" where sensory intrinsic memories are stored. My instructions were that he picture himself as the bowl. When he opened his eyes, he was crying; I asked him to quickly and silently draw himself as the bowl. His drawing was unusual, with large bowl fragments scattered around a small bowl. Then I interviewed him about the cracks and he named the ages at which he experienced trauma throughout his life. He named eight ages, and we agreed to work our way through them to *melt the cracks* starting in the next session. As he cried, he said, "I thought I was over it. I still have work to do. That story is ME. It is like you are in my soul. You KNOW me. I was the green bowl, you were the blue bowl support, not judging me and caring. I didn't want to talk about it, but I decided on my own to get help this time. In the oven, I saw Afghanistan; I felt the heat of the desert on my face. Then I saw myself healing and there was hope. I have had a lot of therapy, you know, and this is different."

This veteran had a breakthrough and felt understood, a clear depiction of what Siegel calls *feeling felt*. I have had similar responses from other veterans, male and female, who experienced combat or sexual trauma or went through circumstances that triggered moral injury.

In sum, creative adaptations contribute positively to trauma-informed care, and it behooves us to study ways in which our treatment might be flexible and integrated for clients of all ages.

5

THE INTEGRATIVE TOOL BAG

INTEGRATIVE PSYCHOTHERAPY

Integrative psychotherapy takes place within a conceptual and theoretical context; it is a flexible approach that combines treatment elements based on client individual and systemic needs. Although I speak to *technique*, it is with the expectation that it takes place in a positive relationship; Norcross (2011) reminds us that "the person of the psychotherapist is inextricably intertwined with the outcome of psychotherapy" (p. 7). He points out that in a large naturalistic study of 6,146 patients being treated by 581 therapists, about 5% of the outcome variation was due to therapist effects and 0% due to specific treatment methods. Therapist effects range from 5% to 9% in their contribution to outcomes. Norcross indicates that "both clinical experience and research findings underscore that the therapy relationship accounts for as much of the outcome variance as particular treatment methods" (p. 8). Also, "the largest variation in therapy outcome is accounted for by pre-existing client factors, such as motivation for change and the like. Therapist personal factors account for the second largest proportion of change, with technique variables coming in a distant third" (p. 8).

The therapy relationship is the "how" of intervention, while techniques are the "what," and it is important to recognize that "in research and theory, we often treat the how and the what- the relationship and the intervention, the interpersonal and the instrumental-as separate categories." "In reality, of course, what one does and how one does it are complementary and inseparable" (Norcross, p. 5). Regarding evidence-based protocols, he points out, "Many practitioners and researchers have found these recent efforts to codify evidence-based treatments seriously incomplete." "While scientifically laudable in their intent, these efforts have largely ignored the therapy relationship and the person of the therapist" (p. 7). When we engage in integrative approaches, especially in trauma intervention, where there is wide variability in client symptoms and presentation, what we provide is more likely to be a "good fit" for our clients.

In his comprehensive edited volume overview of "evidence-based responsiveness," Norcross (2011) discusses such factors as the therapeutic alliance, cohesion (group therapy), empathy, goal consensus/collaboration, positive regard/affirmation, congruence/genuineness, accessing client feedback, repairing ruptures in alliance and managing countertransference. He and the contributing writers stress the need to provide treatment that is a "good fit" for clients based on individual differences across client variables such as reactance/resistance level, stages of change, client preferences, culture, coping style, expectations, attachment style and religion/spirituality. Norcross points out that cultural metaphors, symbols and cultural concepts can contribute to the alliance, and he indicates that culturally sensitive adaptations of EBP results in better outcomes. Stories, art and play contribute to the development of a strong therapeutic alliance as well as to the change process. These modalities are most effective when used in conjunction with, and as components of, culturally sensitive, "good fit," collaborative, evidence-based interventions.

The Tools of the Trade

Most trauma-informed therapists would consider themselves to be integrative practitioners. Unlike "eclecticism," integrative therapy weaves together theory, techniques and common factors across treatments (Norcross & Goldfried, 2005). Clients benefit from integrative therapies that teach coping skills, improve the capacity for attachment and interpersonal relationships and calm physiological arousal by altering neurological pathways (Pernicano, 2014a, 2015a,b).

Langtree and Briere (2017) adopt an integrative approach to addressing complex trauma with children and families, also referred to as Integrative Treatment of Complex Trauma-Child (ITCT-C). Their model integrates a variety of theoretical and clinical approaches in addressing the needs of clients with complex trauma; the approach is systemic, culturally sensitive and relationally based, including aspects of attachment theory and trauma intervention models. Their integrative approach includes a strong emphasis on symbolic and expressive play, individual sessions with the child, as well as collateral and family sessions. Due to cross generational trauma, the caregivers are often provided trauma recovery intervention of their own. These authors discuss factors associated with complex trauma and resultant symptoms, with suggestions for distress reduction and affect regulation. The authors offer ways in which children can learn to delay expression of tension reducing or avoidance behaviors such as aggression, sexual reactivity, self-injurious behaviors, overeating, stealing, sudden and loud disorganized play, etc.

The article *Integrative Play Therapy* (Rocky Mountain Play Therapy Institute, Alberta, Canada, see www.RMPTI.com), describes an integrative approach, the *Play Therapy Dimensions Model*, that provides a framework from which to conceptualize the therapy process and to evaluate interventions when working with children. Yasenik and Gardner (2004) provide a detailed description of this model which allows therapists to examine the "Who, What, Why and How" of therapy; the authors consider it a "decision-making model" whereby interventions are tailored to the client across theories and techniques.

Integrative approaches for adults include some evidence-based treatments such as ACT, with components of mindfulness, metaphor, CBT and affirmation; stages of change models; and the model suggested by Siegel (2010), whereby the entire therapy process is focused on a hierarchy of interventions for neurobiological integration. Siegel speaks to ways in which insecure adult attachment impacts the therapy relationship and the need for the therapist to be flexible, in order to help the client move to a place of regulation and integration. Some adult clients are more chaotic and dysregulated in their cognitive and emotional functioning, while others are over-regulated, rigid, over-controlled and inflexible. Through an attuned relationship and carefully planned therapy activities, the client "moves to the middle" of this continuum.

THE THERAPEUTIC STANCE

Those who provide trauma-informed therapy require resilience, patience and understanding that what has been years in the making, may be changed or lost and is not so simply undone or restored. Woodman and Mellick (p. 15) speak to courage and grieving in the healing process.

> *Healing does not mean wallowing in or identifying with injury. Nor does it mean defensive inaction. It means having the courage to see, acknowledge, grieve and repair the holes ourselves with, if we are fortunate, loving help from others. It means moving on, patches and all.*

From a Jungian perspective, metaphor, dream processing and storytelling are integral to self-growth and therapeutic change; the writings of Woodman and Mellick (p. 27) overflow with wisdom and insight that reflect attitudes and values at the heart of trauma-informed care.

> *Let the metaphors on these pages dance through your imagination. Allow the images to take residence in consciousness, heart and body. Once embraced, they will continue to grow in the chrysalis. One day they will emerge, mature, as butterflies in your psychic life.*

As a bio-psycho-social practitioner of integrative psychotherapy, my clinical work involves attachment development, trance-induction, neurobiological regulation, CBT, interpersonal engagement, mindfulness, playfulness, storytelling, metaphor, narrative and systems thinking

The Integrative Tool Bag

with a pinch of Gestalt tossed in. With my clients, who I am is as important as what I do. We recognize that the therapeutic relationship is a primary agent of change (Norcross, 2011), and more recently it has been suggested that therapist variables of "good fit" to client characteristics are a likely source of unexplained variance in the change process.

Attunement, resonance and appropriate boundaries are components of the therapist-client attachment relationship; regardless of theoretical orientation, the therapist establishes a therapeutic alliance that is a good fit to the client's current functioning (Siegel, 2010). A sensitive therapist follows the client's lead and works within what is referred to as the Zone of Proximal Development, i.e., nudging the client forward "just beyond" where he or she is comfortable now. Per Siegel, the therapist does not stay in "easy-land" (keeping things totally comfortable, backing off out of sympathy or joining the client in his or her views of impossibility), nor does he/she push the client beyond the bounds of current developmental resources.

Our clients *find* aspects of themselves through integrative treatment that includes stories, art and play; identify with those aspects; and then are freed up to communicate more openly about personal trauma. Van der Kolk (2014) compares the mind to a mosaic, providing a good metaphor for inner parts that are wounded and need integration. Trauma contributes to the fragmentation and compartmentalization of self; and stories, art and play are helpful modalities for the representation of these self-parts and with the integration of self. Erickson was a master at unwrapping client "gifts," always with an attitude of kind curiosity and interest. Erickson seemed at times to be a mind-reader with his uncanny sensitivity to what his clients brought him. Like Erickson, we can "wonder" aloud and collaboratively share our tentative hypotheses with our clients.

A client sometimes presents material before he or she understands the full meaning. If the therapist, who is *pleased at being so smart and insightful*, offers an interpretation (before the client is ready to receive it), *it robs the client of self-discovery*. It is satisfying to wait until the client sees the dots in a row, connects them, and exclaims "I think there's a connection here!" Once the client has made a connection, the therapist can help the client put the dots in a row, but it is up to the client, with therapist's help, to connect the dots. Conversely, sometimes the therapist is working his/her own agenda (moving in the wrong direction) and misses some of the client's dots, and at those times, the client is likely to pull the therapist back on track in one way or another.

In developing a strong therapeutic alliance, the therapist speaks the unspeakable truth (gives permission for honesty), models imperfection ("I'm not sure," "I really don't know"), remains curious, shows empathy and compassion, and remains somewhat matter-of-fact in the face of shocking disclosures. Trauma work requires patience, tolerance for personal discomfort and the capacity for "invitation" as well as "gentle nudge." In the face of a dare, we dare to speak up, to challenge and to affirm.

When clients experience a connection with us, they *feel felt* (Siegel, 2010). In *Mindsight* (2010), Siegel discusses how therapy improves neurobiological integration. A well-integrated therapist is adaptable, flexible and organized, able to meet clients where they are. We match our interventions to what an individual can receive. As Siegel notes, due to differences in brain functioning, individuals vary with regards to their degree of rigidity and flexibility, spontaneity and structure. From birth forward, we develop bottom (primitive, survival) to top (abstract, advanced, cognitive), and right (limbic, sensory) to left (executive functioning, planning, sequencing). Trauma and stress can result in rigid reliance on primitive survival modes and on automatic emotional, fight-or-flight limbic reactivity without cognitive control, but it can also result in cognitive rigidity and compulsive attention to detail at the expense of relationships. By meeting the client where he or she is during therapy, we can help that person move toward balance of flexibility with organization.

THE TOOLS THEMSELVES

Mills and Crowley (2014) point out what is lost when we insist that children color within the lines: "We are taught to stay within the lines, yet to be creative and original at the same time" (p. xxi). It can be very perplexing for clients when we ignore or bypass their comments, insights and

The Tools of the Trade

wishes in order to "color within the lines" and lose the opportunity to individualize care. There are those who think inside the box and those who think outside the box, but at times we need to remember that there is no box other than that which we have created. Stories, art and play are the tools with which our clients access, engage with and explore trauma-related material using right brain processes, manage the material with the left brain and find themselves more balanced and integrated. Smyth and Noble suggest that expressive writing, expressive group therapy, mindfulness training and an array of creative interventions such as art, music and body-oriented practices allow representation of trauma without verbal descriptions of the event(s). Visual and auditory materials help clients symbolize the pain and suffering of trauma. Some individuals prefer drawing, sculpting or painting over writing, because less anxiety is aroused. It has been my experience that clients doing story, art, puppet or sand tray work that is directly related to trauma or painful relationship problems display high arousal and anxiety while engaging in those activities, because they remember and re-experience during the activities, but they manage the response through the activity and the therapist's presence. It is easier to talk about something once it has been put to paper, story or sand movie. As noted by one young client, "First I draw it, then I say it!"

Interpreting a child's play or an adult client's metaphor is not unlike dream interpretation, whereby dreams reveal life parallels, emotional intensity, themes and symbolic representation. Dreams may be "parallel" yet not "literal" representations of reality. For example, I recently spoke with a military retiree who, as a teacher, often found the classroom too "noisy," chaotic and overwhelming. He had been having dreams about "taking fire in the chest, as if being pummeled" through his body armor. He had not been wounded while on deployment but his dreams felt "so real." I suggested he might feel verbally pummeled by the kids at school, as if he was taking fire in the form of their rapid-fire comments and questions, resulting in sensory overload. In graduate school, I participated in research on the interpretation of Adlerian Early Recollections, and the process is similar, whereby recollections are analyzed for emotional tone (positive or negative), the nature of the persons in them (authority figures, loved ones) and the expectations or outcomes conveyed by the recollection. In the same manner, art and play may be interpreted based on patterns or themes that emerge and are evaluated for emotional tone (positive, negative, intensity), response to stress, coping ability, interpersonal roles, degree of self-control/impulsivity, expectancy/outcome and barriers to change.

This book is not intended to revisit all the tools and techniques available for trauma-informed treatment, and each therapist will select his or her own. There are numerous publications and schools of thought about sand tray, puppet play, expressive art and storytelling; the reader is directed to the larger literature in these areas. I will highlight some of my "go to" techniques/ tools (ones that I used with the cases in this book) that result in client engagement, facilitate therapeutic rapport and offer information about client problems and progress. A therapist needs a reliable tool bag for use with a variety of clients; these may be used (interpreted, structured, positioned) within the reader's chosen theoretical orientation.

A therapeutic tool bag might include such things as *fiddle* toys, mindful items for distraction (glitter globes, ideally unbreakable), a dry erase board, a variety of toys, some sensory materials (Tibetan singing bowl, sound/noise machine, kinetic sand, etc.), as well as art and expressive materials for children and adults. I have a pretty extensive set of small characters (human, animal, fantasy), fences, trees and weapons that I keep in labeled drawers for use in the sand tray (no shelf space available). Some clients set up stories on the table or floor as opposed to the sand, and other than not being able to "bury" them, the same end is achieved. I also have an extensive puppet collection with many of the animals portrayed in my stories: eagle, kangaroo, black bear, brown bear, dragon, shark, mouse, butterfly, squirrel, turtle, alligator, dogs, cats, ostrich, peacock and lizards, among others. A therapist need not have so many, as clients will select from what is offered. It is important to have specific categories of puppets, such as "vulnerable," "mean," "scary," "lovable," "helper" and "powerful"; in that regard, the provider has an array to set up dialectical stories of good-evil, victim-perpetrator, loving-hurting, etc.

I keep the dry erase board out and markers accessible as clients often spontaneously engage in free drawing or ask to do Squiggles stories. I have a brass mermaid on my desktop, a sign on the wall that says, "Be Still and Know . . .," blankets and a couple of cuddly stuffed animals. I have frozen gel packs for mood regulation, a sound machine (nature and white noise) for focusing

The Integrative Tool Bag

and relaxation, and a Tibetan Singing Bowl on a side table for mindful calming. There are "client books" within reach about anger, trauma, loss, etc., and I have an old xylophone that clients use when they choose to be less verbal in expressing emotions.

Tools help me assess core feelings and concerns, teach or suggest other ways of looking at things, clarify and explore the client's perspective, and/or discover solutions to problems. I tend to use these tools in client-centered supportive interventions and during structured play or cognitive behavioral activities. With individuals and families, I facilitate nurture, self-care and secure attachment development. Using stories, art and play helps me better understand how the client views/feels about the past, what is going on with the client now and what the client anticipates in the future. The reader may use the techniques in different ways and from alternate theoretical perspectives; he or she may find them useful with a wide range of clients, across the lifespan.

Dry Erase Board and Dry Erase Squiggle Stories

Storytelling with dry erase board drawing helps to build rapport, as a session warm up, and for free drawing while I am talking to family members, with or without Squiggles, a small scribble that is turned into a picture (Winnicott, 1953). I use what I refer to as Squiggles Stories(See Appendix for detailed steps of the intervention) for non-directive exploration of feelings and concerns, for problem-solving, to begin trauma narrative work and to evaluate change in attitudes and beliefs, with individual and families.

Dry Erase Squiggles Stories is useful for a number of reasons:

- It is a good icebreaker.
- It is interactive and provides information about client's capacity for shared play and cooperation.
- It is a window into the current state of the client.
- It may provide information about client concerns and emotions.
- It provides clients a little distance to write down or draw what they may not yet be able to talk about.
- It allows for "correction" as the client draws, helpful for the compulsive, perfectionist.
- It has no pre-planned goal and no right or wrong.
- It can be done without artistic ability. It helps to say this up front to client and family members.
- It can be adapted for use with a family. When doing it with a family, the client is the *expert* who introduces family members to the task, with the help of the therapist.
- It allows client to add new details and tell the story a little at a time. Therapist can ask questions throughout.
- It allows the client to relax and find comfort in the "make-believe" aspect of the task.
- It reveals aspects of clients and their family relationships.
- It reveals such things as control/ impulsiveness, developmental level of drawing and coordination (in the drawing itself), emotional intensity (use of color), concerns and wishes.
- It provides new hypotheses. Many clients reveal new information in their drawings or stories.
- It can be preserved by photo for later follow-up. At a later point in time, a drawing or story can be revisited.
- It allows the client to "contain" uncomfortable feelings and thoughts, and client can erase before leaving. This is a cleansing process, as the simple act of erasing leaves the client with a clean slate and opportunity to move on.

If a therapist uses this activity regularly, changes in the client's drawing and stories often reflect current status and "shifts" in the client's functioning. The use of colors and style reflect level of regulation and organization; story themes reflect client's mood and concerns, especially those of an interpersonal nature. Themes, coping and decision-making in the stories will reflect client progress.

In 1980, I saw one of my first child clients, a 6-year-old boy with a bad temper who was defiant with his parents; he struggled with self-control. I had read Richard Gardner's *Stories About the Real World* (1980) after my master's degree training and started using Gardner's mutual storytelling technique (1971). This boy and I often ended our sessions with a Squiggle drawing (Winnicott, 1953). He liked closing his eyes, putting marker to the paper, drawing a simple Squiggle and handing me the marker. This little boy liked telling his own stories to his drawings.

43

The Tools of the Trade

That day, my Squiggle ended up as his dragon. I asked if he might tell me a story about his dragon, and that is how my version of Squiggles Stories was born. His story was about a dragon who was a bully, burned things up and had no friends; he terrorized everyone and blew fire at them "just for fun." The boy had denied the need for friends in earlier sessions, and he was fairly non-compliant at home and school. His story was full of bravado; as the dragon, he was defiant and powerful.

I did not know the source of his reactions, but I recognized his unrealized need for better self-control and suspected he would not "give up" control unless he "gained" something in return; I told a story back to him, attempting a shift. My story was about a dragon that *enjoyed* his fire and didn't want to give it up, *but* he started to be a little lonely. No one liked him because he burned things up, and at first he didn't care. But he wanted other dragons to admire him and to be impressed with his fire. That was not going to happen if no one wanted to hang out around him. The young dragon tells an older dragon that he wants to keep his fire, to impress and to be safe. An older dragon tells him it is not his fire that is bad; rather, it is how he uses it. (At that, the boy's eyes got big and he looked at me curiously.)

I stopped my story there and asked if he had any suggestions for the dragon, ideas about how the dragon could keep his fire but use it in new and different ways. At first he said the dragon "didn't care" and "doesn't want to change." With gentle probing about the dragon being "a little lonely," he was willing to work with me on this.

Together, we came up with "good" things a dragon might do with fire:

- Roasting marshmallows.
- Lighting a campfire.
- Warming people's hands in the cold.
- Clearing a field so they could plant it.
- Letting others roast hotdogs in his mouth.

Next, we came up with fun things the dragon might do to make dragon friends:

- Invite them to play dragon ball with balls of fire.
- Play nicely with them at school during recess.
- Take them for a ride on his back over the mountains and down in the valley (before doing the campfire).

He enjoyed this, so we practiced him being the dragon. I had no play therapy training at that point, but it seemed to work and certainly motivated him to practice between sessions. It was very interesting that as this boy's stories began to change, he became more motivated to work on anger management skills and social communication. His drawing and my counter-story became the first metaphorical story I wrote for children, entitled, *The Dragon's Fire* (Pernicano, 2010a, 2014a), and it is very helpful with children who struggle with anger, sharing or self-control. For other examples of Dry Erase Squiggles Stories, see the case examples.

Recently a fellow psychologist and former graduate student sent me a picture (Figure 5.1) drawn by her 5-year-old client. A mother had been struggling to explain to her daughter why the drug-using father was so unpredictable in his comings and goings. The child missed her father and was sad that she could not count on him to be there for her. "I thought you would like to know," said my colleague, "that I told her the story of Velma Crowe. She drew this after hearing the story. Velma is the pink bird, and the others are her babies. She told me that her Daddy is like Velma."

Velma Crowe's Sticky Situation (2010a, 2014a) is an attachment-based story about a fun-loving yet irresponsible bird that enjoys the nightlife and is not ready to be a mom, but her babies are ready to hatch. She and her babies go through difficult struggles until Velma, with a little help from her friend, finally learns to settle down and put their needs first. My colleague relayed that after hearing and talking about the story, the little girl understood that her daddy was like Velma, wild and free and not ready to be a dad. Velma, upper left, is in bright pink, flying off and "doing her own thing." Her babies on the ground are in brown, purple and green and the ones in the sky are blue and red.

The Integrative Tool Bag

FIGURE 5.1

Puppets and Sand Tray

Puppets are used in directive or non-directive play therapy, mostly with children and families, but the sand tray may be used with clients of all ages. For detailed information about sand tray work, the reader is referred to play therapy books with chapters on sand tray intervention and to other books that are specifically written about sand tray work.

Puppet play is akin to creating a story or play/role play using puppets, and the puppets selected can depict a variety of emotions and actions. Puppet play can be non-scripted or pre-scripted. I may ask the child to select characters from a story I have read or told, then act it out with the child, with caregiver involvement if it is a family session. Puppet play is also a good modality to use in a group for child trauma recovery. Children sometimes spontaneously add new elements, which allow the therapist to form hypotheses. For example, when acting out the story *Safety in Numbers*, one little boy I worked with repeatedly selected a shark puppet for the main character. The shark repeatedly took a small fish puppet into his mouth and spit him out. He explained to me that his dad had been like that, sometimes being nice and sometimes mean.

I have sometimes used puppets to assess how a child depicts adults in his or her life. In that case, I ask the child to select a variety of puppets that represent family members. One child client had previously talked about various aspects of her mother and I asked her to pick puppets to show me what that looked like. She articulated her thoughts and feelings about her mother's behavior and moods; she demonstrated in a puppet show how she wished for things to be different (see *Mom of a Different Color*).

Sand tray work may be a symbolic or literal representation of life, and it is important to photograph a picture of the finished scene (or scenes, if the client tells a story or "shoots a movie" and re-arranges the characters throughout). A sand tray may be used in non-directive or directive ways, to depict such things as a difficult situation, a struggle within the self (battle), family relationships, the past, the present, the future, symbolic representation or conflict resolution. The client has the freedom to select objects and characters to represent what he or she wishes.

The Tools of the Trade

Storytelling can be integrated into both puppet and sand tray play. If a client creates a scene or selects puppets, he or she can be asked to "make a movie" that tells a story and show the therapist the story. Children are uncanny at putting family members into their "movies" and it is a safe way to use the "movie" to communicate something important to the caregiver (see *The Bloody Bats*). Some children involve the therapist in the movie, and others prefer to act it out alone. Cases later in the book give examples of sand and puppet interventions.

Nesting Dolls

Several of the clients described later in this book did excellent therapy work with nesting dolls, a tool I use with both child and adult clients in directive and non-directive ways. Although this is a less frequently used tool in play therapies, I have found it very helpful when getting a life history and establishing a time line for life events. It allows me to address "internal family systems" or "part-self" issues. Over the years, I have collected a variety of doll sets, some animals and some people, most purchased online, and clients can select the ones they wish to work with in session. Clients of all ages are charmed by the nesting dolls, and most can't resist taking a closer look.

The first step is to invite the client to take them apart. Almost without fail, clients say "here's the baby!" (with a smile) when they get to the last doll, then tenderly cradle the "baby." The dolls seem to evoke a natural empathy and emotional response, and awareness of the smallest wooden doll's *vulnerability*. There are many ways in which the dolls may be used, for example, the therapist can ask a client to "anchor" each age before going further and may suggest the age range (birth to your age now, birth to age 12) or leave it open.

Benefits of using nesting dolls include:

- The different sizes lend themselves to being assigned different ages. *Seeing* the size differential can be helpful when the client blames him or herself for the abuse or neglect.
- The dolls can represent different persons or different ages of the same person.
- The dolls pull for symbolic representation of family or abuse relationships.
- The dolls pull for inner representation of self, at different ages and stages of life. Therapist can ask the client to assign each doll an age and describe self at that age. The client may be asked, "What did *she* (point to doll) most need at that age? What was hardest at that age? What was the best/worst thing that happened at that age?"
- The dolls allow some emotional space and distance when working on traumatic material.
- The dolls may be used to tell a story of abuse. Ask which doll(s) carry the pain and what is the pain for each.
- The dolls can be used to clarify developmental details, such as ages at which trauma occurred. Ask the client to pick the five "worst" ages growing up, times you were hurt, ignored, threatened or scared, then point to the dolls and tell me which ages you choose.
- The dolls can be used to teach self-care, internal family systems and empowerment.

I contacted a client's mother about her daughter's case, and the child, now age 10, sent me a message. We terminated treatment about three years ago; the client wanted me to know that she thinks about the nesting doll cats because of the "little mouse" that was inside the last cat. She always laughed, thinking it was so funny to find a mouse inside four cats. Sometimes she protected and nurtured the "little mouse" and other times mouse got eaten by the cat, a symbolic depiction for an abuse victim. Clients respond differently to that nesting set, as some depict the mouse eaten by the cats, and others see it as cleverly outsmarting the cats, hiding beneath their very eyes. I assured her that I still had the cats and thanked her for sharing her memory.

Up the Mountain

I use many techniques that incorporate metaphor and storytelling, and some are applicable to a wide variety of problems with clients across the lifespan. One guided imagery technique I developed is called *Up the Mountain*; it is helpful with clients who struggle with residual

46

The Integrative Tool Bag

emotions and memories that interfere with sleep, coping, etc. See Appendix for the narrative script. This intervention is a form of graduated indirect exposure that combines drawing with guided imagery and is especially useful for anxiety reduction or trauma narrative work. *Up the Mountain* involves purposefully caging "perpetrators," "stress" and/or "bad memories" at the foot of a mountain so that the client can climb the mountain, gain perspective and manage anxiety with perspective. The client can practice and use this technique outside session to relax, cope with anxiety and quickly change perspective when triggered. The task also provides useful information for the therapist about client perception of the problem or problem intensity.

The therapist teaches and practices diaphragmatic breathing and relaxation with the client sometime prior to the climb, because anxiety reduction is a component of the intervention. To begin *Up the Mountain*, instructions are given for the drawing task, after which the client draws his or her picture on the dry erase board. The instructions are somewhat open-ended about the drawing, so the clients add different components to their drawings, and the therapist notes symbolic elements and details that are unique to the client. It is important to ask specifically about the chosen guards (and how many), locks and how many, cage materials, number of chains, means of any restraint inside the cage and safety parameters. Clients have created guards such as lions, leopards, a huge eagle with a sharp beak, alligator with big teeth, snakes, wrestlers or power lifters, Rocky the boxer, police and gorillas that threw poop down on the cage. One client put a fire pit under the cage, just in case. Only the client and the guards have the key to the locks. The cage could be sound proof if needed to block "mean voices" from the angry perpetrators.

By exploring the drawing and asking such questions the therapist can estimate the intensity of affect and residual feelings and thoughts about the trauma. The therapist guides the client through the *climb;* many clients enter a trance state during the climb, and therapist will observe eye movements and deeper breathing. While going *Up the Mountain*, therapist uses language that pulls for visual cues, realization of safety, feeling of relief, feelings of peace, and calming sounds, sights and smells (water, flowers, trees, birds, evergreens, sunshine), as well as calming sensations (feeling a nice breeze, sunshine on the face). The chosen means of climbing by clients have included jet packs, power ski's, motorized bike, bicycle, escalator, beaming up, walking and elevator. Because it is magic, the client can travel quickly if needed.

The client is pointedly directed to distance between "now" and "then" (the cage) and the possibility of relief or relaxation at the changing perspective. Once the drawing is finished, therapist clarifies the elements of the picture with questions as needed and takes a photo of the picture.

I have used this technique with good results with a variety of anxious or traumatized clients, both adults and children, combined with breathing, and guided imagery and relaxation techniques. Clients included a man who had intrusive memories of witnessing a traumatic accident and feared flying (needed for his job); a teen with misophonia (worked in collaboration with her audiologist) and a variety of clients with past trauma.

I had been doing the *Up the Mountain* activity with a brother and sister of a sibling group we were treating. The boy, who had been very closed about his past abuse, drew the first picture below. He put a sea of fire underneath the cage that had 85 locks. He put a giant spider in the cage to guard them, "to suck their blood out if they try to escape." He wrapped his perpetrators in duct tape and deadly snakes were coiled around the chains, "just in case" they ever got out. The cage is suspended with thick chains above a pit of fire. He placed himself and his siblings inside a jet-propelled vehicle with an impenetrable force field, and he operated the controls, representing his caretaking role with his siblings and his feelings of responsibility for their safety. Another guard stood on a fire-proof platform near the cage. His picture clearly portrayed his emotional intensity and fear that so often was displayed as anger. This very angry young trauma victim raged at his memory of helplessness in the face of danger. What is interesting is that face-to-face, he denied fear and would not talk specifically about his abuse at the time he drew this picture. The details of the picture suggest that his abuse elicited significant vulnerability and protective vigilance. (See Appendix for full-color version of this picture.)

47

The Tools of the Trade

FIGURE 5.2 Reprinted with permission from Wiley (see Acknowledgments)

The boy's younger sister drew the next picture. When she drew this and told her story, she said that the cage needed 2,000 locks and 80,000 chains. The cage was "bulletproof." She blindfolded the "mean" perpetrators, saying "They don't deserve to see this beautiful place," and covered their mouths, hands and feet in duct tape "so I won't hear their mean words." She wrapped them up very tight and threw them in the cage, then put a spider in the corner to keep watch, but said she did not want "to hurt them" by yelling or shouting at them. "Let's be nice," she said. The guards are a bear, turtle, eagle (to carry them off if they get out), a lion and a snake. The lion guarded from the left, "to grab them by the throats if they escape." She added a rabbit guard "to yell at them." Next, she put the cage and guards inside another "bulletproof bubble" saying, "If they ever got out, there is one more protection." The details she added to her picture suggest a high level of fear and protective vigilance. She stated, "We are safe at the top of the mountain. They are mean. We are throwing lion, eagle and snake poop down on them."

The girl's mountain captures the perspective and her need for distance—you can see her (and one other unidentified person) at the top of a very tall mountain. Her mountain scene was dreamlike in appearance, with lovely pastel colors, somewhat at odds with the intense fear implied by the details in her drawing, yet at the same time consistent with her dissociative tendencies. It is interesting that in her next session, she asked if we could cut the tape off the perpetrators: "They are out of my mind now. I'll take the tape off; they can stay in the cage. I don't like to hurt anyone." She said she does not like to "feel anger—I want to be nice."

Her description shows ambivalence and discomfort with her own anger toward the abusers, alternately wanting to forgive them/take off the tape/be nice and having a lion present who could "rip their throats out." Her fear is palpable in the protections added to the drawing, at the same time, she retreats into fantasy without fully expressing her fear and anger. See Appendix for full-color version of this picture.

After she drew her mountain, she re-enacted the scene, pulling out a small birdcage, selecting puppet guards and thoroughly wrapping doll house dolls in duct tape. In the foster home, this little girl presented as a pseudo mature child who helped the foster parent, offered advice and kept a cheerful outlook but tended to dissociate when triggered. She loved animals, championed the weak and took up for others who were bullied. Over time, her anger and fear would emerge as the dissociative system revealed itself.

The Integrative Tool Bag

FIGURE 5.3 Reprinted with permission from Wiley (See Acknowledgments)

It needs to be said that artwork and story themes can stir up strong feelings and memories in caregivers or family members who experienced past trauma. Therapists need to be aware that a child's stories and art or play can elicit strong parallel feelings in their caregivers. When the caregiver has past trauma, the child material can be painful and very triggering for the adult under those circumstances. This was the case with the foster mother who, with her husband, cared for these two children; they were part of a large sibling group, each of whom had experienced complex trauma. After sessions, I typically reviewed progress with the foster mother and/or father.

This particular week, after the *Up the Mountain* activity, I showed the foster mother the pictures and pointed out that although the children were given the same instructions, their drawings reflected very different responses to their life experiences. She asked questions about the process and looked at the drawings. When I explained about the cage, she started, visibly blanched and said, in horror,

> Oh my God! I used to draw pictures like that as a child! I always locked my older brother in a cage in my pictures—I was so afraid of him, and he was so mean. I think he sexually abused me.

I helped her calm down and suggested that drawing her brother in a cage did not *mean* she was sexually abused. Over time with her therapist, however, she became more, not less, aware of ways in which her brother had abused her. The picture had triggered strong emotion related to her abuse. Furthermore, her own abuse history made her quite vulnerable to triggered anxiety, sadness and anger as the children continued to deal with their prior abuse and as we worked as a team to ensure family stability.

The mom was empathic and protective of her foster children, and she responded to therapy activities emotionally both as a caring parent and as someone recovering from her own abuse. In the face of aggression directed at her by the children, fear, flight and fight were easily activated, and she had to work hard to self-regulate. This remains for me a powerful example of how cross generational issues can be triggered and addressed.

The Tools of the Trade

Following are some other examples of *Up the Mountain* by clients of varying ages, with individual differences, including varying uses of color and organization, unique to the individual. Once the "something" has been caged, it is much easier for some clients to talk about the fear and vulnerability they experience.

This first client's guards were said to be "invisible." At the foot of the mountain the cage is labeled "RIP." For this adult client, he put to rest his intrusive memories.

Figure 5.5 reflects the client's intense fear and need for self-protection. He surrounded his mountain in a shield of fire. In the middle is a transporter, so that if the perpetrator gets loose

FIGURE 5.4

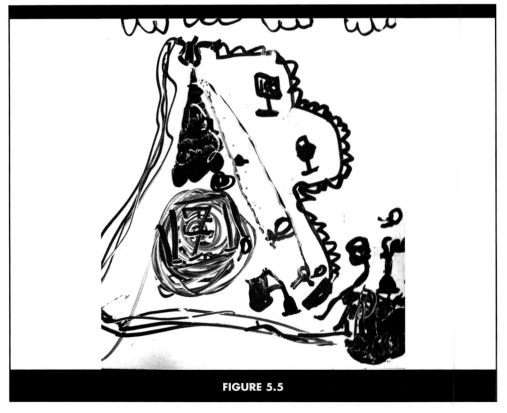

FIGURE 5.5

50

The Integrative Tool Bag

and tries to climb, he gets sucked into a "black hole" to be transported to another universe. He was quite emotionally dysregulated and hyper-aroused.

In Figure 5.6 the cage is depicted as a vault, and the client holds a blade as a backup weapon. Each lookout has a ball of fire beneath it that can be dropped in case of the perpetrator's escape.

Figure 5.7 depicts a mountain that turned into a rainbow after the perpetrators were "gone." The client added a lake "where you can throw bad feelings and memories," and it is marked "No Fishing" (see *The Burden Bag*, Pernicano, 2010a, 2010b, 2014a).

This older client's well-chained cage in Figure 5.8 held very dark memories and was guarded by a combat helicopter and armed soldiers.

A young female client drew the mountain in Figure 5.9. She had experience her mother's death in an accident as well as later sexual abuse. At the top, she shouts, "Ity bite ANT!" in triumph.

FIGURE 5.6

FIGURE 5.7

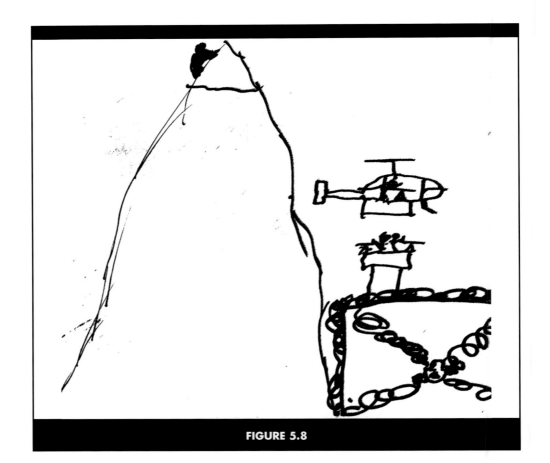

FIGURE 5.8

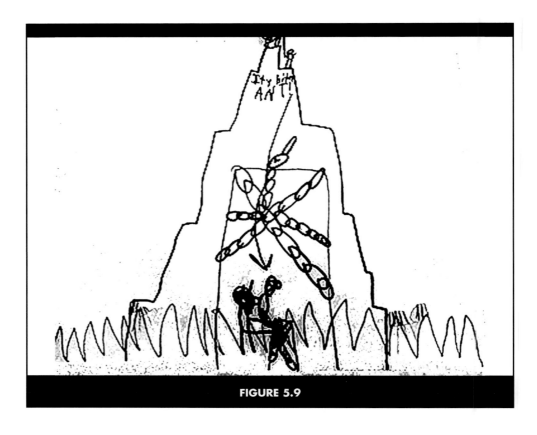

FIGURE 5.9

The little girl who drew the mountain above had witnessed her mother's death in a car accident at age 3, while she sat strapped in a carseat. Her stepfather had been driving when the car skidded out of control. Not long after her mother's death she had been sexually abused on a visit with her biological dad. Her maternal grandparents were now raising her and her older brother who had autism.

This little girl had been "frozen" and in "flight" since moving to her new home, and she tended to "tune out" or dissociate in the face of stress. She did not make eye contact, chewed her lip compulsively and had dificulty making friends at school. Her anxiety prevented her from speaking up about boundary violations and intimidation at the hands of her older developmentally delayed brother. She did not know how to "tell," i.e., use her voice to speak up, nor was she spontaneous in her play.

She responded well to trauma-informed treatment, with playful relaxation exercises, bubble blowing, and drawing on the dry erase board. Together, we played out *The Burden Bag* (see Pernicano, 2010a, 2010b, 2014a), and she threw worries in a lake where the sign said "No Fishing." We developed relaxing, nurturing bedtime routines, and she became more spontaneous in session, with some giggles and laughter. Eventually she was ready, and perhaps eager, to talk more about her lingering fear and anger over the past. The first memories she shared were about the car accident and one day, she drew her mother in the car, red blood all over. For several sessions, she talked about missing her mom and then about the accident and what she remembered; she said, "It was an accident, he didn't mean to crash the car." She was relieved to erase the dry erase board at that session's end.

As her confidence grew, she started telling me about her past abuse by "T." She had intrusive thoughts that he might come back, and she sometimes dreamed about him. The day she did *Up the Mountain* she was bold and empowered as she locked "T" in the cage, saying, "This cage has NO WINDOWS!" As she drew her picture on the dry erase board, she smiled and said, "I'm using my imagination!" She fastened his hands with duct tape and said, "He's frowning. His arms are behind the chair," then added, "There are 13,050 locks." I have found that the number of locks chosen correponds to the degree of client's fear or anger. She stated, "The Security is a Lion and he has Super Paws! The pink is hate, Dr. Pat, chains made out of hate." The perpetrator's cage and feet were secured with the pink chains of hate.

We traveled up the mountain, stopping at each lookout. At the top of the mountain, she said, "I'm adding an extra locked switch on top—just in case." She drew two people at the top of the mountain and then added a third, saying, "We're holding hands. That's me, brother and you." She wrote, "Ity, bitey, ANT!" and said, with a proud smile, "We're shouting it!" I suggested we pretend to do that and we stood up on top of the love seat. Several times we shouted down at the picture on the floor: "You're just an itty bitty ant!" and each time she laughed gleefully as if to say, "So there!" I think of her today as I see pink female empowerment, a great reminder of the progress she made so many years ago.

PART II

CASE EXAMPLES AND APPLICATIONS

6

OVERVIEW OF CASE DEVELOPMENT

It is the therapist's job to recognize that which is meaningful and help our clients discover what is blocking growth, change or personal well-being. Children may mimic or enact exactly what they have seen or experienced, and they also creatively develop their own narratives. What is said and what is *not said* (in art, stories and play) must be received and recognized as meaningful before it can be utilized. Adolescents communicate through their art, music and interests. They are not always clear about that is meaningful for them, and they may openly negate obvious connections when suggested by a therapist or parent. They respond well to interventions that allow them the freedom to maintain autonomy and self-direction. Creative modalities are a good fit for the developmental experiences of adolescents. Adult clients become active, energized and more engaged when I introduce stories or hands-on interventions. As a former part-time associate professor at Spalding University's Clinical Faculty, I remember the hands-on ways in which my students learned and how playful and active they became when tests of reading knowledge included games or contests.

Clients may not have the "words" or cognitive ability to adequately tell us what is going on. Others are so bright and educated that we need to get them out of the "rational" brain in order to access emotions and flexibility. Many clients who have experienced trauma benefit from a gentler or more gradual approach to trauma narrative work, and symptom externalization or story discussion bridges them to more detailed disclosures.

To protect privacy, some details of the cases that follow (names, ages) have been changed for privacy and some have been "reconstructed" from therapist's notes and memories, thus not meant to be literal transcripts of care. Having worked in outpatient and residential settings, I selected cases from each setting. Some case studies that follow will be fairly complete in which the bulk of the treatments included metaphor, stories, art and play. The most relevant details and pertinent details of each case will be shared. Other cases will be "snippets" that will illustrate the power of a particular metaphor, technique or therapeutic story for a specific client.

As I reviewed my case files and documentation, I selected cases with a variety of responses to recent or past traumatic events. Clients or guardians were contacted for permission to share artwork and case details, and I am grateful for the trust and difficult work of my clients. The cases provide a good overview of the work I do and include some of my most memorable clients. When I asked the clients and caregivers about sharing their art or case details, they were eager to do this so that others might benefit. Not every client is artistic or creative in the manner of those in the book; however, techniques such as Dry Erase Squiggle Stories can be used with any client or family regardless of artistic ability.

As always, abuse is troubling and some details in the cases may be disturbing to readers. Self-care is important when working with or hearing the stories of abused children, and readers are advised to keep this in mind. Child cases were selected to provide examples of different developmental ages and stages in response to trauma and because of the wide variety of symptoms and

57

Case Examples and Applications

trauma-manifestations. Some cases include a family therapy component, because adults in these children's worlds became better able to support the child as they became more aware of the child's perception and feelings. Adult cases who experienced trauma were selected to illustrate some of the ways in which stories and art contribute to their progress in treatment.

There is no "one way" to treat trauma. Many interventions are effective, but few interventions are effective without using client material and ascertaining its meaning. By sharing these examples, perhaps new ideas or concepts will be seeded and therapists will have some new tools for their tool bags.

CASE ORGANIZATION

Each case will be organized using more or less the following structure:

- Case Information and Background.
- Problem (and reactions to the problem).
- Conceptualization (including family dynamics).
- Interventions and the Trauma Narrative.
- Shift(s).
  I'm not sure what else to call this, but when a client "gets it" and the intervention proves life-changing or restorative, there is a clear shift in the client's presentation, in a positive direction. Shifts can also occur in a negative direction, due to a struggle, perceived barrier, learned helplessness, reduced self-efficacy, or negative life event that propels a change in perception or motivation.
  As an example, a powerful shift occurred for an older teen client who had lived in fear that her rapist, a former foster father, would come back to hurt her after he got out of jail. It had been a year, and he had not come back, but she still dreamed about him and worried he would seek revenge. We suspended reality one session and told a story about him coming back. We imagined that he came back but she was *ready and prepared*. In the scenario, he broke into her house, and as he said nasty things and menaced, her supports came out from where they were hiding: her best friends, therapist, the police, others he had hurt and adults who had protected her. They threw him down, rolled him in a rug, wrapped him in duct tape, then the police rolled him to the curb. "You take that!" she said. "A little of your own medicine!" Her energy grew, and she displayed a strong righteous indignation. She laughed loudly in glee as we rolled him up in the rug, and she used a whole role of duct tape to wrap him up. This single intervention became her bedtime story, and her anxiety and nightmares dissipated in the face of humor and indignation.
  Similarly, I worked with a college student who started having persistent panic attacks during college classes; he would leave class and go home. He had a "shift" in his anxiety and was able to stay in class after he created a "strong coach" avatar who stood on his shoulder and told the "panic monster" to "fuck off." He laughed at this, utilized it, and his anxiety lessened significantly.
- Progress and Outcomes.

I organized the cases in this manner to provide an opportunity for graduate students and therapists to understand the ways client history and symptoms were connected, also, how I planned and carried out conceptually based treatment. When planning treatment, interventions are not a *shot in the dark*; they are a logical choice given what we know about the client and a *good fit* for that particular client.

CASE EXAMPLES IN TRAUMA-INFORMED CARE

In this section, child cases are presented first, followed by adolescent and adult cases. Child clients generated emotionally laden "material" (through sand tray, Squiggles dry erase, drawing, stories, metaphor, puppets and "games") about the problem and their views of self, others and the world. Adults provided material through metaphor, past-present connections, drawing, nesting dolls and response to stories. Client-generated material was "utilized" and integrated into trauma-informed interventions. I used some of the same interventions with different clients, and the reader will observe the individualized processes that emerged with the same techniques.

The client material, in some cases, helped assess problems and family dynamics; for others, it was the "meat" of trauma identification and trauma narrative work. Some children revisited themes off and on to "show the therapist" their progress. The reader is directed to Pernicano's *Using Trauma-Focused Therapy Stories: Interventions for Therapists, Children and their Caregivers* (2014a) for a full collection of stories and trauma guides, used with the cases in this book.

For each case selected, one or more play, drawing or story activities "shifted" client's perceptions and reactions to their trauma. One of my favorite supervisors once referred to "resistance" as "we haven't figured out what the hell is going on, and we haven't yet offered the right solution from the client's point of view." He pointed out that clients are generally doing the best they can and that judging, blaming or pushing them is unlikely to move things forward. It is up to us to find the relevant key(s) to help clients unblock what is troubling them.

CHILD CASES USING STORIES, ART AND PLAY

7

THE BLOODTHIRSTY BATS

A Case of Child Sexual Abuse

CASE INFORMATION AND BACKGROUND

The first case is about a young elementary school age girl who remained in treatment for about nine months. Her adolescent stepbrother had "molested her" (reportedly one time), and although she was "doing well" her mother wanted to be sure she was adjusting. She was her mother's daughter from an earlier marriage, and the boy who abused her was from her stepdad's first marriage. The boy lived with his mother about 10 miles away and visited every other weekend, some holidays and in the summer.

The abuse was discovered when the mother heard her daughter screaming in the bathroom and went to her. The child was scared to death that she was dying because she was bleeding from her "private." She told her mother that the boy had touched her "down there." Her mother reassured her that she was not dying and they went straight to the ER. The hospital made a CPS report and the girl was scheduled for a forensic interview. The boy "confessed" to what he had done, and both he and his biological parents called it "experimentation" out of "normal curiosity." He said he wanted to know "what girls are like." His dad said he didn't want his son labeled as "some kind of sex offender." The court ordered "no contact" between him and his stepsister, and mandated some brief counseling for the boy (6–10 visits); however no formal juvenile sex offender exam was done. The boy reportedly attended counseling near where he lived, but the counselor was not well trained in trauma intervention or juvenile offending. The biological dad was not convinced that the visits had to stop permanently and minimized the seriousness of what happened, but the girl's mother was adamant. The couple had been in marital counseling prior to this incident, and now the marriage was on even rockier ground.

THE PROBLEMS (AND REACTIONS TO THE PROBLEMS)

The young girl was brought for intake by her mother, who was tearful during much of the session. The child had recently been through a forensic interview, and her mother wanted her to be seen by a psychologist "to be sure she is alright" and "just in case" she had any residual problems following the "one time" sexual abuse at the hands of her adolescent stepbrother. The mother assured me that the boy no longer visited in their home on weekends or holidays, and his dad, the girl's stepdad, visited his son in a location about 10 miles away. The mother believed her daughter had "coped well" with what had happened and "luckily had little damage." The girl had "handled" the forensic interview well, answering questions about the "one" incident they asked about. The little girl put her head down and was silent as her mother talked.

63

Case Examples and Applications

I explained that some children keep their feelings inside rather than talk about them, even when things are bothering them. The girl looked up and met my eyes. I asked the child if she kept things to herself, and she nodded, glancing at her mother then looking away. I asked her a few more questions, and she provided brief responses as she watched her mother carefully while she spoke matter-of-factly in a very quiet voice. She was emotionally constricted and appeared somewhat anxious. When asked directly, the girl said that she was scared of the dark, had been having bad dreams and "bad thoughts," which was all "new" to her mom. "I didn't want to wake you up," she said.

I explained my typical use of play, stories and drawing to help children process trauma. We agreed to work together weekly for a while, and I asked the girl to play in the next room while I talked to her mom.

The mother and I spoke alone for the rest of the session. The mother tearfully said,

> She's doing really well, but I'm not. My husband and I aren't sure we can make this marriage work. I can't stand the thought of that boy hurting her in our home. I think he's minimizing what his son did, and he doesn't understand why the visits have to stop. I don't know if I can stand it if he continues to visit his son. I can't stop thinking about what happened. I never suspected. He played so well with her. They were always together playing, in his room or downstairs.

As mentioned above, the girl's stepbrother had admitted what he had done, and claimed he was "just curious" about sex and how girls were made. He called his behavior "experimentation," insisting that he didn't have any "problem in that area." The court had ordered brief treatment for him but not sex offender treatment, because they felt he was immature but not predatory. His dad and biological mom (who lived elsewhere) said they had not told him much about sex. They didn't think it was unusual for him to do what he did, after all, "most boys his age are curious."

I asked what was reported to have happened. The mother indicated,

> I heard her screaming in the bathroom. I asked her what happened and she said he touched her down there, in his bedroom. When she was on the toilet, she saw the blood and thought she was dying. I reassured her that she was not dying and took her right to the ER. They reported it as sex abuse and that's when the nightmare began.

She said,

> I want you to work with her and make sure everything is OK. We haven't really seen any changes in her. She is pretty anxious at school, afraid to speak up and doesn't have many friends. But she was that way even before this happened. Maybe since kindergarten.

We started therapy the next week. Her mother asked if she should stay and the child said somewhat boldly, "No, you can wait out there. I'll go with Dr. Pat." As it turned out, the precocious second grader transformed into a creative little animated "chatterbox" when her mother left the room. She connected quickly and engaged easily in Dry Erase Squiggles Stories, puppet play and drawing. She had artistic ability and a good sense of humor. I prepared her for what would happen in therapy, that we would eventually talk about what happened with her brother, but for a few weeks, we would use stories, drawing and puppets so that I could get to know her better. She stated clearly that she did not want to talk about "that situation" but that she understood we would be doing so.

She gravitated to stories, drawing, puppets and sand tray. For her, the sand tray was a detailed process of careful, compulsive planning and setup after which she would tell her "story." She liked the idea of "making a movie" with her own characters and story. She would say, "Hmm. Let me think. OK. It's going to be about . . ." She identified small baby animals as the "littles" and "bad guys" as dragon, shark and sea monster. The identified "helpers" were giraffes, "friends," a wizard and protective animals. Her story and play themes were often rather grim, with matter-of-fact victimization of the vulnerable/helpless, and often the perpetrator was portrayed as "sneaky," "acting nice but really mean." She was uncomfortable with her own fear or anger, and she portrayed her mother as a pretty little flower in a small pot hiding behind the enemy or bad guys. She began talking about her nightmares, difficulty sleeping and fear. She worried that the brother might come back and retaliate. She was anxious away from her mother and afraid to speak up at home. She no longer wanted to sleep alone.

After a few sessions I asked her how she was sleeping and feeling. She wrote "happy" on the dry erase board. Then I asked her how her mom was feeling. She wrote "sad" with a frown. We talked about how she did not share her feelings at home because she didn't want to make her mom "more sad."

Then I then told her the story of *The Cracked Glass Bowl* (See Appendix for Guide) in which a lovely bowl is cracked and damaged after surviving a hurricane. She is fragile and anxious after the storm, until her friend suggests that she seek the healing (glassmaker). She is afraid that the healing will hurt, but she goes to the glassmaker. She decides to go through the healing and melt her cracks, healing *from the inside out*. She selects new colors and form and becomes a "new creation." I told the girl that talking about the sex abuse is like that. It hurts, but she can take charge of herself and heal.

My client did not want to draw the bowl and asked me to do it. She told me which colors to use and where to put the cracks (quite a few). She then silently took the black marker and filled in one very large black crack across the entire bowl and said, "It gets better when all the glass melts," then moved to the sand tray. It was a good start but clearly time to shift gears. Doing the trauma narrative a little at a time allows clients to process the memories and experiences gradually and tolerate the process better.

In the sand tray, she carefully put about 50 small farm and zoo animals in layered circles and said, "They don't do anything." She added "bad guys," first a big orange monster with teeth, but commented, "He looks too scary" and replaced him with a dragon ("He acted nice but turned mean and attacked") and a shark.

She placed a small colorful flower in a pot behind the bad guys and said, "It created all the animals. The bad guys want to kill it so all the animals will die and then be extinct because there will be no new animals." She identified the plant as her mother.

The shark carefully and methodically moved through the other animals, politely saying "Excuse me, sorry" right before he ate another unsuspecting small animal. "Excuse me, sorry" then "Yum, yum." I reflected that he and the dragon were very sneaky, acting nice but fooling everybody. She agreed.

She started gathering up the baby animals, saying, "They are the littles" and she grouped them together for protection, but he kept eating them.

The shark had a small turtle in his mouth. She said, with some intensity, "He is not going to ever let it go! He doesn't want to let it go." The shark toyed with the turtle for a long time. Finally, a large antlered animal came to the rescue of the turtle and saved him. "Even though he is beaten and battered," she said, "he is not killed." (This is a clear self-identification.)

In the end, she resolved it when the dragon got a "hurt foot" and died and the shark "got sick and died."

An empowering theme in this sand tray was a group of gorillas she added at the beginning. She laughed repeatedly at their "butts," and pointed out their "cracks." Then, to them, she said sternly, "You need to put on some clothes. NO ONE WANTS TO LOOK AT THAT!" She laughed each time she said that, but she did not touch them again until the end of the session. (This was a clear symbolic communication about her brother.)

At the end, all the other animals pounced on the gorillas, telling them they needed to put on some clothes. This raised up a cloud of sand, everyone was in a tumble, and she laughed as she said, "The story is over."

THE CONCEPTUALIZATION

A child's trauma response, as noted earlier in this manuscript, can range anywhere along the trauma continuum, and this child had lived in "freeze" and "flight" in part because she was "protecting" her mother from knowing "the rest of the story." She had been abused on a regular basis for two years, not once as her parents had believed. Reportedly, the forensic interviewer only addressed the more recent incident; she was not asked what he made her do to him, just what he did to her. She had *contained* a significant amount of troubling information since kindergarten.

Her social anxiety, withdrawal, inability to speak up at school, lack of close friends, lack of much if any visible emotional response and fear of sleeping alone had been going on since

Case Examples and Applications

kindergarten and were likely at least in part related to her trauma. She was afraid of her older stepbrother; he had threatened her about what he would do if she told.

The child was very perceptive. She was aware of her mother's depression and anger, and she felt a burden of responsibility to "not make it worse." That is one reason she did not want her mother in the therapy room initially, except to give limited feedback at the end of each session. I think she knew that she could work on her abuse better without her mother in the room, and she trusted me to help her mother cope with the truth because "you are a grown up, you can tell her." She also believed when starting treatment, to some extent, that since she had not told or "stopped" the abuse earlier in time, it must be her fault. She did not want to be "responsible" for the breakup of the family and her parents' marriage.

Her play and stories, from the beginning, conveyed anxiety and perceived helplessness with some sense of futility. She did not have a "safe place" at home for her emotions, and she was aware of her stepfather's ambivalence. She was uncomfortable with her own strong emotions, shame, fear and anger (at her brother, herself and her parents). She needed to understand that the abuse was not her fault, even though she had not told anyone. At the same time, she showed a fierce determination to use the therapy to conquer her fears. She struggled but never shut down, and she trusted that if we "did the work," she would get over "the situation."

Her mother needed to become a more stable and reliable "holding place" for the child. I met individually with the mother, serving as a "holding place" for her sadness, pain and guilt while preparing her to be more involved in her child's therapy. The mother was intelligent, observant and compassionate. As she sat in, silently at first, on sessions (once the child indicated she was "ready" and invited her), she quickly "soaked up" her child's communications. Then, between sessions, she became the "strong mom" and encouraged interactions that would boost confidence and reduce avoidance.

INTERVENTIONS AND THE TRAUMA NARRATIVE

When working with trauma, after the client completes any forensic process, I usually go through a "head to toe touch interview" to clarify the nature of what sorts of touch happened, prior to working on a trauma narrative. It requires naming/labeling parts of the body, then pointing to where the child was touched and where the child was asked to touch someone else. This provides much detail about what the child experienced. I have a set of forensic drawings (basically naked bodies, front and back, of different developmental levels), and the child picks one that best matches him or her and one that matches the other person. She picked a pre-pubescent girl for herself and an early adolescent male for her stepbrother, going "ewww" at the nakedness.

We go head to toe, from hair to feet, and I ask what the part is called. Then I ask the child to point at parts of him/her that were touched by the perpetrator. For example, she pointed to her "butt," "chest" and "private." Then I asked her to point to the part of the brother that touched her. She pointed to his penis and indicated it had touched her "butt" and "hand." She pointed to his hand and said it had touched her private and arms. She pointed to her hand and said he tried to make her put a finger up his butt and make her touch his penis "but I said no." I asked if his penis was soft like limp spaghetti or got hard and stuck out. She described an erect penis. I asked if he touched her clothes on or clothes off and she said "both."

Then I asked what grade she was in when he first touched her: "kindergarten." She was now in 2nd grade. I asked if it happened once or more than once and she said "more than once—almost every time he visited." She indicated she answered the CPS questions about the "one time" but "that was that."

We shared the drawings and information with her mother, who was very upset. She felt terrible that they had not known and told her daughter she would inform CPS and the court that the sex abuse had gone on for two years, many times. She praised her daughter for being brave, and we did some breathing while we listened to the Tibetan singing bowl to "calm down." She finished the session with a rainbow drawing that depicted the sun trying to break through the clouds.

A few weeks later, the client was ready to tackle the full story of her own cracked glass bowl. I asked her to help me label each crack on her bowl before the healing. She identified the things he had done, made her do and tried to make her do. She identified him molesting her "in the closet," "in the bathroom" and "in his room." She talked about "the first time," the "worst time" (when she bled) and the times in between. She described her feelings and her shame at the nakedness. As her anxiety increased, she moved around to manage it. She expressed her righteous indignation several times that he "acted so nice, especially in front of my parents, but he was really mean." I provided appropriate support throughout.

THE SHIFT

A shift began to occur when she began her work on the "cracked glass bowl," talked back to the "bad guys" in the sand tray and told the gorillas to put on some clothes. She was clearly feeling empowered to speak up and able to rely on helpers, so as to not be alone with her problems. She was starting to challenge things her brother had told her, and she was talking more openly with her mother. She was practicing her breathing and relaxation at bedtime.

The next session, she invited her mother into the playroom at the beginning of the session. She directed her to "sit on the other side of the room, watch and listen and don't cry." This was a clear shift.

The client selected the "littles," cows, dragon, lizard, seal and giraffe. She then picked up a wizard and said, "The wizard got separated from his magic, so he has no power and all the animals will die. Then there will be no way to make new animals." She then identified "bad guys" as dragon, gorilla and two pretty ponies. They attacked the unsuspecting good guys and buried them in "a pile of doom." She said, "The lizard bites the dragon and he becomes bad. He is a very powerful bad guy. He acts nice but he's really bad." She commented on the gorilla, to her mother, "He really needs to put on some clothes. No one wants to see THAT!"

After some deliberation, she finished her story and a solution arose. The giraffe unburied and led everyone to safety, then led the wizard "to his magic." With the wizard's help, they filled the lizard up with "good magic, twice, to change his colors and fill him with good. First, he is just a little good, finally he is all good." This seemed to be her wish for her brother to change. I reflected that she also seemed "a little mad" and she said strongly, "YES, at HIM!"

As we started to clean up, she picked up a whale and said, "He's sad." She then showed her mother the small potted flower she had used in the last session and said, "I picked this to be you. It was sad BECAUSE OF THE SITUATION." Her mother asked, "So you think I'm sad and you're mad?" The girl replied, "YES, you're sad because of THE SITUATION." Her mother's eyes grew big with amazement at what she had observed that session, but she did not cry. I said, "I think your mom and you are both sad and mad over the SITUATION, and we are both very proud of you."

I asked her then how the lizard felt, since he represented her brother and her hope that he might get some "good magic" and be "good" again. She said in a matter-of-fact voice, "He doesn't feel anything. He pretended to be nice, but he did not care about hurting others. He was mean and wanted his way." She walked out hand in hand with her mother.

THE PROGRESS AND OUTCOMES

A summary title for this little girl's progress and outcomes might be *The New Creation and Defeating the Bats*, although there were a number of steps we went through in achieving these outcomes.

As we worked together, she continued to be open and talkative as soon as her mother left the room. She remained overly careful about her mother's feelings and watched her for signs of emotional upset. Her mother was very nurturing and supportive of her daughter, and she had always been protective; however, she had never anticipated that her husband's son would do anything to hurt her daughter. He was described as "very immature" and "young for his age." The mother was depressed early in treatment and struggling with guilt that such a horrible thing had happened to her daughter "under my own roof, and I didn't know!" Her mother cried easily, which bothered my client, and as her mother gained better control over her own emotions, the client included her more in the sessions.

Case Examples and Applications

This delightful little girl particularly loved the set of nesting doll cats. Each cat was a different color and style, and inside the smallest cat was a little mouse. We pretended that the cats were a family, and she revealed in her play that she wanted her mother to take charge but viewed her as somewhat fragile. She wanted her mother to be stronger and to protect her. She was protective of the mouse but also laughed sometimes that the cat "ate him." I asked the largest cat to "call a truce and protect" the mouse because it wasn't a "fair fight" with four against one tiny mouse. The largest cat put the mouse inside the smallest cat and said, "There you go, all safe and sound, tucked inside."

We did some Cognitive Behavioral Therapy (CBT) work for her social and separation anxiety at school as we prepared to terminate treatment, and then she revisited the cracked glass bowl

FIGURE 7.1

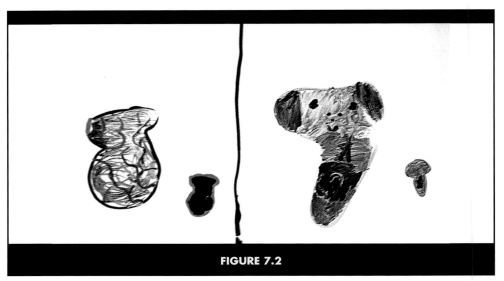

FIGURE 7.2

one more time. She drew the pre- and post-versions herself, using bright colors on the dry erase board. (See Appendix for full-color version of this picture.)

"Look, Dr. Pat," she said, "I made this one a blue bowl." The first bowl on the left was outlined in brown and full of cracks. "That's all the sex abuse," she said, "and my mom crying and I couldn't talk to anyone at school." She added, "Look, Dr. Pat, she has a friend with her, see the small bowl?" The "after" was a mushroom shaped glass and was no longer a bowl. It had beautiful colors and was decorated with a star and a heart. She announced, "You know, it feels bad, but then you heal inside." She added, "Her friend decided to join her in some changes" and pointed out the new green color of the "friend."

I asked her how she could tell that she was different. She said, "I talked about what my brother did even though I didn't want to. I stopped worrying that he would come back and hurt me." She proudly announced that she had "talked back to the nervous voice" that week at school and raised her hand to answer a question. She was sleeping in her own bed and no longer having nightmares. She hoped her stepbrother would get help but "first he has to admit that what he did was wrong. Sexual abuse is wrong." As an aside she said, "My mom's different too. I like talking to her in therapy, and she doesn't cry as much."

She came prepared for the final session, inviting her mother to join us, and she asked if we could do Dry Erase Squiggle Story one more time. She had me do the Squiggle (purple line below) and then she drew her picture, creating the scene below. It was a bat cave with a pond outside. The pond had rocks in it and smudges of dark red. (See Appendix for full-color version of this picture.)

She thought for a minute or two, smiled at me and told this story:

Once upon a time, there was a bat cave. And the bat that lives in it is a very mean vampire bat. He acts nice but he isn't nice at all. He tricks you to get you to come into his cave. It isn't safe to go in there but no one knows that. If you go in his cave, he sucks your blood and you die. See the red in the water? That's the blood of those that didn't make it.

She pointed to the lake and the red smudges in the water. Then she pointed to the largest bat.

He uses a fake voice and lures you to his cave and says, "got you!" Then you are trapped. After he sucks your blood he dumps you in the water. No survivors! One day a little centipede came to the bat cave. She wanted to get out of the rain so she went inside. She didn't know it wasn't safe. The mean bat said, "I'm going to pluck off all your legs and eat you!" 100-pluck-99-pluck-98 . . . Down to the last leg—pluck! No more legs! The centipede knew he was a goner.

"Oh no!" I said, with concern. She looked at me intently and paused. I waited to see how she would resolve it.

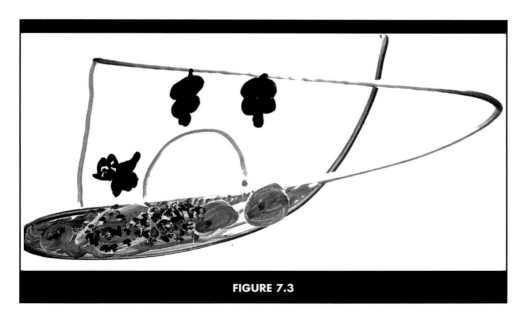

FIGURE 7.3

Case Examples and Applications

She said, with an impish grin,

AND NOW FOR THE REST OF THE STORY! Her friend saw her go in the cave and knew she needed help. Her friend went in the cave. The bat said, "I'll suck your blood too!" But he didn't know that the friend had GREAT MAGIC and 1–2–3 used the GREAT MAGIC. POOF! All the legs came back. The centipede ran free, and together they killed the bat. No more bat. No more blood sucking! THE END!

This story was the first time in the course of her treatment that she directly referred to blood. Her bleeding had terrified her after he touched her, because she thought she was dying. Now, she was very much alive. The blood was in a pond, where it might be contained and eventually cleansed and washed away. She had all her legs back: by utilizing her creativity and drawing from the "GREAT MAGIC" of her therapist, her confidence, her safety, her personal power and her feelings were restored. She is no longer "alone" in dealing with her fears, and there is some degree of security and hope.

TERMINATION PROGRESS AND OUTCOME

We ended treatment when I was moving to a new location, and she continued for a few sessions with another psychologist. She made significant changes at home and school during treatment, and although she sometimes had social anxiety, she was working to conquer it.

The following rainbow pictures, one early in treatment and one later, show the reader some of the changes in her mood and thinking that became visible at home and school. The first shows dark coloring, around the sun and over the tree, and splotches of rain. The tree is standing firm and tall, somewhat rigidly, but the top (head, brain) is filled with dark dots of worry and fear. The rainbow is emerging after/during the storm, but the storm, for her, is not yet over.

The reader will see the before and after contrast between the two pictures, representing mood change. The first picture depicts stress and an attempt to stand firm in the midst of stress. There is a row of black clouds under the blue sky at the top. There is a black ring around the sun. There

FIGURE 7.4

are raindrops falling around the tree. The rainbow does depict some hopefulness. (See Appendix for full-color version of this picture.)

This second picture is of a happy well-developed flower, after the storm. There is no dark or black color in this picture, and it represents an overall optimism. The center of the flower is rainbow colors, the sun is no longer blocked, and the rainbow is in a clear sky. It was drawn close to our termination of treatment. (See Appendix for full-color version of this picture.)

The following Dry Erase Squiggle Story drawing depicts the client's more secure and protective relationship with her mother and stepfather, and the three flowers inside the green seem

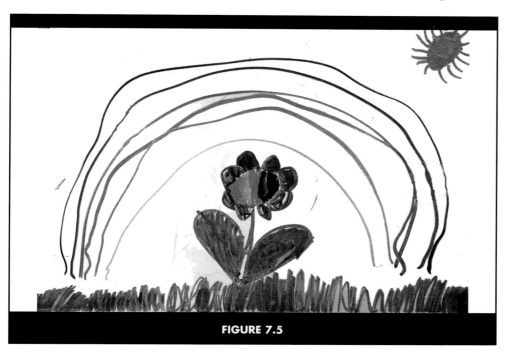

FIGURE 7.5

FIGURE 7.6

Case Examples and Applications

safely and securely sheltered. The picture may also represent the positive alliance in our therapy relationship, as she drew a girl and an adult outside the family in their own realm. The red below the clouds is the original "Squiggle" I presented to her and had to be left in the picture (I didn't ask her about it), but it could be "powerful magic" as in the bats story or even the awareness that things are mostly *good* in her world, but there is lingering memory of the *bad*.

QUESTIONS FOR CASE DISCUSSION

1. The child's mother said her daughter had "handled" the abuse very well. What (symptoms or therapy interactions) suggested the child was troubled or bothered by what had happened to her?
2. From a family systems perspective, children sometimes "protect" their parents by not talking about their abuse. In what ways do you think this child was protecting her mother or family by keeping things to herself?
3. What changes (mood, thinking or behavior) did you notice that suggested the child was learning new ways to cope and reducing her anxiety?
4. Select a metaphor from this case and state how it represented the child's concerns, feelings, relationships or therapy process.

8

THE ALLIGATOR EYES

A Case of Complicated Grief

CASE INFORMATION AND BACKGROUND

An 8-year-old girl was brought in by her adoptive parents for therapy because she was having nightmares and not sleeping well. When she was between 2 and 3 years of age, her biological dad had died of a drug overdose while she slept with him. At that time, she was treated for symptoms of acute stress and grief for three to six months, and the symptoms resolved. Relatives in the extended family had adopted her and her sister. She had adjusted well to the home and was doing well in school. Emotionally, she was struggling again, with nightmares that *made no sense*.

The girl was a talkative, expressive child who articulated what happened when she was 3. She had fallen asleep on her daddy's chest when he laid down on the family room sofa to watch TV. He had taken drugs that evening and died of an overdose while they slept. She woke up on his chest with his arms around her, not realizing he was dead. She could not move and cried for her mom; the next thing she knew EMTs were there, and *daddy* was taken away in an ambulance, never to come home again.

THE PROBLEMS (AND REACTIONS TO THE PROBLEMS)

She had recently started talking more about her dad and her life before the adoption. The girl's biological mom had "shown up out of the blue" at a grandmother's house and was making inquiries to extended family members about having supervised visits with her children. The adoptive parents set some expectation for the birth mother, as she had a history of substance abuse and had not kept in touch with the adoptive family, apparently resenting that they had stepped in and "taken" her children. She had made promises (did not follow through), and they had not known her whereabouts until she reappeared. They did not want her to disrupt the children's stability and asked that she do a couple of things before they would allow visits: have a meeting with the adoptive parents (without the children) to discuss her plans to work and support herself, have weekly speaker-phone calls initiated by her (a specific day and time) and be able to see where she was living. They were open with the children about what was going on and their decisions. As of yet, the birth mother had not contacted them to set up a meeting. The little girl was aware that her birth mother was back in the area, and around that time she started showing signs of increased anxiety, mood swings and nightmares.

Case Examples and Applications

INITIAL INTERVENTIONS AND NEW PROBLEMS

The child was open and trusting, as well as very frank about her feelings. We revisited her dad's death, especially the circumstances around the night he died. She shared her feelings about her parents using drugs, her dad dying (essentially leaving her) and her mother's unreliability as a parent. She indicated some of the memories from her early childhood had faded and that she still cried sometimes because she missed her dad.

We talked about her dad in each session—she drew pictures of him and wrote letters to him. She made a list of questions she would like to ask her mom if they had a conversation. Her questions showed insight, and I helped her expand the list with clarifying questions. Finally, I asked her to write down what bothered her the most at this point in time.

She wrote, "I'm afraid I killed my daddy."

THE CONCEPTUALIZATION

The child's past memories and feelings of loss were triggered by learning her mom was back in the area. She found herself thinking more about her birth parents and how different her life would have been if she grew up in that home. She voiced ambivalent feelings about her mother. She talked about wanting and not wanting to see her. She and her sister had not been well cared for after the dad's death, and she felt abandoned in the years since, due to lack of contact. She was very attached to her adoptive parents and didn't want to hurt their feelings by showing interest in a visit. She wondered about her birth mom and whether she had changed; *deep down*, she always hoped her mother would change and regret the past life of substance abuse, child neglect and irresponsibility.

An important factor in her symptom emergence and coming back to treatment was being at a totally different developmental stage. When her dad died, she had been a preschool child without the ability to make cause-effect connections. She had lacked the capacity for insight and experienced the sense of emotional loss, without being aware of "why."

This problem (fear she had killed her daddy) had not emerged during her last therapy; she had not been old enough to mentally process the circumstances of his death. Now, thinking more about her daddy dying, she worried that her weight on his chest had caused his death; she felt guilt and fear. It was an "unspeakable" possible "truth" for her, and she had not wanted to tell her adoptive parents about these fears. For children, speaking something makes it more "real."

INTERVENTION WITH A SHIFT

"Let's do an experiment," I suggested. "Let's see what the facts tell us." I brought in a scale. We estimated the weight of a 2-year-old, and her adoptive mother showed her a picture of herself at that age. We then found some things that weighed the same amount. I laid down on the carpet and asked her to pile those things on me. She did so, but looked very anxious. I breathed up and down lightly, then I huffed and puffed and the things moved around. Her eyes widened.

Next, with her adoptive mother in the room, I said, "OK, now sit on my chest." She giggled and did what I asked and she noticed that I had no trouble breathing. We did the same thing with her and her mother.

Next, she lay down on the carpet and we she piled the things on her. As she breathed, the things moved around and did not weigh her down. None of us had trouble breathing or talking with the added weight.

I asked her, "What do you think?"

She looked at me, seriously, and said, "I didn't kill him."

"You are so smart!" I replied. "That's right. You didn't kill him."

Then I asked, "So what killed him?"

She thought for a moment and answered, "The drugs killed him. And he took them, so he killed himself." I nodded in agreement.

She teared up. "I really miss him." Her mother pulled the child into her lap and held her close. I said, "You loved him and he loved you—of course you miss him!"

She paused and said, "But he didn't want to die. It wasn't on purpose. He didn't want to leave me."

"No," I said. "He didn't want to die. He didn't want to leave you. He took drugs, and they killed him."

After this session, her anxiety was much lower and she concentrated better on her schoolwork. But the nightmares continued, so we made a plan to work on them more directly.

THE TRAUMA NARRATIVE AND NEW SHIFT

Her recurring nightmares were about an alligator. I asked her to tell me her dream and act it out with the alligator puppet. In her dreams the alligator had big eyes and was staring at her. He looked "mean" and was watching her, as if he was going to attack and bite her. She felt acute fear but could not get away. When she had the dream, her mother heard her screaming and crying in her sleep. She would then go to her daughter's room to comfort her; after the child woke up, she had trouble falling back to sleep.

I assessed for recent stressors or events that might be intruding into her dreams. She was not being bullied at school or in her neighborhood; she was not being abused by anyone. The dreams had started "out of the blue" and were happening two to three times a week. Together we drew alligators, talked about alligators and played with the alligator puppet. She talked to the alligator puppet and told him to leave her alone.

As I looked closely at the alligator puppet after one session—the big eyes, the open mouth, the teeth—I got a shiver. Suddenly I realized what she might have seen when she woke up on her daddy's chest that night long ago, trapped by his arms. She was face to face with her daddy in death: big, open eyes, fixed and staring at her. Open mouth with teeth showing. Scary, not like the daddy she had known and loved.

At the next session, I suggested that maybe the alligator meant her no harm, and that he couldn't help it that he looked scary with his big eyes, open mouth and teeth showing. Perhaps he was even a vegetarian and didn't eat meat (like her daddy). I said, "Take a good look at him. Up close."

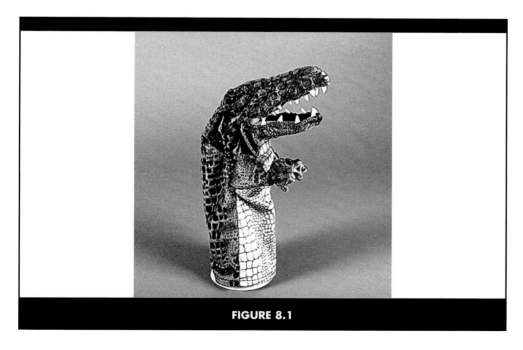

FIGURE 8.1

Case Examples and Applications

She somewhat reluctantly pulled the puppet closer to her face. Face to face, she stared at the alligator and grimaced. "What's scary?" I asked. "His eyes, his open mouth, his teeth!" she said.

I played the alligator. I said, "I'm sorry I scared you. I have big eyes and a big mouth, lots of teeth, but I am a vegetarian, and I don't eat meat. I would never want to scare or hurt you. I'm so sorry."

She teared up, took the alligator and held it close to her in a hug. After a moment of silence, she said, "Thanks, Dr. Pat." With metaphor and puppets, words sometimes don't have to be spoken.

PROGRESS AND OUTCOMES

Who knows why she stopped dreaming about alligators after this session? Certainly, the intervention may have gone right to her heart and to the "meaning" of why she dreamed about alligators; perhaps the intervention lowered her anxiety about alligators and changed her perception.

With children, metaphor and play do not always have to be interpreted. I think it certainly might have exacerbated her past trauma to point out that the alligator face, mouth and eyes resembled her dead daddy in her dreams. Intervening symbolically provided a big shift for her, a positive resolution, and the treatment ended soon after.

When we terminated treatment, her caregiver noticed positive changes at home and school. She had resolved her guilt, found the source of her dreams and revisited the trauma she had first worked on during preschool. Now, at a later stage of development, she had gained new meaning and understanding.

QUESTIONS FOR CASE DISCUSSION

1. Clients can process an issue at one developmental stage and then have the issue re-emerge later in development in a new way. What are some reasons this happens?
2. Give an example of how a CBT play intervention helped this client change her thinking about an aspect of her dad's death. Also, describe how thoughts, feelings and behaviors are connected and what therapist did to change these connections.
3. Collaborative empiricism is a CBT technique, the term coined by Dr. Donald Meichenbaum, and refers to a process whereby a client and therapist work together through CBT to "test hypotheses" with data and facts. Give an example of this technique being used with this client.
4. How did the child's "play" with the alligator help her resolve her grief and nightmares?

9

THE BOY WHOSE SISTER SAID "FUCK"

A Case of Parental Drug Overdose

CASE INFORMATION AND BACKGROUND

The 6-year-old boy and his mother came for intake soon after the accidental death of his father to a Fentanyl overdose. The mother worked full time and was a reliable head of household, but she had been overwhelmed since the untimely death of her husband. She had two children, one about age 6 and one in her early teens, both very changed by the traumatic event they experienced as a family. The mom was in therapy as was her older daughter, but she wanted help for the changes she saw in her young son.

I gathered family history from the boy's mother, seeking to understand the circumstances of the death and the context of the family home prior to the dad's death. Before you can evaluate the nature of grief, you *first must assess the quality of the family relationships before death*, because complicated relationships result in complicated grief work. She described the events prior to and on the night of the father's death.

The mother indicated that her *disabled* husband had struggled with addiction for years; he was a stay-at-home dad before his death. The parents struggled in their marriage long before the night the dad died. He allegedly abused Ambien, his wife's pain medication, his own opioid medication for chronic pain, and was recently prescribed a Fentanyl patch. He had sleep apnea and had been hospitalized for mental health problems about six months prior.

The boy had been in bed sleeping between his parents the night his dad died. His dad had taken both his old medication (oral opioid pain meds) and his newly prescribed medication (Fentanyl patch). His wife recalled how she tried to keep him awake that night because he was snoring heavily and his breathing was slower, but she finally fell asleep and he did as well. When she woke up, he was non-responsive, with fixed pupils and no pulse or heartbeat.

THE PROBLEMS (AND REACTIONS TO THE PROBLEMS)

Since that night, the household had been in chaos. "Fuck," as noted in the title, had become a household word. The mother was angry at her husband for not entering detox or pain management; his addiction to pain medication was not new. He had *gotten off* narcotics twice in the past but relapsed both times. The mother was the family breadwinner, working long hours; her grief prevented her from being fully attentive to her children. All three were traumatized and *existing day to day*.

A year prior to this, the family had survived a tornado while the mother was out of town; the boy struggled afterward with sleep problems and anxiety, especially when there were storms.

77

Case Examples and Applications

The dad had taken the kids to a back room at Circle K as the *first storm passed*. But another storm approached, and instead of taking the children home to safety, the dad took them with him in the truck, *to help others*, with objects flying around and wind roaring. A baseball sized chunk of hail hit the dad on the head, drawing blood, and he did not seek medical help until later; both the boy and his sister had been terrified. During that storm, many homes in the immediate area were destroyed and people died. In the aftermath of the tornado, the family's home became full of mold, and they moved.

This traumatic event of the dad's death was about a year later. The night his dad died, the boy said that he had called 911 three times; he became very distressed when they did not come "right away." The mother had screamed for her teenage daughter who was sleeping down the hall when she saw her unresponsive husband. By the mom's description, the dad was already dead at that point, but she did CPR. The mom also said that EMTs did not come quickly; when they arrived, the boy watched silently as EMTs "worked on" his dad then took him away in the ambulance.

Since that night, the three survivors lived like ghosts in the house, each somewhat invisible to the others. The mother and sister were fighting, the boy and his sister were fighting, and the mother wanted "help" so that her son could sleep and "settle down." The mom didn't like it that her daughter and son were cursing *all the time*, the daughter shouting "fuck," the little boy copying her, and the mother "on them" to stop fighting. She was overwhelmed with her own grief and subsequent life changes. Her son could not sleep alone, least of all in his own bed. He was obsessed with EMTs—going over and over whether daddy would have lived had they come sooner, and questioning why he did not wake up earlier to get his mother. He talked incessantly about daddy not moving or breathing, hearing the ambulance, and going to the hospital. He was upset that his mom and sister had been screaming loudly that night. The panic and anxiety he felt that night were most likely layered with the helplessness he had experienced during the tornado. His mother did not want to talk about it, because for her, it was *too much too soon*. She didn't know how to "reach him" and he didn't want to upset her with the intensity of his anger and grief.

I encouraged her to bring her son regularly for trauma therapy and invited her to be involved in the therapy. They lived quite a distance from the counseling agency, which prevented her full involvement, so sometimes she scheduled her own therapy at the same time as her son's.

THE CONCEPTUALIZATION

When a client goes through multiple traumatic events in a short period of time, it challenges available coping resources. Trauma activates fear and anxiety, which also activates what is referred to as the Attachment Behavioral System. For both adults and children, the attachment behavioral system is activated when safety and security are threatened, such as during illness, loss, separation, potential injury, abuse or neglect. We turn to our primary or secondary attachment figures at such times, seeking to re-establish equilibrium and maintain security.

For victims of trauma, it is very difficult to meet one's attachment security needs, because the source of attachment and security (primary or secondary attachment figure) is the same person causing confusion, fear or insecurity. There is thus no one to turn to when the attachment behavioral system is activated. Also, depending on the prior response of the attachment figure, the attachment may not be secure. Some attachment figures expect the child to be "strong" or "tough," may punish or ridicule the child for seeking help, may be non-accessible, may not notice the child's needs and/or may trigger anxiety in the child.

In this child's case, his dad had not been a reliable person with whom to seek comfort, because his judgment put his children in danger rather than protecting or buffering them. The dad's disability and drug addiction resulted in unpredictable and inconsistent responses to his children. At the same time, the little boy loved his daddy and could not reconcile his ambivalent feelings.

This client had experienced two life events that threatened life, safety, security and health. After the tornado, he was very anxious and had an acute trauma response. It is not clear how his dad responded to this, but his mother likely felt overwhelmed. They were unable to remain in their home due to the mold. When the father died, it pushed each remaining family member over the edge. She had been considering divorce prior to the overdose, and now she had to deal with her own conflicting emotions as well as her children's grief. The boy noticed the emotional changes in his mother, who was able to do little more than go to work each day then spend the evening alone in her room. At this point in time, she did not provide the nurturing behaviors he needed to ground himself and feel secure. His world had been turned upside down, and his primary attachment figure, equally traumatized, was not available; the child was drowning, without a life jacket.

It is likely that his dad's death re-activated the fear and anxiety the boy experienced during the tornado; now he had a whole new set of fears. He feared he had let his dad down, and he was afraid that he might die, especially while sleeping. He wanted to sleep by his mom, but that meant sleeping where the trauma occurred; the bed itself was a trigger of nightmares. At his age, he did not have a good understanding of life and death, and he was worried that someone else (mom, sister, him) might die in their sleep. The boy's reactions to the sights and sounds of that night were visible in his verbalizations, moods and behaviors, with nightmares, intrusive thoughts, guilt and troubling memories. He was aware that his mother was not "all there" and turned to his sister for many of his attachment needs/security, but she had become angry and distant. He was alone in the middle of an emotional storm.

INTERVENTIONS AND THE TRAUMA NARRATIVE

At intake and subsequently, the boy could not sit still. He was a hyper-aroused, agitated, emotionally frozen, acutely traumatized child. He avoided eye contact, did not seek comfort from his mother and gravitated to the therapist as he touched things, played with toys and told creative stories. He was very talkative and in constant motion in the waiting room and in my office throughout early sessions.

It was clear that he was very intelligent, and his work at school showed advanced reading and a keen understanding of math. At school, he was not "listening" to the teacher and would get up and move around the room, touching things and talking as if no one else was in the room. His eyes had the "far away" look of dissociation. The teacher could not redirect him, but she was patient and kind.

Had someone not known his history, they might have missed the frantic anxiety that accompanied his hyperactivity and labeled him ADHD, or diagnosed him as having an autistic spectrum disorder, due to his mechanical play and avoidance of eye contact. They might have missed the themes that emerged in his stories and drawings that pointed to PTSD and depression.

This child was angry, scared, needy and agitated in sessions; he "latched onto" me as if dying of thirst and I was the only water available. My role was to become a temporary attachment figure, a nurturing secure base with predictability (therapy) and open acceptance of his very complicated thoughts and feelings. He trusted me to help and from the beginning showed a willingness to gradually broach his feelings. He seemed to recognize that I could hold his anger, and he never became physically aggressive. It was a "fight-flight" response of enormous proportions.

We had to work first on calming his agitation and easily triggered anxiety before we could do trauma work. We adopted a ritual order to the therapy session that often started with 1. practicing deep breathing with a helper (stuffed animal on his chest, make it move up and down); 2. sitting still like a frog while listening to the singing bowl; and 3. using the sound machine to play water running (waves or brook). At the beginning of each session, he went straight to the sound machine to turn on the water sounds then rang the Tibetan singing bowl to breathe and calm down. He often rang the bell during sessions when he was becoming anxious or nervous.

Sitting Still Like a Frog (Snel, 2013) provides a good introduction to mindfulness practices. A frog sits quietly and moves only his eyes, and if he sees a fly, his tongue quickly grabs it. He only jumps when he wants to go into the water or jump to a different lily pad. My client and I practiced sitting cross-legged like frogs as we did our breathing.

I decided to engage in non-directive play at first, to allow the child to find modalities that were a "good fit" and allow him to best communicate. He sometimes "bounced" from one thing to the next, but it was clear that his choices were not random. He played out scenes of hospital and rescue. His favorite activity was the dry erase board, either free drawing or doing Squiggles and telling stories. He engaged in this activity to express strong, uncomfortable feelings and to show

Case Examples and Applications

FIGURE 9.1

me things that bothered him. Regardless of which Squiggle I offered him, his stories were about danger and rescue, fear and safety, good and evil.

One small toy he liked was a movie character whose face would contort into anger when you pushed down on him. One minute the character seemed to be calm and then he was yelling. The boy would push on it, let out a ferocious yell, then laugh uproariously. He once commented that a hungry monster was trying to eat a favorite toy cow. He hesitated, looked at me and seemed pleased when I offered the monster something else to eat. I commented, "We can feed him when he's hungry, but we don't have to let him eat your friend the cow." He was afraid of his own anger and sometimes doubted his impulse control; at those times he would turn to me for containment.

With regard to his dad, the child "popped in and out" with spontaneous commentary, at first with some anxiety and trepidation, sort of like someone who hesitates before pulling his own tooth. He would suddenly say things like, "My dad talked like this a lot" (then demonstrate his dad's slurred speech) or, "Sometimes he was wide awake and then he was snoring sound asleep" (which is what happened the night his dad died after struggling to stay awake). We talked about the impact of drugs on the brain and filled a sponge with muddy-colored water. He tended to avert his eyes when interacting and mostly maintained proximity with me. His comments were usually an "invitation" for my comments.

Early in treatment, he talked quite a bit about the tornado that had devastated the area about a year prior. The damage to their home had required that they move, and he was still not comfortable sleeping in the new house. The memory was triggered whenever they had a storm with strong wind, and when that happened, he became talkative and hyperactive. He learned about tornadoes and could tell me the warning signs and what you do in a tornado to stay safe. It was a complicated memory—his dad had been with the kids and "helping" other people, but at the same time he had endangered his kids by not taking them to a safe shelter. He remembered houses collapsing and trees flying, and he remembered his dad bleeding after getting hit on the head by flying debris. He drew the house below (Figure 9.2) as a free drawing, and outside the house, someone is calling, "dad." "It's in a tornado," he said. "See how the wind is knocking it down?"

Much of his communication was through metaphor. Early in treatment, he painted the next house (Figure 9.3) in water-colors, saying, "This is an angry house. It has a mind of its own. That is why it's red (angry). It turns from happy to mad. It has chicken feet—it's strange . . . The roof is the house's brain."

This was a transparent metaphor, an "open invitation" to talk about how angry everyone got at his house. Certainly, everyone in his household was turning "from happy to mad," including the boy, and I was sure this house represented him.

I reflected that it was OK to have a mind of your own; I asked some questions about what made the house mad, and what made it turn from happy to mad. After we talked about the house, he told me he was having nightmares "but not about my dad." I suggested that his brain was like a sponge and that right now, it was probably full of bad memories. He was still sleeping with his

The Boy Whose Sister Said "Fuck"

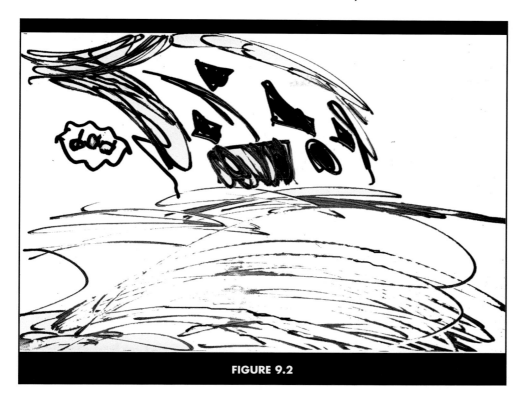

FIGURE 9.2

FIGURE 9.3

mother in the bed in which his dad died, and he feared he might die in his sleep. He said, "You know, I'm mad at my dad. He took too many drugs and pills!"

This was a shift for him, opening up about his out-of-control anger and his dad's drug use. At most sessions, he talked about his big sister saying "fuck." He would write it and draw it and tell me she said it. He said, "B is mean to me, and she says fuck so I say fuck back." Then he whispered secretively, "Dr. Pat, fuck was my dad's favorite word." Ah, this word did not have an entirely negative connotation. For him and his sister, it was a link to their father, a form of identification.

Case Examples and Applications

A creative child, he often used color to show his feelings, and the typical 6-year-old "bad-good" dichotomy. In the picture below, the yellow sunshine at the top was the "happy boy." Under the sun was the pouring rain, and that was the "bad boy." Flowers and grass were the "happy boy." And the pure black poop was a "very bad boy." He thought he was "bad" when he said "fuck" and got in trouble for cursing at his sister or mother. The night his dad died, he had called 911 three times and grew more and more frantic as he made his calls. Perhaps he blamed himself for not waking up before dad died.

The theme of "good" and "bad" continued (see picture below) as he began to work on feeling identification and the types of things that triggered his mood changes.

FIGURE 9.4

FIGURE 9.5

82

The Boy Whose Sister Said "Fuck"

His mother was not always consistent in joining him for sessions, because in her own grief she could only tolerate so much of his; I believe she did the best she could by participating in his treatment whenever she could, and after about two months, she noticed some changes in his anger and agitation at home.

I "reframed" his "bad" to "brave"; when I saw him write "bad" I queried, "Bad? I don't know about that . . ." I would say, "What a brave boy you are! You went through a tornado, and you helped your mom the night your dad died!" He soon started saying, "I am a brave boy, right Dr. Pat?" "Yes," I replied, "You are very brave to go through such things!"

When he commented that his sister (and he) said "fuck!" I said, "Of course you are angry. Fuck tells people how angry you are!" We talked about not using that word in public and also about finding some new words for "I" messages that could express anger and frustration.

In sessions, he began to be more focused and less agitated. He was planful in his therapy activities and more goal oriented. I continued to engage in much client-centered work, with some redirection and suggestion, and followed his direction and pace. I trusted him to communicate what he needed and to let me know when he was ready to talk more directly about his father's death.

SHIFT

He settled into a regular routine for sessions and was less agitated during the activities. His chosen routine included:

- Turn on the sounds and listen.
- Sit still like a frog.
- Ring the bell and listen.
- Breathe.
- Read a book.
- Talk about school, his mother and sister.
- Draw or do sand tray.
- Clean up the room.

At the 3rd or 4th session, the boy walked in, turned on the sound machine to rushing water and started drawing what he said was a waterfall. He finished drawing his waterfall, which was *calm*, then drew the *not-calm* of his sister saying "fuck" and his mother saying "bitch." He said that when they got really upset like that, it made him upset and he went to his room to be alone.

He asked me to photograph his drawing of the waterfall and asked, "Do you hear it?"

"Yes, I hear it," I replied, as we both listened to the sound machine in the background.

FIGURE 9.6

Case Examples and Applications

It seemed like an innocuous drawing of a waterfall until he said, "Watch." He added a circle for a head, then open eyes and a mouth. "Oh," I said, "now it's a face." He nodded.

I said, "The waterfall is the nose." He nodded.

Then he wrote his dad's name on the face. He wrote "Yes" when I noted it was his dad. He asked me to photograph it. He said, "Dr. Pat, see, eyes open." I nodded.

He asked me, "What do you hear?" I thought it had been water, but now perhaps I thought it was snoring or gurgling, through the nose . . . He had been sleeping beside his dad the night he snored, stopped breathing and died. I tried to picture what he would have heard as he lay there in bed. Before I could answer his question with a, "What do you hear?" he picked up the marker and went back to his drawing. I waited.

"Watch," he said. He erased the open eyes and drew what he said was eyes closed. "That's dead," he said. See Appendix for full-color version of this picture.

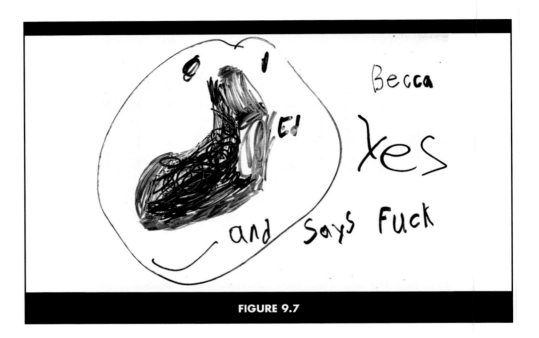

FIGURE 9.7

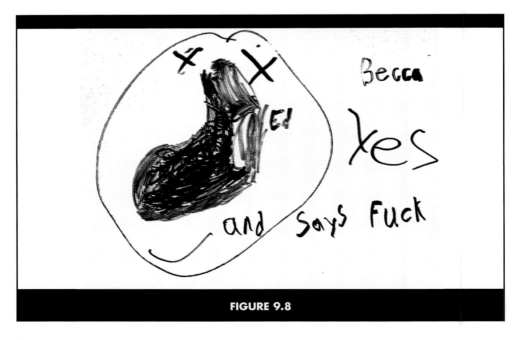

FIGURE 9.8

84

The Boy Whose Sister Said "Fuck"

I was momentarily taken aback at his openness. I saw this series of drawings as an invitation to further process his dad's death. "That's your dad dead," I commented. "Take a picture," he said, and I did as he requested.

We looked together at the "dead daddy," and I said, "That's scary. The faces are really different. First, he's alive. Then he's dead. Just like that!" He nodded and moved closer to me. We talked about what it was like to go to sleep with daddy alive and wake up with daddy dead. Like a *bad dream*? He nodded and said, "I called 911 four times." "I know," I replied, "You tried so hard to save your dad. I'm *so sorry* your dad died."

He erased the board. Then he jumped up and bolted to the singing bowl, gave it a ring, came to sit beside me, took my hand, closed his eyes and breathed deeply. I did the same.

To calm down and distract himself after doing these three drawings, he played with several sets of nesting dolls, speedily constructing and taking them apart, laying them all down on the carpet.

He erased the daddy picture and wrote a word on the board, "police," and then he said it aloud. He commented, "I write it first and then I can say it."

"Yes, like you draw it first and then we can talk about it?" He nodded. He was saying that it made it easier to talk about his dad's death by first drawing it for me.

Not long after that session, I told him the story of *Poop in the Barnyard* (Pernicano, 2012, 2014a). He had alluded to being angry at his mom (for being so unavailable emotionally since dad's death), at his sister (for changing so much toward him) and at his dad (for leaving him and using drugs). He laughed uproariously as only 6-year-old boys can over "poop." The story's metaphor is about flinging "poop" (words or literally) at others when you are angry. The main character was a little girl who lived on a farm and got angry when she stepped on poop in the barnyard. She had neglected to do her chores (clean up the poop), and rather than take responsibility, she blamed the animals. In her anger, she flung poop at the animals.

He did not need any interpretation of this story. His Squiggle drawing turned into a colorful "poop monster" being flung by an unidentifiable hand at a "poop horse." He giggled as he drew, and we talked about how he, his mother and his sister flung words at one another.

He showed his mother this drawing and said,

> In the story, the girl doesn't do her chores. She's supposed to take care of the animals, so now they are hungry and poopy. She gets poop on her shoes when she goes out in the rain to feed them. It's her own fault but she gets mad at the animals and throws poop at them.

I asked him to explain to his mother how people throw "poop" at one another. "We all say 'fuck' and we get mad at each other. We yell or say mean things. Mean words are like POOP!" He

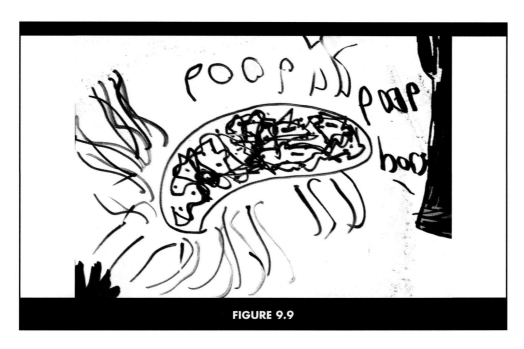

FIGURE 9.9

Case Examples and Applications

FIGURE 9.10

laughed. She laughed with him, and then we identified other things you could do when you feel like flinging poop. See Appendix for full-color version of this picture.

There are a number of good books that help children talk about anger, including *Ahn's Anger* written by Silver, where a boy's anger turns into a monster, and he learns to meditate, dance and sit *with* his anger. The story has a mindfulness component, as it suggests that anger gets smaller when you sit with it calmly. I decided to read this story with my client.

As we read the story together, my client said, "I bet his grandfather dies and he puts all his anger in his head."

"Like you?" I asked. "NO!" he shouted, like "Ahn!"

As the anger monster appeared in the book, my client went to the dry erase board and started drawing a picture. "This is Ahn and his anger, which is bigger and blacker." Then he wrote "Fuck you" and "Bitch" and said, "That's Ahn's anger talking, not me. His anger is talking to my sister." He paused and asked my permission to read "the F word" out loud to me. I told him he could read and say just about anything in our sessions as long as he did not hurt himself or anyone else.

He then said, "I'm not talking to my mom about my feelings—she's too sad and mad. I put my bed next to my mom's. I'm not sleeping up there anymore." It was another "communication," this time about his decision to change where he slept and about how strong his anger was.

He drew the Dry Erase Squiggle Story picture above and told a story about two people on a boat, on the waves. It represents his still-precarious stance, trying to balance, but not alone. He was able to bring his feelings to therapy because he was aware his mom was struggling to contain her own.

SHIFT AND TRAUMA NARRATIVE

In the next session, I felt he was ready to use the sand tray, because he now had enough control that most of the sand could remain in the box. I introduced him to it and invited his mom to watch quietly. I suggested he make a movie, with his own story and characters. He planned carefully and selected the characters and props that he wanted. He did "takes" like a movie, and several times he started over with a "new take." During each take, the mom dragon was captured and taken to the "bad guy side." Each time she was rescued by "good guys." He added more bad guys and said, "It won't be easy" (to rescue her). Two little dragons stayed on the other side

The Boy Whose Sister Said "Fuck"

and cried for their mother when she was captured. He put a row of rescue vehicles and a wizard prepared and ready for the rescue. He requested my help and gave me a helicopter and a net. However, during his first take, a big guy tried to carry out the rescue all alone. He was aggressive and smashed the bad guys. Sand was stirred up and there was a chaotic pile of dead soldiers.

I suggested it was very hard to fight bad things alone. I wondered if the team of characters he assembled could help. He did another "take" and his action included lots of teamwork and shared rescue. He showed high energy and motivation as he told and played out a well-planned and orchestrated story; then he invited me to come in with helpers. When it was over, he created a "zoo-jail" for the bad guys (soldiers, tank and shark). He said, "Cut!" and clapped for himself (see Figure 9.11).

His mom asked him how the mother dragon felt when they took her away and he gave her a funny look. She had missed that he was worried about the babies being without their mother (they needed her and felt abandoned), and I wanted to communicate that it wasn't his responsibility to worry about her feelings, as that had been a problem since the death of his dad. I quickly noted that she must have felt terrible to be taken away and not able to be there to protect her babies, then I asked him how the babies felt all alone in the middle of a battle, without their mother. He quickly came up with "mad" and "sad."

Then I tentatively asked about "scared," and first he said, "They aren't scared because their mom said to never be afraid of anything." His mom looked sheepish. I noted that most anyone would be scared in that situation. His mom said that maybe the dragon children were also mad because she left. He agreed.

I commented that she had not been able to stop it from happening. He got very upset and dysregulated, loudly saying "No!" and turning red. We had gone a little too far, come too close to his "real" mom not being able to stop his dad from dying. I said it was not the mom's fault and she wished she could have stopped it—at that he calmed back down and he rang the singing bowl before we cleaned up.

At the next session I told him a trauma narrative story called *Bear of a Different Color* and he started acting it out as I read. In this story, a small bear gets hurt due to lack of adult protection. He falls in a deep pit of black goop, is injured, and when he is finally rescued his fur is no longer brown. The traumatic event changes him and he wants to be the way he used to be, so he goes to a healer. The story illustrates trauma narrative work at a 3rd grade reading level.

My client chose puppets to act out the story: bear, squirrel, puppy and Ninja. He created props and was very engaged. He selected puppets to be the guards who were supposed to keep watch at a deep pit full of black goop; instead they fall asleep.

FIGURE 9.11

87

Case Examples and Applications

The little boy became very agitated when he realized the guards were not going to wake up, not going to keep the bear safe. My client shouted at the guards, "You should stay awake! You need to wake up!" He then gave the bear glasses "to see better," but bear still fell in the pit. He yelled at the guards, "It's all your fault! You needed to wake up!" He was very upset that the bear got hurt.

We took the bear by ambulance to the healing center. The boy's puppy puppet told the bear, "You should go to therapy to get it all out. It hurts, but then you will feel better." In the boy's own adapted version of the story, the bear's sister also fell in the pit and then an owl puppet put a protective wall around the pit. The boy said, of the sister's fall, "She got all full of the black stuff and can't talk—she is filled from head to toe!" He put her in a hot tub to soak off the goop—"She needs a long time." This was a very good understanding of his sister's emotional injury from their father's death and his recognition that it would take a while to heal.

He then announced, "My sister is still saying 'fuck,' Dr. Pat." He chose to end the session by reading part of a book where a dad hurt his son's feelings. My client stated, "My dad said bad words that hurt me inside. Like the black goop. You have to get it out. It's in his (the boy's) brain, in his memory." He was clearly making connections and verbalizing his own feelings, which was a shift in his therapy process.

In the session that followed he talked openly about his dad, saying, "He took my mom's medicine, A LOT!" He added, "When my dad died at first I was shocked and sad. Now I'm feeling a little bit better." He said his mom was doing "not too good." He was upset at how messy the house was and that "Mom sits and watches TV." He drew a picture (below) of what looked like a giant raindrop that turned out to be a "tear of a crying giant." There was also rain and two growing flowers (him and his sister?) around a red person with a "penis" (dad?). He announced, "He (crying giant) holds in his feelings at school. Kids at school wouldn't want to know, I'm sure. Some of them have lost their dads." I commented that "it is OK to share feelings, because losing your dad is a very sad thing to happen." He nodded.

This client often moved to the sand tray to help him regulate after doing a Dry Erase Squiggle that brought strong feelings. In the playroom that day, after he talked about missing his dad, he announced he would do "the same movie as before" but with different protectors. He used mommy and child alligators. Before he left, he wrote on the dry erase board, "I love you Mrs. Pat. My sister is both bad and good. So am I," then told me not to erase it.

Many child trauma victims go through a period where they display a super-hero magical thinking or grandiose power-control themes. They are hyper-aroused and can't self-regulate. This may

FIGURE 9.12

The Boy Whose Sister Said "Fuck"

FIGURE 9.13

appear in the form of make-believe play, such as playing super-hero, a form of healthy adaptation and a means of *conquering the past, feeling safe and experiencing self-efficacy*. Some children become overly bossy and "want their own way," which is understandable given their lack of control during the abuse or neglect. They also may decompensate and display out-of-control rage, aggression and reactivity, and at those times, they are seeking inner and external limits, but they need the adults in their world to provide structure and safety limits.

This little boy went through a period like this of bossy, loud, angry, cursing anger, and he found himself unable to contain it. His mother and sister were equally dysregulated, and he felt even more helpless in his grandiose *powerfulness*. He responded quickly and *with some relief* to structure and limits in therapy, as he felt safe and secure in my presence.

The Dry Erase Squiggle Story picture above was drawn during the period he struggled with anger and experienced mixed emotions. You can see the large, black mouth (probably saying "fuck!") and the clouds are mixed, with black closest to the creature, most of them frowning. There is hope in the blue clouds above and the sun is shining and smiling. The character is huge, and it is the black stuff in the mouth that suggests a lack of verbal control, likely a mouth full of "fuck." See Appendix for full-color version of this picture.

THE PROGRESS AND OUTCOMES

It is notable that one of the first things his mother had said at discovering her husband dead was, "Fuck! I didn't sign up for THIS!" In a strange way, the family that says "fuck" together sticks together. The genuine expression of anger for all three was a piece of glue (emotional intensity)

Case Examples and Applications

that helped them survive and move on as each found a way to deal with the family stress before the dad's death, the loss of a loved one and the subsequent changes in their lives.

Before we had our last session, my young client said that his sister still said "fuck" but was *nicer* to him. He quietly said, "But I'm not nicer to her yet." I asked him why he thought she said it, and he said, "She's mad." What is she mad about? "Dad." Who is she mad at? "Mom. Dad. Me." He talked about his sister being mad; her anger bothered and hurt him, because she had cared for him in a nurturing way before the dad's death. I said that he also said "fuck" and that perhaps he was "mad" too, about Mom, Dad and Sister. About how much everything had changed. He nodded. As therapy continued, he talked a little more about the night his dad died and his anger that the EMT was "slow." He played out his wish where the EMT saved his dad, and the ambulance got him to the hospital on time.

I wish we could have continued our treatment until his issues were fully resolved, but his mother said he was doing "so much better" and, using the life insurance, moved the family to a

FIGURE 9.14

FIGURE 9.15

The Boy Whose Sister Said "Fuck"

FIGURE 9.16

new home in a rural area, terminating his treatment as well as her own. She thought the move would help him think less about his dad's death. Although I wondered if he was "ready" to terminate treatment, his artwork above may have suggested otherwise. This picture of him holding a friendly looking kite in the sunshine suggests no storms; he understood that he could take his internalized supports with him. This is a low stress, cheerful picture with better grounding and a tone of optimism.

He said goodbye without fear or anxiety. Rainbows are drawn as a symbol of hope, an "after the storm" metaphor. He was sad, which is normal for children who have developed a strong alliance with the therapist, and the reader will note the alliance below, with no storms, a brightly colored rainbow and a large sun in the corner.

Working with children is satisfying in so many ways, as they wear their feelings on their sleeves and they do not hesitate to express them. He said, "Dr. Pat, don't look!" as he drew the following. He said I could look at it after he went to the waiting room to join his mother.

QUESTIONS FOR DISCUSSION

1. Agitation due to autonomic hyperarousal is common in trauma victims, both adults and children, and it can be mistaken for the hyperactivity of ADHD or even hypo-mania. What were the clues that this child's agitation was due to trauma and not ADHD? How does agitation interfere with a client's ability to think, plan and process?
2. TF-CBT (for kids) and CPT (for adults) include a phase of treatment that teaches relaxation. Why is that so?
3. How did the client's art parallel his mood and reaction to life experiences?
4. What did "fuck" represent in this family?

10

FEED THE ALLIGATOR

A Case of Sibling Trauma Intervention

CASE INFORMATION AND BACKGROUND

Many years ago, I worked with a family that was court ordered to treatment after a CPS investigation. The children, other than the baby, received individual and sibling therapy in the playroom; both parents attended individual therapy. Family therapy occurred weekly in the home; parents received parenting instruction, in-home case management and self-sufficiency classes in addition to the therapy.

The mother was of small stature, about 5 feet in height, weighing perhaps 90 pounds. She had serious health problems, including cardiac issues, which had left her unable to work, and her husband had quit his job. Their five children ranged in age from pre-teen to 1 year old. The mother was in her late 20s and looked much younger than her age. The man I will refer to as "father" was father to the youngest children and stepdad to the oldest. He was much older than the mother, over 6 feet tall and weighed over 250 pounds. He met her in his 20s while working for her father. As a young pregnant teen, they "got together" and married, with her parents' permission, not long after they met.

Several high-risk problems were identified at the time of the court referral. The children were removed because the family was "temporarily" living in a car, and the children, who looked disheveled, were not attending school regularly. The father smoked pot regularly and had difficulty maintaining employment. He had been arrested for domestic violence but was allowed to do "anger management" in lieu of jail time.

THE PROBLEMS (AND REACTIONS TO THE PROBLEMS)

There was a long history of domestic violence. The father had been raised in an abusive household. He had attended a few sessions of "anger management" but complained bitterly about being referred for treatment. He indicated, "She attacked me. What was I to do to keep her from hurting me?" The children had witnessed the dad hurting their mother on many occasions, and they cowered in his presence. He bragged to therapists about a porn website he liked, where women reportedly posed as pre-pubertal girls.

There was a history of coercive, controlling child "discipline" in the family, such as children made to stand on tiptoes in the corner for long periods of time, being "whupped," being cursed at and berated, and being made to stay alone in a bedroom for hours. The dad was particularly harsh toward one of the younger boys, who got up in the middle of the night to "take" food from the refrigerator and who had "accidents" for which he was spanked. Persons outside the family frequently heard the father screaming at the mother and the children.

92

THE CONCEPTUALIZATION

The mother's treatment focused on her inability to be emotionally and physically protective of her children, and the need to change dynamics within the adult relationships. Like many victims of violence, she was emotionally dependent on her husband; she had gone straight from her father's home to her much older husband's. In many respects he had become a new father figure.

The father had started a relationship with the children's mother when she was barely through puberty. The oldest daughter was now nearing puberty, and the treatment team wanted her to be safe from harm. His narcissism required that his wife remain helpless, weak, "childlike" and dependent on him to maintain their roles in the relationship. By keeping her dependent, he maintained power and control. She had grown up in poverty and at a very young age walked to work and took care of herself. Things changed when she married. In many ways, her husband competed with the children for her attention and was jealous, behaving like an overgrown teenage boy. He was overly harsh with the children and resented their needs; his expectations for them were developmentally inappropriate. School personnel had called CPS on more than one occasion, but the cycle of abuse continued.

The mother "loved" the father and could not envision raising children without him. The more marijuana the father smoked the less he wanted to get and keep a job. Onset of serious health problems during a pregnancy left the mother unable to work as she had in the past, and soon they were homeless. The mother would have been happy to get a job, but subsidized housing and child care were difficult to secure. The mother risked losing her Medicaid insurance plan if she went back to work, especially with her pre-existing conditions. At times, the barriers to success seemed insurmountable.

INTERVENTIONS AND THE TRAUMA NARRATIVE

The treating therapists were concerned about the risks to the children; however, the providers had difficulty getting child welfare to set limits on the father. The treatment team focused on psychoeducation about abuse and appropriate family interactions, to help the mother set limits with the father and be more protective of her children; treatment also gave the children an opportunity to process trauma and develop new coping resources.

The mother's therapist educated her about the cycle of violence, because she repeatedly returned to her partner. The mother at first minimized how her husband treated her and remained emotionally dependent on him, but with her therapist's help, she started to notice how the stepdad's behavior affected the children, and she began to assert herself. She soon realized how much they cried when she did not protect them and how angry they became in his presence.

In a pivotal therapy session with the mother, the therapist asked how her husband's interest in the porn site might put the kids at risk. The therapist pointed out that their daughter was about the age the mom had been when he showed interest in her. Her face turned red and she appeared very uncomfortable. The mom said that he liked her to "look young," without makeup. The mother had looked like a child when he married her, and she started to worry that her pre-teen daughter, who looked so much like her, could be at risk. In terms of the stages of change, she moved briefly to contemplation with regards to their marriage relationship and how he treated her.

The program staff was finally successful at getting a no-contact order against the father while he attended anger management, but the mother snuck him in and out of the home, for sexual contact. She was not able or willing to refuse him entrance, although she risked losing the children.

The mother indicated that the children missed him and were more "defiant" after his "visits." She found it difficult to parent alone, saying that they "misbehaved" and "I can't get them to mind." They cried more when he was there, and they clung to their mother or were isolated in their rooms. During his visits, discipline was harsh and the couple continued to argue loudly on a regular basis. He was physically controlling with the mother, pushing her away (to "protect" himself "when she attacked me") and grabbing her wrists.

The children had varying types of problems, including anger, social avoidance, non-compliance, taking and hoarding food, mood dysregulation, depressed mood, anxiety, sleep difficulties, fear of the dark, and relationship trust difficulties. They were treated by a team of therapists who used CBT, play therapy, therapy stories and metaphor; the siblings were expressive in their play and began to share their concerns. The children were offered a safety plan (how to get help by phone, at school or in person from program staff), because the mother was not a reliably protective parent. The sibling group often engaged in play that paralleled or mimicked family interactions.

THE PROGRESS AND OUTCOMES

The children used their safety planning, by telling their teachers at school when something "bad" happened, and telling their mother that they did not want their father to move back home. The biggest change was their insight into their stepdad and realization that they were not to blame for his anger and abuse.

The children gravitated to playing with an alligator puppet with very big teeth and a mouth that opened and closed. They were offered a variety of puppets to choose from, but this puppet became the "bad guy." He acted like a bully and went from nice to mean in an instant.

Sometimes a younger child, as the alligator, would pounce on an older child and "bite" with the teeth. The therapist would ask, "Why did he do that?" The answer, "He's mad." Question, "When is he mad?" Answer, "All the time." Question, "What gets him in a bad mood?" Answer, "Everyone gets on his nerves." Question, "When is he nice?" Answer, "When he drinks beer and eats pizza." When alligator "misbehaved," the children put him in time out as they giggled. There was a lockable birdcage (see below) that the children used as a jail, zoo and time out cage. Sometimes when he was in the cage, alligator "begged to come out." He said he was sorry and promised to behave; when he got out, he started biting again.

We identified that it is not safe to play with an alligator or to try to fight an alligator. The children understood that you can't get "too close to" an alligator. We talked about zoos as safe places where dangerous animals can live and be fed. We talked about what it would be like if zoo animals were let out of their cages and allowed to roam the grounds.

When the alligator was in the cage, we would not give in to his promises to be nice. We agreed that we didn't need to kill him or starve him; we fed him play food from the toy kitchen. The children would gather a pile of hotdogs, hamburgers, French fries, watermelon, cheese,

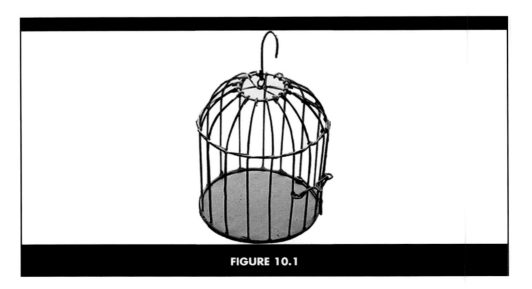

FIGURE 10.1

etc., and throw food into the cage to the alligator. Eventually, the children got "brave" and told the alligator that he had to stop biting. The therapist told him, "Sorry alligator, you're not allowed to bite or eat these children. We don't eat our friends. We don't eat family. And we only hunt for food."

THE SHIFT

Drawing on their play with the alligator puppet, I wrote a story for this family titled, *The Hungry Alligator and the Mean Snake* (see Pernicano, 2010a, 2012, 2014b) in which a nurturing kangaroo protects a group of younger animals from an alligator and a mean snake. The alligator has the reputation for being a sneaky bully, and his friend the snake is known for suffocating others. In this story, the hungry alligator and mean snake approach Kanga and her small friends, pretending to be nice and extending a dinner invitation. The animals do not understand why anyone would want to hurt them on purpose; they are overly trusting. The kangaroo tells the animals that if they go to an alligator's house for dinner, they are likely to *be* the dinner. She tricks the alligator and snake by inviting them to dinner in the park near the zoo. They lure the alligator and snake into a zoo cage by throwing in lots of yummy food. The two dangerous animals are trapped when they go into the zoo cage for the food. The kangaroo and animals continue to feed the alligator and snake, but they do not let them out of the cage. The message is that vulnerable individuals need a plan and strategies to protect themselves, and not to trust those that might take advantage of them.

The therapist read the story, and the children cheered when Kanga and her friends trapped the alligator and snake. They did not need to be *told or educated* directly about the story's message. They looked at each other as if sharing a secret, as if they thought we did not understand that there was more to the story. For the next few weeks, they played out this story nearly every session; they grew bolder in standing up to the alligator and snake. In their play, the alligator would beg to leave the zoo and promise not to hurt the therapist or children, and the children would throw food in the "zoo cage," refuse and say such things as, "You're mean. You haven't learned your lesson! It's too soon! We can't trust you! You just want to eat us!"

In the home, they had overheard their father make promises to change when the mother threatened to make him leave (after abuse or harsh punishment). He would apologize and at the same time blame them or their mother for setting him off or making him mad. The older siblings helped the younger children understand the difference between false promises and real change. One day a younger child let the alligator out after he promised to "be nice" and he "bit" one of the children; they promptly returned him to the zoo. Through their interactions and play as a sibling group, they learned lessons about safety and self-protection and supported each other in speaking up.

Therapists did not make any comparisons between the alligator, snake and their father. One week, the children invited their mother to a session to read her the story and show her the "zoo" where they fed the alligator and the snake. No one mentioned the father. She looked visibly uncomfortable but remained silent.

Soon after the session when they read the story with their mother, one of the children looked at the alligator in the cage, *in the middle of play*, and said, "You're mean like my dad!" The other children giggled and agreed. The therapist acted "surprised" and asked them how the dad was like the alligator. They did not need prompting to share their observations: "He's a bully." "He lies to you." "He acts nice and then he turns mean fast." "He promises to be good and breaks his promises." "He buys himself beer (and pot) but we run out of food and diapers." "He promises to change and doesn't." "He cares more about himself than about us." "He says he loves you but it's not true." A final comment was, "He shouldn't act like that!" Therapists asked how that made them feel and they voiced fear, anger, anxiety and disappointment.

One morning soon after that, the mother stormed into the therapy office and insisted on talking to the therapists. "You're putting ideas in my kids' heads. You're turning them against their dad!" We asked what she meant. It turned out that the night before she had snuck her husband into their apartment. One of the kids confronted him and said, "You're not supposed to be here.

Case Examples and Applications

You should leave." The father was angry and said, "I can go wherever I please. I don't care about the stupid rules." Then he made the child go to his room until bedtime.

The next morning, the dad tried to sneak out early so no one would know he had been at the apartment. He ran right back into the house and shouted, "What the hell is this? Who did this?" He took the mother out to his van. There was a good assortment of food from the cupboards, freezer and refrigerator stuffed under and piled on top of the rear seat of his van. None of the children would confess to doing it, and after they all put the food back in the house, the dad left in a huff.

That is why the mother had stormed into the therapy room. I looked at the treating psychologist and started to laugh after the mom returned home. She looked a little confused. "You know what they were doing? They were *feeding the alligator!*"

She "got it" too and we laughed at the childlike transparency, but it was clear that the children felt unprotected and sad that they needed to act on their own. In their childlike minds, maybe if they fed him well he would go away and never come back. Maybe they would finally be safe. It was important that they realized it was not their job to "take care of" the alligator. In the next family session, the children told their mother, when she asked, that they were afraid of the dad and they did not like it when he pushed her or yelled at her and at them. They did not like the way he punished them. They thought the home was "better" and "more happy" when he was not there. Each time he left, they hoped he would not come back, but they gradually understood that they had no control over whether he stayed or left. The therapy team communicated ways the children could stick together, communicate feelings to their mother, protect themselves (resist the urge to argue with dad, go to their room, tell a teacher) and seek safety (call 911, go to a neighbor).

PROGRESS AND OUTCOMES

Our treatment ended with the family because, during the time we knew her, the mother did not become adequately protective of her children, nor did child welfare place the children out of her care. Prognosis was considered guarded from the treatment team's perspective. The state seemed to think it was easier to leave the big family together than to split them up in foster care.

After leaving the program, the mother briefly separated from the father, and one weekend on a visit to her family, he stalked and assaulted her and left her in the cold. She contacted the therapy program, who stepped in, and she pressed charges. The mother appreciated the support from treatment staff after the assault, and she stayed in touch for a while. It was encouraging that at least on that one occasion, she had been able to leave him and set some expectations for him prior to returning to the home (domestic violence perpetrator group and therapy). She allowed her children to talk more about their feelings and assured them that she would remain protective. The children became more assertive in their feelings with her, and they had good support at school and from their extended family. The mother apparently lived with family members while her husband started his own court ordered treatment. The last we heard was that she reunified with her husband soon after he finished court ordered domestic violence classes. It seemed too soon for him to have moved from pre-contemplation to action, especially since his attitude toward women and children was very entrenched, but perhaps it was a step toward change.

Families like this, who struggle with barriers to change, may need something said or done with the mother and her children that may prove useful or helpful later on, and perhaps the future will bring a better life for all. However, in reality, this family may require another serious "wake up call" before they have the courage to change and live a safe, protective life.

QUESTIONS FOR DISCUSSION

1. What were some of the barriers to this family's progress?
2. In terms of the Stages of Change, at what stage of change was the mother? The father? The children?
3. How can children benefit from therapy when the parents are not ready to change?
4. Why did the children put food in the father's van? What message were they sending?

96

11

THE HOUSE WITH MANY ROOMS

A Case of Child Dissociation

CASE INFORMATION AND BACKGROUND

I selected this case as an example of long-term treatment with a young girl who struggled with trauma-related dissociation and family complex trauma. She was a middle child in a sibling group whose lives and memories were like a house with many rooms, separate and disconnected, yet at the same time intertwined. This sibling group had been placed together in a foster home willing to care for all six children, their third out-of-home placement. They had first been placed in foster care due to neglect, physical abuse and domestic violence between the mother and her boyfriend. There also had been sexual victimization at the hands of teenage male cousins who watched the children after school.

This elementary school-aged girl, and two of her older siblings, were my individual clients. Another therapist treated the younger children, and we did frequent co-therapy with the children as a sibling group as well as family sessions with the foster parents. There were signs of trauma-related symptoms in each child, including rage outbursts, fear, threatening, numbing, dissociation, sexual acting out, toileting struggles and agitation. This little girl initially presented with somatic complaints, "tuning out," sleep difficulties, overeating and low self-esteem.

THE PROBLEMS (AND REACTIONS TO THE PROBLEMS)

The "problems" were many and layered with this child; new issues continued to emerge through treatment. She held secrets for her sibling group and protected them like a mother hen, when what she needed was to join the sibling group and be more of a child. She carried the burden of memories from the past and did not ask for or seek help; she blamed herself for what happened to her and her siblings, and she implied that she did not *deserve* a loving family or home. Her older sister was emotionally disengaged and had lived apart from her siblings for several years; my client felt responsible, in an overly grown up manner, to care for and protect her siblings from a very young age.

THE CONCEPTUALIZATION

An observer might have thought that all the children in this family had ADHD at the time of placement, due to hyperactivity and inattention, however these symptoms were trauma driven. Given my client's absence of memories for specific events and periods of time, the dissociative

Case Examples and Applications

process likely began in early childhood. She had witnessed abuse of her mother, knew about abuse of her siblings, may have witnessed sexual abuse of her younger sister and experienced sexual abuse at the hands of male cousins. There were holes in her memory for events that had not yet been accessed, and over time, she revealed a highly organized inner world that was consistent with her past abuse and neglect.

This client's history and presenting symptoms were consistent with complex trauma from chronic abuse and neglect that resulted in "frozen" emotions, suicidal ideation, emotional avoidance, anxiety and dissociation. Of the six children, she was initially the most regulated, until an incident with her foster father triggered high fear, protective anger and dissociation. The dissociative process had been somewhat dormant in a prior foster home, with symptoms of overeating, "tuning out," poor focus/concentration at school and "parentified" behavior toward siblings.

Many writers have written about the dissociative continuum. The process of dissociation ranges from normal daydreaming, fantasizing while reading a good book or experiencing brief periods of highway hypnosis while driving to full Dissociative Identity Disorder (DID), with compartmentalized separate personalities living separate lives without full awareness. Dissociative amnesia can occur after a head injury, and time limited dissociation may occur during or after high stress events, such as a severe car accident.

With complex trauma, dissociation serves as a protective coping mechanism and can become a "habit" or "automatic response," because some things are *too terrible to know*. Dissociative symptoms develop as an adaptive coping response when one or more aspects of reality overwhelm the client. Clients with dissociation display significant "inconsistencies" of information and history, eye contact, facial expression, memory, reported symptoms and play/art content with an otherwise honest and genuine client. As a result of the dissociative process, memories are neurobiologically compartmentalized, with associated or related emotions and experience.

Dissociated-off states hold different memories, roles and functions for the client. Once the client trusts the therapist, the inner world starts to reveal itself, which happened with this child. A therapist may feel at a loss when a new set of eyes presents with curiosity, fear or challenge; through engagement and "welcoming," the therapist gains access to new information. Eventually, with the "help" of the inner world, the puzzle of the client's history and trauma experience is pieced together.

Once my client was removed from her home and living in a safe environment, it was no longer adaptive for her to cope through dissociation (what she called "tuning out"); however, the automatic neurobiological process of dissociation is easily triggered in the face of threatening events. An event with her foster father activated memories, high arousal and fear. At first we thought my client was experiencing a protective "flight" response, because trauma victims, when triggered by anything from loud voices to environmental threat, may freeze and "tune out." Calming and grounding will eventually bring the client "back" and orient to the present. For this child, it was as if this triggering event awakened the past, and the compartmentalization in her mood and behavior from that point forward suggested we were dealing with more than a transient trauma reaction.

INTERVENTIONS: PSYCHOEDUCATION ABOUT TRAUMA

The psychoeducation about trauma takes place throughout treatment, however, early on, it is necessary to talk about the impact of trauma i.e., common symptoms and outcomes. Pernicano, in *Using Trauma-Focused Therapy Stories* (2014a), provides two guides to trauma, one for children and one for caregivers.

With this family, the therapy team used stories and activities to provide psychoeducation about trauma that would help the children regulate their emotions and control behavior and guide the foster parents in their parent-child interactions; these parents needed to become aware of the ways in which their behaviors triggered the children. In a very early co-therapy family session, we read *Lucky the Junkyard Dog* (Pernicano, 2010a, 2012, 2014a), a story about an abused dog who does not know how to respond to a caring, nurturing home once he is rescued from the junkyard

The House With Many Rooms

where he has been a guard dog. Lucky no longer trusts humans after his abuse, and even in the face of kindness, he shows his teeth, has urinary *accidents*, expects to be hurt and misinterprets cues. The story educates clients and families about the process of trauma in a non-threatening manner through the "mind" of the dog. It elicits empathy, identification and protectiveness as clients discuss the impact of trauma.

INTERVENTIONS

While living in the previous foster home, the children reportedly had "therapy" that amounted to case management and talking about school and sibling arguments. There had been no trauma-focused work, although their exposure to traumatic events had been significant. Prior to their first out-of-home placement, the children experienced threat, maliciousness (one of the children had been put in a clothes dryer), violence (saw a man abuse their mother), physical/sexual abuse and neglect (nothing to eat). The youngest girl had an "accident" while sleeping with mother's boyfriend on the couch. We decided to take a more trauma-informed approach during this episode of treatment, because we viewed their poor social skills, high arousal, developmental delays, inability to self-soothe and overactivity to be at least partly due to trauma.

The children and their foster parents attended therapy regularly. The children shared secrets, and all of the children engaged in some degree of dissociation; each displayed fear and anger, silly/angry reactivity, agitation and attachment difficulties. It was initially difficult to work with the children together in the same room, even with tag-teaming. We engaged in many calming activities before or during sessions. The family and sibling sessions had to be very structured, with a story or theme, a hands-on activity with a goal, a family processing time, regrouping/settling time and closure. The therapy process was like the ocean tide, sometimes going out and pulling you with it and other times flooding in with high waves.

BEGINNING TRAUMA NARRATIVE

After reading Lucky's story together, we discussed the dog's situation and what his needs might be; the children talked about Lucky as well as their own needs. My client wanted to add to the story, saying, "They go on a walk and find Lucky's siblings who were homeless because their mother left them." They labeled the characters in the story with family member names and identified what would have to change for Lucky to trust others.

Early in treatment, this little girl presented as highly verbal, artistic, creative and motivated. At home, she offered advice to the foster mom in a *pseudo mature* way, and in session, she was articulate, artistic and insightful. Her foster parents and I first saw a persistent "switch" in mood and behavior after an incident where the little girl had been physically fighting with her brother; the foster dad intervened forcefully to stop the argument. She had been very close to the foster dad and turned to him for affection and nurture. That day, she cut off interactions with him at home, said she hated him, declared that she knew he wanted to hurt her and insisted that he could not be trusted. She spoke as if "he" had also been in her past. She was "different" during her next session and revealed that because she "hated" the dad, she would not be in the same room with him or talk to him during session.

I asked to meet with both of them to process what had happened at home and offered to mediate. She agreed, and she presented quite differently with me that day, turning her chair away and speaking in an angry voice, which I first chalked up to a situational loss of trust. With encouragement, she told him how he had scared her and made her "mad." We did things to validate her fear and tried to "restore" trust with an agreement, but the interaction had triggered memories of physical abuse, and she was convinced that she was no longer safe.

Then, while sitting with her back to me, she took a rabbit puppet she enjoyed playing with, cuddled it and spoke to me *through it*, asking in a different, childlike voice, "Do you understand me?"

99

Case Examples and Applications

SHIFT: SHARING THE INNER WORLD

I was not sure what she was asking but in hindsight, I think she was introducing herself and asking if I understood who she was. She was telling me that the interaction with the father had triggered dissociation and *her* emergence. I did understand the protective nature of her anger and fear and reflected as much. Each question for the rest of that session was responded to with a "whine" and "LEAVE ME ALOOONE!" I gave her a little time; then she said she felt "old" (even though she was acting young) and commented "I don't want to be a child!" I then asked her to draw or write what she wanted me to understand about her. She described "flashbacks" and drew a "bug catcher" that would catch her flashbacks "when they come quickly into my brain so they don't all escape."

Around the same time, my client struggled to behave appropriately in family sessions and her behavior became less consistent across settings. One week she was a compliant helper, and the next week she would hide under a table in defiant rejecting anger; later she engaged in regressed behavior and baby talk for the first time.

Dissociation became apparent in her artwork, behavior and play, revealing her inner world. One week, without prompting, she drew some of her "scary memories" and said, "They flow in and then they flow out before I can catch them." She said she did not want to hold onto the memories of her cousins. I used her words and asked her what it might take to catch them; could we get the memories to stay a little longer? Was there something we might do to *stop the flow*? Could we *slow down the flow*?

She and I discussed the processes of *keeping in, letting out and opening* (the compartments within her). She dropped "hints" about her inner experience, saying she had seen "a movie where there is a hunt for five keys that will open something." She announced, "My feelings are like that, in a box, and they need keys to open them." She then relayed somewhat matter-of-factly, "It's scary when your mother threatens to cut your fingers off. My mom had an Army knife. She threatened to cut off my fingers and cut out my tongue." I realized that the tongue threat might have been about not telling and maintaining secrecy. She added, "My cousins kept a knife in their room, too." She started to share another memory, dissociated briefly and said it was "gone."

We created a *bug catcher*, i.e., something that could catch the fleeting dissociative thoughts. Discontinuities in her mood and behavior became more prominent. She usually loved to draw, but one week she said, "I HATE drawing. I HATE stories." I asked what she would like to do, and she chose to play with sand tray characters, refusing to tell a story. At the next session, she set up an elaborate sand tray and told a very detailed story, unaware that she had refused the week prior. It was hard to know what to do therapeutically one week to the next, because what "worked" one week was "ineffective" the next. When I reviewed her drawings, I saw distinct differences in developmental ability, content/ themes and emotional tone. I had originally thought her pictures reflected conscious mood changes or states, but it became clear that her inner world was much more complicated.

See below, a picture of Mrs. Grim Reaper with the "Beware" sign, drawn in forbidding black with a weapon; the horse she called Romeo was done in pastel colors, childlike and playful in nature. These drawings, and others, accompanied changes in her mood, behavior and verbal communication in sessions. The "Beware" drawing was done soon after the less cooperative, angry side of her appeared at home and in sessions. This drawing turned out to be a self-representation of herself as "evil," "unlovable" and "harmful to others." That side of her believed she was beyond help and should not be living with the other children in the foster home. She blamed herself for not protecting the other children from abuse.

Conversely, the side of her that drew the horse below was cheerful and talkative. She thought "love" was the answer and did not want to be angry at the teen boys who assaulted her, because they were "family." She was loving toward animals and engaged in caretaking behavior, and she felt it was her "job" to help the foster mother when the mother was under stress. She was affectionate, compliant and loved to draw.

After drawing Romeo, she asked to borrow my fake roses and silently arranged them this way on my table. This side of her was quiet and loving.

FIGURE 11.1

FIGURE 11.2

FIGURE 11.3

Case Examples and Applications

FIGURE 11.4

She drew this last picture above to explain a phrase she used during a session: "Tackle with Love." She described it as an emotional tackle done with "kind tings." In this drawing, a kind woman is sending hearts to a female skeleton and surrounding her with love. She agreed that it was sad for the skeleton to feel dead and empty, and maybe love could restore her and her life. See Appendix for full-color version of this picture.

NEW SHIFT AND CONTINUED TRAUMA INTERVENTION

Dissociative clients do not easily or quickly disclose their inner experiences. They feel different, "one of a kind," and sometimes even "crazy." Their "normal" is "abnormal" to the rest of the world. At the same time, they do not present in therapy as seriously mentally ill or psychotic. They are usually aware that their inner reality is out of the ordinary, and there is often some secrecy, due to fear of not being believed or being treated medically as if psychotic. Certainly a therapist would rule out a psychotic condition when a client hears voices, but this client's academic performance, verbal communication, good eye contact and social network outside therapy were inconsistent with psychosis.

The dissociative process continued to emerge, a *little at a time*, until one session, she said, "You know I hear voices, someone saying my name." She watched me to see what my reaction would be. I explained that some abused children hear voices. There was enough evidence at this point to hypothesize that her symptoms were those of a dissociative disorder and that the holes in her memories were likely related to more severe trauma that had not yet been disclosed.

I decided to "test the water" and read her a story during our next session. *A Safe Place to Call Home* (2012, 2014a) is helpful in assessing and treating clients with dissociative conditions. Non-dissociative clients tend to react to this story as they would a fairy tale, but dissociative clients "get" the story, know that I "know" and start to share more details of their inner experiences.

The story is about a woman who had lived "with mean people as far back as she could remember" (Pernicano, 2012, p. 80). She wanted *to find a safe place to call home*. Her grandmother, who had

The House With Many Rooms

cared for her from the age of 8, was like a Disney villain who does bad things and you hope she will suffer in the end. The woman doesn't remember much from the time when she lived with her parents. The woman finally moves into her own house; the rooms inside the house are "locked" and she doesn't have a key to open them. She lives in the rooms that are "open" to her. At night, the woman hears voices behind the locked doors, and some wake her from sleep during the night. She thinks she is crazy but she is not. One voice is that of an angry teen, and the others are scared younger children, of varying ages. They want the woman to let them out of their "dark" rooms. The girl is finally able to find the key to the rooms, meet the persons inside and give the house a "total makeover." The restored house has an alarm system and lots of light. It is open, without locked doors. The beds and rooms in the house are "safe." A line in the story says, "*As you might guess, each of them had feelings and memories to share. It was as if they had known each other a very long time.*"

I finished the story and sat silently. Her first question was, "Are they all parts of her?" followed quickly by, "Are the ages her memories of the past? Are they locked inside her? Does she need a safe place to call home before she could listen to them?" I asked her what she thought, and she said that it was like in the story, i.e., that the girl's memories were locked behind the doors but she was maybe ready to listen to them. Later in that session, she said, "You know I have imaginary friends?" She told me that the friends talked to her. I validated her openness and willingness to share this with me.

Many young children have imaginary friends; at younger ages, many bright, creative children create imaginary playmates or friends as part of healthy development. Dissociative "friends" are different as they present with different ages, genders and intentions and often emerge at a time of non-tolerable abuse or traumatic exposure.

From this point forward, my client began to open up about past abuse, both experienced and witnessed (abuse to her mother and siblings; abuse to her), and her therapy progressed, with other sides of her presenting themselves to me. She used puppets to identify her "imaginary friends" and the "voices in my head," and at one point described the voices as a negative 8-year-old boy, a 2-year-old toddler who hits, a mean teenager, a nice 8-year-old girl and a "mixed" voice. She said that the voices criticized her clothes, told her not to trust her foster dad (the side of that got hurt by him) and seemed real. I suggested she find a way to "open the doors" and invite them to tell her their stories. During our work together, she started to do so.

MAJOR SHIFT

At a subsequent session, I asked her to develop a sequel to *A Safe Place to Call Home*, because she was a good storyteller. She was very invested in this task and drew the colorful house below, narrating a story as she drew. In her story, a girl "a little younger than me" was in one room and watched TV all day. The "baby" needed food, holding and kindness. One room held an angry girl who said, "No!" and would not come out. That room had fire in it. The key to that room had been hidden in a series of places, by the rabbit, birds (guarded by an eagle) and dogs. It was now hidden under rabbit poop. The girl did not want the key to be found. In the end it was found and the others let her out of the room. They surrounded her and healed her anger with love. But at the end of the story, all the doors locked again.

A therapist would not take her story *literally*, but might infer abuse at a young age, a reluctance to reveal some of the past (the key was hidden *under rabbit poop*, to deter someone who wishes to touch it) and hope that one day the doors would open and she would come out to tell her story. She was aware of angry feelings and believed that love would heal her, like the "kind tings" were healing the skeleton with love.

The ending of the story suggests that the doors are not ready to stay open, that her mind closes back up and is locked again, after something emerges. There are still doors that are locked, some to which she has limited access.

I decided to expand our modalities of treatment and introduced her to the sand tray in a subsequent session; she was a very organized player. She set up a story (Figure 11.6) she referred to as *snakes versus frogs*. The frogs would try to hide, but parts of them were *showing* and the snakes bit them. "Bit the dust!" she said. She removed dead frogs as they were killed, saying, "They will stink up the

Case Examples and Applications

FIGURE 11.5

desert." Eventually the snakes left. The frogs gathered to talk about what they might do if the snakes came back. The lizards arrived to help. Only a few frogs were "smart enough to survive." In her world, it was hard to survive, because you could not hide from the "bad guys," who found you and hurt you. This sand tray (see Figure 11.6) reflected the experiences she and her siblings had with the older abusive cousins, trying to come up with plans to protect themselves.

We reached a point in therapy where she suggested she draw her own house, to tell me what she knew about her dissociation, and show me who lives in each room. She had said, "I know all my people. They are the parts of me from my past. One is a nice teenager who looks out for me. The angry one is 7, and she wants her way." She (the one I met with that day) had good understanding of the "others" and talked with them. With regard to dissociation, we call this co-consciousness and inner awareness. I had not "met" this side of her before. I asked, "Do the people in the rooms draw different things? And talk about different things in therapy?" She nodded. "Ah," I said, "So

The House With Many Rooms

FIGURE 11.6

the person that draws the hearts is not the same as the person that draws the skeletons?" She confirmed this, and the look she gave me was "Duh, can't you tell?"

She drew the house and labeled the rooms (see Figure 11.7); together we pieced together the information that she could access. This activity followed up on her previous story sequel. She pointed out which doors are "open," "closed" or "stuck." She indicated that "some things happened to the kids that they haven't talked about yet." I thanked her for telling me this and commented, "I guess there are some things that you don't want to talk about yet either." She nodded. It was clear that some pieces of the puzzle were still missing.

CONTINUED TRAUMA INTERVENTION

As treatment progressed, the little girl revealed more about her and her siblings' past abuse. We talked about how to create emotional distance from the things in the past that were so hard to talk about. She went with me *Up the Mountain* (a Narnia-like pastel drawing shown earlier in the book), and during that activity, she told me that she remembered a time when her older male cousins lured her to a bedroom "with candy and money," then exposed themselves sexually to her and her sister. She was "spaced out" talking about it, a sign of dissociation. She remembered her brother coming to the door to "protect" her but then drew a blank. Her memories ended there in the room, the older boys telling her to touch them and perform oral sex. In her mind, she said "no" and stopped the boys from "doing anything" but she did not have any memories of "what happened next." She remembered that one had cut her with his knife, and one grabbed her "down here, outside my clothes."

She said she felt bad for going in the room and asked, "Wouldn't any kid go in? Wouldn't any little kid want candy and money? I didn't know what they were going to do!" I mirrored what she had said, "Of course, any little kid would trust them and go in for candy and money. They were

105

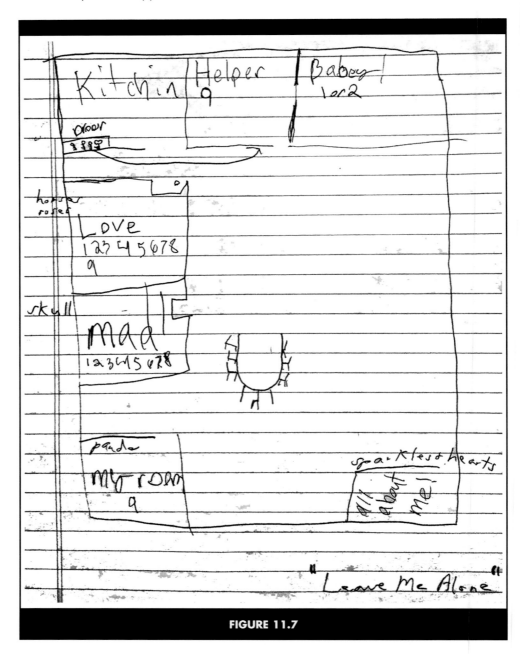

FIGURE 11.7

tricking you!" She seemed relieved but continued to revisit her strong sense of self-blame and responsibility. It was not clear exactly what had happened in that room, but at a later point in her therapy, she reported she had been sexually abused "one time" when alone with the boys (would not speak about it), and they "tried" the other time, but her brother walked in. She continued to play out themes of being "tricked" and hurt.

My client's art and sand tray work continued to reveal possible details of her previous sexual abuse. Like many sexual abuse victims, she had a weight and eating problem, and for her this may have proved protective. During a very involved sand tray, she portrayed herself as a panda. There was quite a battle, and this time, the allies defeated the enemy. Her story indicated that during the battle, a *hungry panda* was *caught* in a *net trap*. She said, "It was too heavy for their net. This is the first time that being too heavy saved him. He thought he was too fat, but it kept him from being trapped and eaten."

The House With Many Rooms

FIGURE 11.8

This is a good example of potentially meaningful material provided during play. In hearing this, I suspected that her weight and strength might have eventually contributed to an escape from the older boys, and perhaps her tendency to still hoard food and candy served a protective function. She ended that sand tray story with, "You see that they built a place where each one could be happy. Each one needed a home that was the right place to live." Panda got a very pretty place with a "nice bed and covered up." I reflected that she deserves a safe home that is the right place for her and she nodded her head. Before she left the playroom she wrote on the dry erase board, "Love is important. So are you. And Dogs." She put a heart around the word "Dogs" and signed it with both our names.

When working with siblings, it is beneficial to notice what metaphors are revealed in their selection of toys, puppet play and stories. This client and her brother had a sibling session, and he, the angry brother, selected a shark for his puppet, then indicated shark was vegetarian. This was consistent with another drawing he did of an armored individual who was "fighting for Peace." In his play, the shark said he was angry "because I got stung by two million jellyfish and by thousands of spiny sea urchins." Shark said he had scars from it.

This sounded like a ferocious attack. It made me think about the cousins who kept a knife in their room and about him walking in on them sexually abusing his sister. I wondered silently what he might have experienced at their hands. This boy's demeanor was one of toughness, bravery and anger, which can point to fear and protective anger following abuse.

Suddenly, *after the shark disclosed his pain and injuries*, the boy withdrew from the play, as this was hitting too close to home. It was his first "admission" of fear and vulnerability, and he was uncomfortable letting down his guard.

His sister then selected her puppets for the play and said that one of her puppets was "unique. It needs a family to accept that it is one of a kind and not like the others, and to understand." The parallel to her work with the iris and roses was very clear (iris placed in the middle of a bunch of roses). She was aware that her dissociation made her "different" and she wanted to be accepted and understood. She was "different" than the others who lived inside her and different than her siblings.

Each of the siblings was telling the other something very personal, and I reflected that it is hard to let go of anger after being stung by 2,000,000 jellyfish and thousands of spiny sea urchins,

107

Case Examples and Applications

just as it is hard to be unique and one of a kind unless you also have love and understanding. They were close as siblings go, but they also shared trauma, which complicated the trust in their relationship. It seemed possible, if not likely, that the brother had taken on the abuser role with his younger siblings, to avoid his feelings of vulnerability and to feel powerful and in control.

Shortly before our therapy ended, my client went through another change. A new "side" of her told her foster mother she had suicidal ideation and wanted to die. Around the same time, she started taking candy and showing anger and defiance. I was not clear about the source of the suicidal ideation, but I suspected that traumatic memories were emerging. She and I went to the sand tray, and I asked her to pick one character that wanted to die and one that wanted to live, then to do a story with them. She picked *a flying fish* for the one that wanted to die and put it in the mouth of a *vegetarian white whale*.

She said, "It is 3 years old and living in a dangerous place. Its mom called it 'stupid' and said, 'You should never have been born.'" She picked up a panda who also wanted to live, and the panda invited the flying fish to live with it in a safe place. The flying fish first went to see a foster mom giraffe and the client said, "It loves the giraffe." The client became visibly sad at this point. In her story, the foster mom giraffe was nice, sweet and "she loved the fish and took good care of it." My client had dearly loved her first foster mom and still talked about wanting to go back. In the end of her story, the fish went to live with panda. "It will be safe and happy," she said. As she finished this sand tray, she told me the side of her that wants to die is 3. At age 3, her parents were no longer together and she stopped being happy.

I reflected on her loss and sadness, as well as her desire to be loved and accepted. I offered, "A 3-year-old is too little to protect herself in a dangerous place. How insensitive and hurtful for the mom to call it stupid!" She nodded her head *emphatically*. I added, "The 3-year-old wanted to die because bad things happened and there was no one to protect her. She needs to know that she is safe now." She reflected on that, as our session ended.

During our next session, in response to something I said, she turned her chair away and said, "Leave me alone" in an angry defiant voice. The *angry one was back. This one had been taking candy at home and stealing small items.* She announced, "I'm not a child. You don't know me. And I'm not going to tell you anything about me. I'm nothing." Her facial expressions and tone of voice were very different from earlier in the session. This side continued to present during two to three subsequent sessions and mentioned that people did things, "just for money" and hinted about taking money for favors. At the time I thought she was talking about foster parents, and didn't realize she was probably also referring to the boys who baited her with promised money and candy. I suspected that this side of her was an angry protector who could piece together some of the holes in my client's memory.

THE PROGRESS AND OUTCOMES

The little girl presented differently from session to session, and sometimes when you looked in her eyes they were vacant and blank. Other times she presented with a warm smile and open trust.

At one of our final sessions, she was open and receptive, and I read her the story of *The Cracked Glass Bowl*. Without a word, she started drawing her own cracked bowl as I finished the story. She said, "It's like therapy. The person gets to heal and get over the past—become what she wants to be. She is in charge. The therapist helps her figure things out."

It is encouraging when a child tells the therapist that he or she understands the therapy process and is doing better. To heal, all the parts have to be put together. She *knew I was referring to more than the cracked glass*, and she drew her new creation(s), one that incorporated some of her therapy symbols. She first drew a glass dolphin with a reformed piece of the original glass; then added a beautiful vase with roses; and a lily pad with a happy frog, commenting that he was "plump." Finally, she added an iris to the vase, like the flowers she had put together in my office, saying, "I will be an iris and my foster mom can be a rose."

She added, "Sometimes DCS thinks they are saving kids. Sometimes they do that and sometimes they ruin their lives." I asked which it was for her, and she said that they "did a good thing" for her and her siblings.

108

The House With Many Rooms

FIGURE 11.9

My young client continued to experience ambivalence during sessions, and sometimes said she was "bad" for "doing terrible things" and "I don't deserve to stay" in the foster home. Other times she said she could not be "enough" for the foster mother, because she was empty inside and couldn't be there for her in the way she (foster mom) wanted. At times she had to "take care of" the foster mom and it was "too much." She was very sensitive to changes in the foster mother's moods and behavior (which had on occasion been dramatic and volatile), and she grieved the loss of the other foster mother with whom she had lived since she was very young. A persistent theme in therapy was that she could not share "all" her feelings with the current foster mother.

After each session she told her foster mother the stories we had worked on and commented, "She cries to hear the stories." I commented that she seemed to be trying to help the foster mom feel better, and she said, "Yes, like mini therapy" and she drew a picture of herself as a bird (see above) that was a "helper." I commented that usually the parent helps the child with his or her feelings and that it is stressful for a child to carry that load. I talked with her about the bird also needing to accept help for itself, especially when it had a problem, that we all need to help and be helped.

It took me a long time to figure out that I was dealing with different "people," and toward the end of our time together, she presented again with the angry defiant side and remained in that state from week to week. I did not recognize that this side was "not a child," even though she had told me previously, and I suspect that this side that said, "Leave me alone!" had likely been present during an episode of sexual abuse. While angry and defiant, she stopped "hanging out with" her closest friend at school, became socially withdrawn, erupted in anger at home and had very tight walls around her feelings. This side of her "hated" drawing and refused to engage in storytelling. She acted disdainful and scorned my efforts. She called her child welfare worker and said she wanted to be moved. This was a different person, well defended and not easily accessible. But the angry side was there for a reason, and undoubtedly, had her own story to tell. I did not get the opportunity to find out what she wanted to tell me.

Not long after the appearance of the defiant side, child welfare made a sudden decision to place most of the children in a different foster-to-adopt home in a distant rural location. They

109

Case Examples and Applications

decided that the older boy presented risks to the younger children because of his anger and heightened sexual reactivity; welfare moved him to a separate home. They were skeptical of the 9-year-old's mental health diagnosis and questioned why the symptoms had remained underground until this foster home. However, it made sense to the treatment team that the symptoms and memories of trauma only emerged after the children were far away from the source of the trauma and in a safe place.

The day I went to say goodbye, I was not able to "find" my client, and she would not speak to me. Her eyes were vacant, she sat angrily on the steps and repeated, "Leave me alone!" She was angry and defiant, saying she wanted to go. This was a side of her I had not yet worked with closely and had only encountered a few times.

I sat near and stayed until they were picked up by child welfare. She would not look at me. "I'll miss you," I said, for the sake of whoever else inside might be listening.

"No," I thought. "I don't know *you* nearly as well as I would like to. I'm sorry I didn't get to work with you longer to hear your story."

This girl's prognosis was uncertain when she moved to the new home. Her future depended in part on her new therapist's understanding of trauma, her using of coping skills and the degree to which she remained "underground" or "ventured out" in a new foster family. She had many strengths and an ageless wisdom. An iris in the middle of roses, she deserved a permanent home in which she would be loved and accepted. I wonder about her to this day.

QUESTIONS FOR DISCUSSION

1. Do you think that this child had PTSD? Why or why not?
2. How did the foster father "trigger" the little girl when he put hands on her?
3. What were some signs that this client was dissociating?
4. How did this child's stories, art and play reflect her trauma experiences?

12

THE MOM OF MANY COLORS

A Case of the Impact of Parental Substance Abuse

CASE INFORMATION AND BACKGROUND

This case is about a resilient child who was brought to therapy at age 6 due to "possible ADHD." I include this case so that the reader will see how life events result in escalation of symptoms at times of high stress, noticeable in stories, art and play. At the same time, the use of stories, art and play resulted in steady progress in terms of self-esteem and acceptance of what this client could not change. The reader will remember this client as the creative child who presented the gift of the flowers. She was a precocious and artistic child, and her family was actively involved in her treatment. I worked with her for about a year until I moved away, and during that year her great-grandmother, who lived with them, died and her mother relapsed several times.

The family history came out bit by bit. Her mother had used opiates during pregnancy, and there had been repeated domestic abuse between her and the child's father. My client and her parents lived with her maternal grandmother (who she calls "M") after she was born. The mother was in and out of jail and rehabilitation for her abuse of alcohol, opiates and methamphetamine; the father also had substance abuse problems. "M" eventually assumed custody of the child due to the family instability and high risk lifestyle. The parents eventually split up and the father "left for good" in 2014. During periods when her mom was stable "M" allowed the mother to live with them. Each time she relapsed she was asked to move out because she was not being kind or attentive to her daughter. This "roller coaster" life took its toll on the girl; at the same time, she developed coping skills to deal with family and personal stress.

At the time we began treatment, "M" still had trouble setting limits with her adult daughter; "M's" husband was alcoholic and in poor health, and "M" cared for her own mother who had dementia and lived with them.

THE PROBLEMS (AND REACTIONS TO THE PROBLEMS)

When this child first came for treatment, she was in kindergarten; her teacher believed she might have ADHD. The child got angry easily at school, had trouble accepting "no" and could not sit still. She liked to be "in charge" and had difficulty regulating her moods. She was ashamed of her occasional aggressive behaviors at school and tried to keep "M" from sharing those with me. She was scared to sleep alone (had bad dreams) and usually slept with her mother or "M." At intake she was overly clingy and affectionate with the therapist, also quite talkative with many questions

111

Case Examples and Applications

about therapy. We spoke about her mother's substance abuse ("I don't like it, she promises not to do it and then she does it again") and when I asked her about bad memories, she said, "Dr. Pat, I remember my dad hurting my mom when I was 4. It was scary." There was much to work on, and I decided to follow her lead and go at her pace, at least to start.

THE CONCEPTUALIZATION

Although the client has clear symptoms of ADHD, her anxiety, intense moods and strong attachment needs stemmed from past abuse, neglect, lack of consistent parenting, witnessing domestic violence from a very young age and the in-and-out relationship she continued to have with her mother. She did not trust her mother to safely care for her and had strong ambivalent feelings about her mother's behavior, yet did not want to alienate or lose her. She "bossed" adults because she was impulsive and did not think before she spoke or reacted. Even "M" did not fully understand that the child needed more stability and predictability in her world. "I'm codependent," she said, "I always have been." The child craved a nurturing relationship with her inconsistent mother, and she worried too much about her mother's substance use and the men in her life. "M" was not consistent in her expectations for her daughter, and the "roller coaster" family life was having a negative impact on the child.

The child liked having a safe, consistent relationship with a therapist so that she could freely express her thoughts, feelings and concerns, and develop coping skills for dealing with the strong emotions she carried. She needed some help with focusing, taking turns, tolerating distress, being less "bossy" with adults and engaging in conversation without interrupting.

INTERVENTIONS

I began therapy with psychoeducation about trauma, substance abuse, feeling identification and expression; we engaged in activities to calm her arousal. I used a concept I refer to as *The Sponge* to communicate about feelings and about the impact of drugs and alcohol.

> *A sponge can hold a lot of water and clean up dirty things. But if it gets too full of dirty water, it can't clean very well. When a sponge is too full of dirty water, you have to squeeze out the dirty water. Well, if a brain gets full of drugs or alcohol, it is like the sponge. It can't think and the person acts different. Until they get the drugs/alcohol out of the brain, get clean, they have problems.*

We talked about how a person can fill up with bad feelings, like a sponge. They get so full of bad feelings they have to squeeze them out. We drew a sponge and she filled in the holes with colors. Each color represented a bad feeling. She identified her feelings as anger, guilt, fear, sadness and jealousy. She indicted who in her life filled her with those feelings. She was jealous of the men her mom brought home and of the baby her mom sometimes watched. She was scared that her great-grandma, who had dementia and was sometimes "mean," would die. She was sad that her grandpa had to go to the hospital for his drinking and scared that her dad had hit her mom. She was mad at her mom for drinking and mad at her cousin for bossing her. Next, we "squeezed out" the sponge (she erased it), and she drew a new sponge. She colored in positive feelings, each a different color. Then she wrote who in her life filled her with those good feelings. "M" made her feel loved, happy and safe. Her mom sometimes made her feel loved. When her teacher praised her artwork, she was proud. When she went swimming in their pool she felt fun and happy.

The little girl initially displayed hyperarousal and agitation when we talked about past violence in the home or about her mom's unpredictable behaviors and moods. She had trouble sitting still, and, after a challenging week at home, she showed visible changes in her mood, focus and behavior. She would sometimes get "silly" or change the subject suddenly. It cued me to "back off" a little and give her time to regulate and calm down. We practiced relaxing, listening to nature sounds, and breathing to the Tibetan Singing Bowl, closing our eyes and trying to open them together at the same time, only when the sound had stopped.

112

The Mom of Many Colors

Her mother's instability and family problems continued to keep her a little "off balance," and as a result, she sometimes managed her anxiety by bossing or taking charge. She loved creating Squiggles Stories and using the dry erase board, puppets or sand tray. She also enjoyed having me tell her a story, and afterwards, she would spontaneously act something out or draw. We engaged in a variety of activities to increase her focus, help her use words to communicate and relinquish control to "M."

SHIFT AND BEGINNING TRAUMA NARRATIVE

Early on, we used a clam puppet to talk about closing vs. opening. Clam did not want to open up about his feelings. And once he closed you could not force him open. She said, "I'm like clam, I don't like to talk about my deep sad feelings, because they make me feel bad." She added, "I don't like it when my mom screams at me when I mess up. I say I'm sorry and she says sorry doesn't count. Sorry should count for something . . ." She looked up at me and added, "I'm afraid my mom's boyfriend will hurt her like my dad did. I don't trust him yet."

We talked about her fear and recalled "four memories" of dad hurting mom. She shared a memory of her mom locking her in a bathroom to keep her safe. She heard screaming in the other room; she thought of her mom hugging her to feel safe. She announced, "Next week our story can be the spider who was scared!" Her mother was surprised her daughter remembered this, as she had been very young. Mom expressed regret at exposing her daughter to this.

One week, the girl got into trouble at school for biting someone who accidentally bumped into her on the playground. When "M" started telling me about the biting, the little girl appeared to dissociate and became very dysregulated, whining and saying in a much younger voice, "I'm scared." I reassured her that she was not in trouble and I wanted to help her, not punish her. Biting is a typical behavior for an infant or toddler, the age at which she had experienced the most trauma in her life. For most of that session, she was regressed, "whiny," anxious and upset. She suggested we use the puppets as our therapy intervention. She chose a "biting alligator" and said, "He needs to be put in jail by the ocean police," represented by an octopus puppet. She also selected a variety of other ocean "friends" and helpers (grownups). I wondered hypothetically if the story was about her and the recent biting. Perhaps she was ready to work on her fear at witnessing domestic violence toward her mom by her mom's boyfriend and her own physical abuse as a toddler by her bio dad. Perhaps "all of the above."

She put the alligator in the birdcage jail and was ambivalent about letting him out when he begged. The octopus told him, "You can't bite your friends. You won't have friends if you bite people in your class." We practiced "bumping" to show the alligator the difference between "on purpose" and "accident." This targeted her symptom of hypervigilance about physical harm, due to early experiences of violence and abuse. I casually noted that babies and toddlers bite when they are scared. "M" shared that when the child was insecure at home, she clung to her and followed her around a lot, afraid to be alone. The child told "M," "I'm afraid to be alone. I'm afraid of the dark. Maybe when I'm alone in the dark, people (you and mom) will disappear."

Around this same time, her mom relapsed twice on alcohol, and the child became more anxious and dysregulated in therapy. "M" told the mother she would have to move out because she had been angry and "mean" toward the little girl. I asked my client, "How does that make you feel?" She replied, "scared . . . and a *little* angry."

This was the session where she drew the flowers in the waiting room. She wanted to communicate how much she was thinking about the past and about how her mother's drinking upset her. She wanted me to know that therapy was helping her.

Later in the session after the flower discussion, the client went to the sand tray, created a scene and told a story. "That's a baby castle," she said, "and that's a big poison frog sitting there." She placed the poison frog close to the babies who sat on the sand castle and said, "They need help. This guy is a poisoned frog. He's the enemy." Toward the end of her story, almost as an afterthought, she brought in the parents of the babies and sat them down. Next, she brought in "the help," saying, "These are two wizards Bandolf and Gandolf, this is Grandma." She identified other helpers and supports, adding other babies, older children, a protective monster, protective

Case Examples and Applications

FIGURE 12.1

snakes, a protective cat and a friend turtle. She added "lookouts." In the end, the "good" characters defeated the poison frog, but the parents never became part of the protection. They sat and watched (out of picture).

About six weeks into therapy, her teacher wrote home that the child's attention and mood were "much better"; this was a good indication that we were moving in the right direction. The child, direct and open, was responding well to the transparency of the therapist and benefiting from sharing her thoughts and feelings.

NEW SHIFTS

This child's treatment took shifts both forward and backward. Forward shifts were evidenced in her improved mood and more open communication about family roles and about her relationship with her mom. She had a strong "voice" but learned to temper it, and she learned to share "unacceptable" feelings and urges. She settled down at school and listened better at home, but when she experienced family stress or loss, there were clear backward shifts in mood and focus.

Soon after the "flowers" session, she brought in another picture of a bowl saying, "Dr. Pat, this is me. This is good feelings (pink on the right) and this is bad feelings (blue-green on the left)—see, now there is more good than bad."

This type of statement provides an opportunity to explore further. I asked, "What sort of things make you have good and bad feelings?" She replied, "Good feelings are my art, my grandma, swimming in the pool. Bad feelings are bullies, my mom yelling, missing my dad." Her dad had visited that week so we talked further about her contact with him. "I think he really came to see my mom. He slept on the couch and he talked about how his girlfriend had left him. It wasn't a good daddy visit." I asked what would make a "good daddy visit." She stated that her dad didn't "act like a dad," he broke his promises, and he drank alcohol. It was clear she felt anxious talking about the stressors; to manage it, she changed the subject and said, "I'll do a puppet show about bullies." She selected the puppets and announced, "This is Bird King of the Jungle, a mean crocodile, and a poison frog, he's planning how to be mean." She played out her own story, with the angry and aggressive puppets, with no clear resolution. At some level, she knew that the problems with her parents were unlikely to be easily resolved.

The Mom of Many Colors

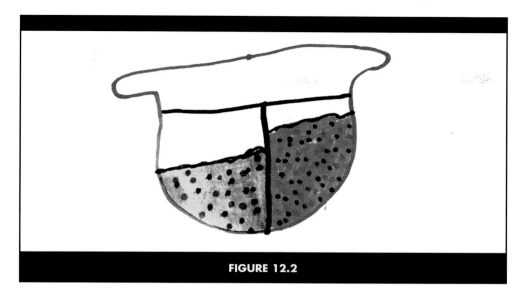

FIGURE 12.2

As this client became more self-regulated and turned to "M" (custodial guardian) for support, she became more direct telling her mom how she felt. After one relapse, she blurted out, "When my mom drinks and gets mean, she needs to go somewhere and explain it to me!" She was referring to her mother *coming and going so unpredictably*. One night, she was upset that her mom did not come tuck her in (mom's boyfriend was there). She said (to mom), "Come do what moms are supposed to do. I matter more than him." Her mother apologized for confusing her priorities, and "M" realized the mom needed to make some changes if she was going to live there.

INTERVENTIONS ABOUT PARENT-CHILD ISSUES

During one family session, we talked about the mother coming and going, and my client created another "castle" scene in the sand tray (Figure 12.3). "There are two babies in the top of the castle. There are grownups below, watching them, to keep them safe." She put in many "guards" including a panda and a tiger. Then a sea monster came, and he got too close. "He was hungry, so the babies threw him sweets, from afar."

The babies were taking care of themselves—the grownups just sat there. The animal guards helped. I asked, "Where are those grownups? It's their job to take care of the baby!" She laughed and said, "They're hanging out. They don't do anything." This was an accurate portrayal of her life before she came to live with "M." She used the sand tray to portray her avoidant/anxious attachment, whereby she took care of herself rather than counting on adults to be reliable caregivers. See the picture below of her sand tray with the grownups "hanging out."

Then she said, "The babies grow up. Now they are big, and they can lookout for themselves. They taught the monster manners. He started to get a little nice." I pointed out that growing up takes a long time, and asked if the monster would really change. She said, "Maybe he will and maybe he won't." She did not want to clean up that day. She said, "I'll come back. Each time, I'll talk about my feelings!"

I decided to explore her perceptions of her mother. First, I asked her to pick out puppets that reminded her of her mom at different times: she called them the angry mom (spider), the nice caring mom (eagle), the "boyfriend mom" (a loud noisy bird), the drunk mom (alligator), the therapist (rainbow fish), the grandma (squirrel) and the child herself (small mouse).

Once she selected the puppets I asked her to create a story and we decided to do a puppet show. In her "script," the alligator and spider showed aggression and mouse fought back. The girl hugged the mouse and then the eagle wrapped the mouse in a wing-hug (clear wishes for

115

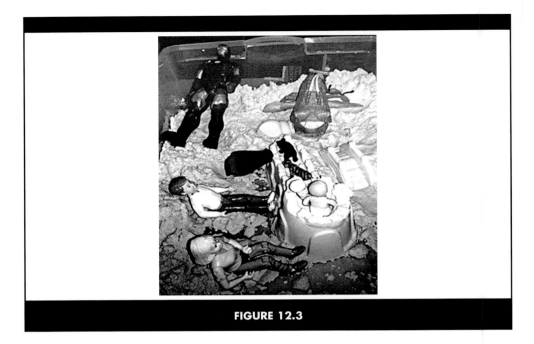

FIGURE 12.3

FIGURE 12.4

affection from her mom). The child helped the mouse accept a hug from the squirrel who had offered a hug. The squirrel suggested the mouse stop trying to get hugs from alligator and spider. The child brought two aggressive male dragons into the story (dad and boyfriend), and they had to be locked in the cage to protect everyone. The story ended with eagle embracing mouse, more of a wish than a reality in her life.

I asked her for the lesson to the story and she replied, "Don't try to get a hug from an alligator (drunk mom) or spider (angry mom)!"

The Mom of Many Colors

As we worked together, she came to an understanding "acceptance" of her mother. She knew she could not change her; she also knew that relapse and men got in the way of her mom's consistency and often said so. She relied on "M" for her basic needs and turned to art and play for self-expression.

Above is a spontaneous drawing that portrays the push-pull relationship she has with her mother. She commented, "They're turning away from each other." I asked what was going on and she said, "I really don't know." I reflected that they were frowning and turning away while they said, "I love you." I said, "It must be hard to love someone and have them turn away so much." She sighed deeply and looked very sad at that moment. This picture spoke more loudly than words.

INTERVENTIONS: PERCEPTIONS OF MOM

In the next session, the girl was quietly drawing while I talked to "M." She was drawing a woman with multicolored hair, some thick areas, some thin; she was very deliberate in selecting the colors. I stopped my "adult" conversation and asked her to tell me about her drawing. She said, "Dr. Pat, this is my mom. Her hair is all different colors, like she is all different. Each color is a different mom. See, some parts are bigger and some are smaller."

She had transferred the concepts from the previous session's puppet show and picked a new way to communicate her feelings about her "different moms." I sat across from her and asked her to tell me about each color while I labeled them on the board, which is why the labels are upside down. See 'The *Meaning* of Color' from page 202 for full-color version of this picture.

We used this drawing for the rest of the session, so that she could describe the types of interactions she had with her mother, present and past. She explained each aspect of her mother, and when I asked how each aspect of her mom made her feel, she said she was sad, frustrated and hurt by many of the interactions. We talked about how the drugs and alcohol brought out different moms.

FIGURE 12.5

Case Examples and Applications

The Colors of "Mom"

Colors on the Left (Bottom to Top)	Colors on the Right (Bottom to Top)
Brown = Drunk Mom	Red = Mad Mom
Dark Purple = Upset Mom	Light Purple = Happy Mom
Light Green = Yuck, Disgust (sexual mom?)	Blue = Sad
Orange = "I loved you as a baby"	Bright Green = "I'll do it later" (when asked to do something, says "later")
Pink = "I missed you" (says this after being gone and returning)	Turquoise = "I'll walk you home from school"
	Black = "I'm too tired/I can't get up"
	Yellow = "Maybe" we can do that/go there

I asked, "Which parts do you want to grow bigger?" and she replied, "The happy/loving, the walk you home from school, the play a game with you, the tuck you in part." "M" interjected that the mom isolated herself in her bedroom a lot and expected "M" to get the child's snacks and do the bedtime routine. If the girl wanted to see her mom, she went in and slept in the mom's room. We set a goal that once a week, mom would do the snack and go to the child's room to tuck her in at bedtime. It was hard for her mother to do even this small thing on a consistent basis for very long.

I asked which parts she wanted to be smaller in the hair, and the girl said, "the drunk mom, angry mom, the leave me alone, the maybe, the come back later, the I'm tired, and the I'm too busy sides." I suggested that she was 6 and couldn't make her mom change. She could tell her mom her feelings and wishes, but it was up to her mom to decide to change her priorities and habits.

When a child presents material like this, it is important to "stay in the middle" and not be perceived as *against* the caregiver; rather, to empathize with and stay focused on the child's feelings, validating all aspects. A child's ambivalence is like a see-saw, with up and down feelings, longings and love balanced with anger, hurt and sadness. It is not our role to judge, but to reflect and help the child tolerate the ambivalence. It is the dialect of the "and" of feelings, not "either-or."

Stress often results in changes in a child's play (themes, degree of organization, interactions or intensity) and drawing (colors, themes or organization). Regression in functioning occurred when her great-grandma died, when her mom brought boyfriends home, when her grandpa went in the hospital, when she was jealous over a young child her mother babysat, when her mother relapsed on alcohol or drugs, and when an older boy in the neighborhood showed her graphic porn and violent movie clips. Her art was usually the first indication she was upset and it became an "invitation" to talk about what was bothering her. The reader will see below that the quality of her drawings became very chaotic when she struggled with strong feelings or aggressive urges.

She had a good sense of humor, and we spent two sessions processing her feelings of jealous hurt and anger over her mother babysitting a 2-year-old. In the first session, she told a story of "The Evil Baby Monster." I asked her how a baby could be evil. She replied, "He's taking away my mother's love. My mom was using her voice, getting all cuddly with him and saying things she used to say to me! *I'm* her baby!" I invited her to talk about what it was like when she was a baby. There had been violence and substance abuse in the home as well as inconsistent caregiving. She was jealous of seeing her mother give another "baby" what she had not given the client.

At the next session, "M" and child's mother joined us. I found out that her mother had relapsed and wasn't going to meetings, claiming she didn't have time. The mother said, "She's a hard child to deal with you know," as if her daughter were not in the room. "M" and I saw the hurt in the child's eyes and "M" quickly disagreed saying, "She may be opinionated and moody, but she's a very easy child. You spend too much time watching TV and sleeping to notice that." I suggested

The Mom of Many Colors

FIGURE 12.6

that parenting was not an easy job; at the same time, we can't blame children for our moods and behavior. Her mother returned to the waiting room, and the child requested to play family Squiggles with "M." We took turns finishing the drawing and telling the story. When it was her turn, the child took charge, drew the picture above from a simple Squiggle, and told the first story (see drawing below), with a big grin.

Here's that *e-vile* baby again. I'm riding a dragon. The dragon uses its fire to turn this baby into a duck. The girl said, "See you." The duck-baby falls off and says, "Noooooo!"

See 'The *Meaning* of Color' from page 202 for full-color version of this picture. The reader will clearly see the intensity of her feelings and the anger toward the baby, with humor interspersed. After she told her story, the girl looked at me, and said, "Dr. Pat, it's just a story. He's not really evil. He's just a baby, but I don't like him one bit." We all smiled, and I validated her feelings that she sometimes yearned to be a baby again to get what she had missed. Therapists need to remember that urges, fantasies and negative feelings may not equate with behavioral risk, and this child was mastering her feelings through drawing and story. She was angry and hurt that her mother did not show her the kind nurturing behavior she showed the other child and felt safe to openly communicate without judgment.

A change in a child's typical play presentation can indicate an attempt to cope with stressful life events as well as a "bid" for help. One week, this client engaged in disorganized play the entire session. She could not maintain eye contact, and she buried and unburied characters in the sand tray, saying they were her great-grandparents, both of whom had lived with the client and died in the last two years. She moved from one activity to the next and was much less focused, with a "silly" mood and high-intensity play. I suspected something had increased her stress and anxiety and suggested we play Dry Erase Squiggle Story. I did a simple Squiggle (purple up-and-down line below), and she competed the drawing. It is common for this up and down pattern to be turned into mountains, but her Squiggles Story was full of danger and uncontrollable events. She presented the concept of "quick-ice." When I asked what that was, she replied, "Dr. Pat, quick-ice is like quicksand, if you slide into it you never come out."

We talked about the precarious ice and the danger of the growling polar bear. Everyone on the ice mountain seemed "up in the air" and dangerous. I asked her how someone might survive by wearing ice cleats. She remained agitated and said, "It's no good, once you slip down the quick-ice

Case Examples and Applications

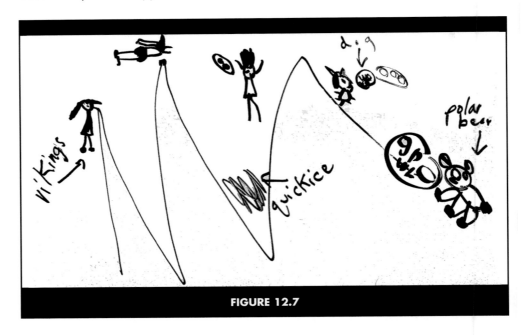

FIGURE 12.7

you are a goner." This was a notable difference, as she usually developed solutions or resolutions in her stories. Her session activities clearly reflected concerns about danger or even death.

After she and I finished, I asked "M" if anything had changed that week, or if something had raised her anxiety given the nature of the drawing. As it turned out, her beloved grandfather, "M's" husband, was in the hospital because of health problems due to his drinking. The girl had visited him at the hospital and told him he needed to stop drinking or he was going to die. She told him she loved him and he teared up and told her he would try to stop, that he loved her too. Before we ended our session that day, we talked about how scary it was for her that he was sick again and she couldn't really do anything but love him.

SHIFT

During times when her family was more stable, this client's artwork was organized and showed positive self-representation. I was concerned when, after a period of good stability, she again displayed agitation and dysregulated behavior, this time lasting across two sessions. She avoided my questions, remaining closed and at times flippant. I wondered what might be going on. Then a picture was confiscated at school from her desk, and her grandma forwarded it to me.

She initially denied drawing it and for several days stuck to her story that it just "appeared" on her desk. Then she admitted she had drawn it, and said it was a picture about her scary dream. When her teacher, "M" and I saw the picture, we were concerned about some type of sexual exposure or assault. I was concerned about the bloody object that looked like a penis, but she vehemently insisted that the bloody tool was a knife. I asked her to describe the picture: there was a male with a bloody "knife" confronting a girl in a purple dress (holding her bloody abdomen), a baby in a crib in the background, and an older female in underwear or bathing suit. He was saying "shut up," and a girl was crying for help.

She announced that she would not talk about the picture or the dream with "M" in the room but agreed to go in the playroom and talk with me. Piece by piece some details emerged—a young male teen in the neighborhood had shown her a scary video game, aggressive videos on YouTube and at least one pornographic clip. She said the scariest thing he showed her was about a girl who killed others at school and put them in boxes. The neighbor boy told her it was a simulator game

The Mom of Many Colors

FIGURE 12.8

FIGURE 12.9

and that when you played it "you have to BE her!" The drawing that follows depicts this video. The choice of dark black and the red of the blood communicates her distress. In this picture, the larger girl's face, body and legs are in red. There is a red cloud surrounding the smaller girl, and a red stab mark in the center of her chest. The knife has red blood coming off it.

121

Case Examples and Applications

She did not want to talk about the other video he showed her. I pressed a bit, and she admitted he had shown her a picture or video, on his tablet, of a man and woman having sex. "The guy had clothes on and the girl was naked." She said it really bothered her, because the man "had his hand up her." She was quite embarrassed by it all.

She denied that the neighbor boy (or anyone else) touched her or made her touch him. But his behavior had made her very uncomfortable. She agreed to tell "M" with me, because it was a "need to know" situation. "M" followed up and later texted me that the girl and her male cousin had been caught on a "bad" website on which adults were known to have exploited kids. On this site, "cartoon characters" get naked and there was some sexually explicit activity. Both the children's guardians put blocks on the site and monitored closely.

FURTHER CONCEPTUALIZATION

We continued to work on the "peer nature" of her relationship with her mother. When her mother was tired, depressed, upset about a boyfriend, or irritable and unmotivated due to drugs/alcohol, she expected the child to tolerate the changes in her moods and to "excuse" her lack of consistent parenting. The child had taken on the role of "parenting" her mother when she was home. "M" was the legal custodian, but the bio mom acted more like the child's "older sister" than a responsible adult. Certainly, the roles were very unclear, and the "M" had enabled her daughter to continue in a dependent, *adolescent* role for many years, coming and going as she pleased, not contributing financially to the household. This created a high level of stress for the child, who felt responsible for her mother and "bossed her around."

THE PROGRESS AND OUTCOMES

This spunky, creative, resilient child made steady progress in therapy over the year we worked together. We moved into maintenance treatment then towards termination when I moved from the area. But recently "M" called me. The girl's mother had relapsed on alcohol and methamphetamine, and she had been jailed for 14 days. Also, after a long hospital stay, the child's grandfather had died. During this time, the child's "behavior" at school had resulted in "Needs Improvement" and her teacher said she wasn't paying attention or finishing her work. She was struggling to deal

FIGURE 12.10

The Mom of Many Colors

with her mother's return home from jail and the loss of her grandfather, after having lost her great-grandmother the prior year. I agreed to see her for a few monthly telehealth sessions and we revisited the flower theme at the end of our first session. She remembered the first drawing when she was 6 and that it had represented her at various life stages. I asked her to draw me her "now flower" at age 7.

The flower has leaves and a full yellow center, but it is not fully open and lacks large petals. "The sun is asleep," she said, "and the flower is trying to wake him up." This accurately reflects her sadness after her grandfather's death, her efforts to "wake up" her mom who has pulled away from her and her desire to get back in the sunshine. It is a hopeful drawing but represents the effort it takes her to feel good. It reflects her awareness that her mother, from whom she desires nurture and care, has been "asleep" in recent months and that "M" had not been as available due to her own grief at the loss of her husband. She verbalized that she was "upset" with her mother but "glad" mom was out of jail again. She said, of "M," "She's 100% there for me." She seemed to have maintained much of her progress from earlier treatment.

Toward the end of a recent session, she spontaneously drew the following picture. The mermaid's tail is rainbow-colored, the octopus bright pink with a red tongue sticking out, black dirt spots on the tail, and a blue shark. She told her own story, as follows:

> *A mermaid with a beautiful rainbow-colored tail was swimming in the ocean. She has spots on her tail. Shark had dirt on him, and when he bumped into her he got dirt on her. Now she has dirt on her tail. [I asked if he would hurt her.] No, he won't bite her, he's coming to help. The jellyfish tried to hug her and stung her on the tail; 3 tentacles stuck to her. The shark saved her by biting away one tentacle that was hugging her too tight. The shark ate that tentacle. Some parts of the tentacles are still stuck to her. Now that she is freed, she is going to take a bath to get the dirt off.*

I reflected that the mermaid lived in water. "I know," she said, "but she feels dirty. After her bath, then she can hug the jellyfish again." I wondered aloud if the girl needed to protect herself from the stingers. I asked, "Perhaps she could wear a protective covering?" The child said, "Yes, rubber." This picture suggested that affection (hugs) and pain (getting stung) are intertwined, and that there is risk in affection. It may refer to repeated disappointments and hurt by her mother's inconsistent behavior; she is aware, based on this drawing, of the need to protect herself. The language of "dirt" is a strong metaphor, and the character must take a bath to feel clean. I found "rubber" to be an unusual choice of protection for someone her age. Dirt/cleaning imagery is

FIGURE 12.11

Case Examples and Applications

sometimes present in sex abuse victim; I talked with "M" (a protective caregiver), who assured me she did not leave the child alone with the mom or mom's boyfriend. It was clear that the client felt "freed" by a protective "other," a shark that would not bite. At the next session, a month later, we reviewed the previous drawing and story. I suggested I play a talk show host and ask her questions about her picture, so she could tell the "audience" ("M") a little more about the picture, and she agreed to play "TV interview."

During our "talk show" she revealed that the jellyfish was a male friend (age 9) and that the mermaid was 9 years old. The jellyfish "didn't mean to hurt her." When asked how the mermaid felt when she got stung, the client said, "*HORRIBLE! PLEASE GET ME LOOSE, IT HURTS!*" The shark was a friend, and he got dirt on him from the jellyfish who had been "playing around in the sand"; then he got it on the mermaid. She said, "Now the shark has to go brush his teeth again." I commented, "I see, after he bit the tentacles to free the mermaid, he had to go brush his teeth." The rubber protection was described as a wetsuit, and the mermaid put it on because, "She didn't want to get stung again." Then I asked, "What did the mermaid do when the jellyfish came to give her another 'hug'?" The client's response: "She said, 'Wait, I have to get on my rubber suit.'" She said that she would play the part of the mermaid if we acted it out; I commented, "I thought so, because of all the colors and you know how to protect yourself." "Yes," she replied.

NEW SHIFT

The client's picture and interview suggested that she was feeling "stung" (hurt) and needed to protect herself from pain. I checked in about her daily after-school routine to see if anything had changed. She typically had a snack after school before "M" got home, so I asked, "Does Mom join you in your snack?" She put her head down. "No," she said. "She goes to her room and locks the door."

"Why does she lock the door?" I asked. Her voice grew intense. "Because she wants to be alone and she doesn't want to be beside ME! And I'm OK with that!"

"M" gave her a look, and she looked back. I said, "I see the looks. 'M' doesn't believe you. I'm not sure I do either."

"It's the truth!" she said. "My mom doesn't want to be with me!"

"That may be true. Sometimes your mom acts like a mom, and other times, she does her own thing." I looked her in the eyes and added, "I don't believe the other part. I think you really do care when she leaves you alone and doesn't spend time with you."

"Yes," she admitted. "I do care."

I told her I was proud of her for being honest. "It's OK to say how you really feel even when you know it won't change, at least right now."

"I'm used to it," said the client. "That's what she does."

I commented, "That's what she has always done, sometimes act like a mom and sometimes do her own thing." "Yes," she replied.

"Before we end our session, let me tell you a story," I suggested.

I made up this story to reinforce the nurture from "M" and permission to let her mother remain on the emotional banks. As I told the story, I watched and listened for their reactions, to "adjust" if needed. I wanted to leave them both with a "gift" to take home.

Stuck on the River

Once upon a time, there was a little girl. She wanted to take a raft trip down the river. She got in the raft, pushed off and started to float along. The river current guided the raft. But there was a problem. As the river started to get a little rough, with rocks and splashing, the girl realized that she was missing three things in her raft: a lunch, a LIFE JACKET (interjected the client), yes, and a paddle.

"Oh no!" said the client and "M."

Then a woman came along, paddling in another raft. The girl told her, "My raft was empty, and it doesn't have a lifejacket, a lunch and a paddle."

The Mom of Many Colors

"That IS a problem," said the woman. "What good is a raft without the life jacket, lunch and paddle? I have an extra life jacket and you are welcome to borrow it. I have an extra paddle I can loan you. I can even share my lunch. But it might make more sense to have you get in my raft. We could paddle together, share the lunch, and you would have a life jacket. The raft trip would be easier if we did it together."

The girl had to think about that for a minute. She really liked doing things on her own because she was very independent. She knew she could take care of herself and wasn't sure she wanted any help. At this the client grinned at "M" as if to say, "That girl is like me!" and she leaned sideways into her, her head on "M's" shoulder.

They decided to finish the river journey together. But first they had to put the girl's raft on the riverbanks, because it was of no help to them. They were careful to pull it up on the banks without any damage. They left it there and paddled on down the river.

The girl added, "They paddled to Starbucks to eat their lunch" and "M" added, "and they bought a treat to share."

We all laughed and "M" wiped a tear from her eye as the girl leaned in for a hug. They would get through this time in their lives, together, and they recognized that sometimes you must leave behind what is no longer helpful on your journey.

PROGRESS AND OUTCOMES

After the last session, "M" realized that the mother was using again and gave her (and the boyfriend) a deadline to move out. "Ah," I thought. "Ready to put the raft on the river bank . . ." They have since moved out and at our most recent session, I asked the little girl to draw a sponge and label her "now" feelings; she filled in the "now sponge" with "love" and said, "That's because my mom is gone and I'm happy again. I can love her but I don't trust her. She stayed in her room all the time. She was mean and yelled. She didn't say she loved me. I love M and I'm doing good."

Her grades came up on this report card and her behavior improved as well, so this episode of care is winding down. I will continue to do maintenance checkups with this client and her family due to the recent family losses, but we will soon phase out. The little girl has coping resources she did not have when we started, and her drawings and stories will continue to be an outlet.

QUESTIONS FOR DISCUSSION

1. Describe how this client's flower story was a life-representation.
2. In what ways does this client's use of art and stories reflect her developmental functioning (insight capacity, cognitive, emotional and visual-motor abilities)?
3. Give some examples of how this child used symbols in art or play.
4. How did therapist stories or interventions result in a shift for this client and "M"?

13

THE BOY WITH A HUNGRY HEART

A Case of Maternal Neglect and Abandonment

CASE INFORMATION AND BACKGROUND

A 3-year-old boy arrived at his new home where his extended family had agreed to care for him, "until his parents get their act together." His mother had a drug problem and his dad had a prior brain injury, and his biological mom might have used drugs or alcohol during pregnancy. He had been severely neglected and physically abused from birth; he had witnessed the abuse of his biological mother. I will refer to his caregivers as "mom" and "dad" in this case.

At age 3, the boy had very little speech and his preschool teacher reported he did not engage with the other children. By the time his caregivers brought him to therapy at age 4, he had lived in the new home about a year, they were concerned about developmental delays and about what they referred to as habitual "lying." They wondered if he had autism, due to the speech delay and lack of reciprocal social interaction, but he showed none of the repetitive or ritualized behaviors seen in children with autism. He watched his environment carefully, as if ready to hide or flee. He was being held back in the preschool because he was not ready for kindergarten. He did not know his colors, could not say his ABCs and clung to adults.

THE PROBLEMS (AND REACTIONS TO THE PROBLEMS)

When he first arrived at his new home, the child was not interpersonally responsive and walked around "as if in his own world." His hearing was checked, but it was within normal limits. This child turned out to have many of the developmental delays that can occur without nurture, consistency, stimulation and attention to basic needs. A cognitive assessment indicated deficits in expressive and receptive language as well as visual-motor delays. He often stared blankly at adults when they spoke to him. He sometimes hoarded food and took things that belonged to others. He had a very short attention span and bounced from once activity to the next. He was about two years delayed in adaptive and communication skills, yet his bright eyes and ability to connect emotionally with a ready smile suggested his delays were due to neglect and not to something like autism.

At home, he would not let his new mom out of his sight, especially when she returned home from work. He followed her around the house, hugged on her leg and became distressed at any separation. She was patient with him and with the therapist's help, she educated herself about the impact of trauma on attachment development. The older children in the home engaged the

126

The Boy With a Hungry Heart

child in play and talked to him quite a bit. He warmed to them and soon became part of the family. His new mother was kind and patient, and when she got home from work she tried to spend time with him. He was still clingy; we talked about attachment disruption that results in a child basically "starting over" with attachment development. I helped mom understand his need for proximity, constancy, consistent response and, at the same time, encouragement to venture further from her presence and play more independently.

His new dad was not patient. He thought that the boy should "snap out of it" now that he was in a stable home. He misinterpreted "tuning out" as defiance and thought the boy was disrespectful for ignoring him. He also thought that his wife was "babying" the child and became impatient with the boy when the child appeared to not listen. When he raised his voice, the boy cowered, *tuned out and stared straight ahead*. The dad had grown up with harsh discipline in a family where you did not complain. Children were expected to do promptly what they were told, and his loud voice triggered a stress response in the child.

A year after the boy arrived at his new home his biological parents remained unstable in their lives, were without a permanent place to live and continued drug involvement. It became clear that his biological parents might not ever be capable of raising him. The new family and the child had grown attached. The boy was now only a year behind cognitively and developmentally, a testament to the love and stability in the home. He was preparing to enter kindergarten that fall with special education resources for his slow processing speed, communication delays and challenged social interaction.

THE CONCEPTUALIZATION

This child had significant attachment delays in addition to his developmental lags. It takes a long time to remediate the impact of severe neglect and abuse in the first two years of life. Dr. Bruce Perry refers to the functional impact of abuse and living in fear with concomitant cognitive, emotional and social maladaptation. He proposes that children need interventions that match their current neurobiological functioning. In this manner, we can "match" interventions to a child's capabilities. He developed a mapping process for identifying a child's strengths and limitations and how those correspond to neurobiological development. This child's brain formation had been impacted by his abuse and severe neglect, and as such, his right brain (emotional, sensory) was better developed than his left (verbal, executive functioning, planning). He had coped through dissociation, which is common when trauma occurs through infancy, and he continued to live in fear. With environmental stimulation and love, he was emotionally "catching up" and even developing a sense of humor, but he would likely continue to have problems with expressive and receptive communication until his cognitive brain caught up. As part of developing a more secure attachment, he needed to know that no one was going to abandon him, and in that aspect his development was more like that of a toddler than a 4-year-old. He clung to his new mom because that was his attachment development level.

INTERVENTIONS AND TRAUMA NARRATIVE

At first, this little boy had no capacity for make-believe play, which was consistent with his "toddler" stage. He used objects in non-meaningful ways, naming them and touching them, without emotional display. He would set out dishes, pull play food out of drawers, move dolls and furniture around in the doll house, without any role playing or goal to the play. He did not have the ability to tell a story or generate a puppet story.

Initially, he had an extremely short attention span, bouncing from sand, to kitchen, to dry erase, to toy cars, to doll house in a period of minutes at each activity, and he sometimes seemed to forget what he was doing then move on to the next. Like a sensorimotor-stage player, he touched and moved things without purpose.

What he liked to do most was cook and bake. He wanted to "bake a cake" and at home his new mom let him help her "bake." This was novel to him. Baking = Love. Cooking = Not going

127

Case Examples and Applications

hungry. At that session, I taught him to play and joined him at the stove. We talked about the steps of baking a cake and I taught him how to pretend. At first, he was very literal. "What's this, Dr. Pat?" "That's salt." "No, it's not. It's a wooden block." "See, on the outside, that word is salt. It's pretend salt." "Why?" "Because we don't have real salt, flour, stove here, we make-believe." "Why?" "Just because we do."

He was drawn to the baby doll and each session he cuddled her and fed her. I began some reflection, "Oh, she's crying, you pick her up and take good care of her." One session, he answered: "Yes, I'm a good daddy."

In play therapy, after about four months, he could focus for longer periods of time and was starting to engage in some rudimentary make-believe on his own, self-initiated play using the sand tray and the kitchen. I began doing some feeling identification with him, and sometimes he talked about his memories of his birth mom.

THE SHIFT

About this time, the boy started to show better emotional understanding. He told people he loved them, and he showed remorse when he made a mistake. He still didn't seem to understand the difference between truth and lies, as his reality and fantasy were still undifferentiated. The boy periodically asked about his biological mother, and his family noticed that he was starting to express feelings about her. She contacted his guardians somewhat unexpectedly and requested a supervised visit with him. He wanted to see her, and he made a list of questions he wanted to ask. Throughout the visit, however, she paid little attention to him and showed little interest in his life. After this visit, he seemed very sad. That week in session, he showed his first display of anger.

"Dr. Pat, my mom isn't nice." I asked how he felt after the visit. "Sad," he replied as he went to pick up the baby doll. Then, "Mad," as he slid out two beanbag chairs. He added, "She's mean" as he urged me to sit with him on the floor.

"So you feel sad and mad after your visit with your mom?"

He cuddled the baby doll and curled up next to me on a beanbag chair. "But I want her to be nice!" he said in a loud voice.

"Yes, you want her to be nice," I reflected. "In your make-believe, she *turns into* nice, like a happily ever after story, but when you see her that is not true."

"YES!" he retorted. "A mom should be nice. A mom should take care of her kids."

He also started asking questions about whether he would have to *go back to her* or stay where he was. "I don't want to live with her!" he said. "I like my school. Aunt M cooks good." It was clear that he needed reassurance, to feel secure about staying in his current home and know that he would continue to be nurtured and cared for.

I told his guardians, during an update after the session, "You know, he probably needs to know your intentions. He sees himself as temporary. A little like the Velveteen Rabbit. He wants to know that he is 'real' to you, like your other kids."

The parents both said, with some surprise, "He's part of our family and with us for the long haul. At this point we can't imagine ever returning him to that home. And nothing has really changed." They said that they loved him and had committed to keeping him in their home. They told him so that same week, and he settled in a little more securely.

At the same time, the boy's dad was still impatient and skeptical. He did not really seem to grasp the profound impact of the child's early experiences on his attachment style (anxious and insecure), and on communication, social and emotional development that would take time to remediate. He expected the child to respond promptly, to stop taking things, to tell the truth 100% of the time and to stop following the mom around the house. I explained that the boy's behaviors had meaning and purpose (to meet his needs for survival, security and nurture) but were not *thought out* (he lacked the capacity to plan/sequence) or done *on purpose*. His behavior had been *adaptive* within an abusive/neglectful environment but was no longer adaptive. The dad was aware that his frustration and criticism sometimes caused the boy to *shut down*. It was no surprise that this ex-military man, who had been raised in a harsh, controlling, punitive family, had difficulty understanding the emotional impact of this child's early development; he found it

128

The Boy With a Hungry Heart

hard to summon empathy for the child's current behavior. He loved the child and could be quite nurturing, but his quick anger was a barrier to the child's trauma recovery.

I decided to write a story for them to help the dad better understand the child's situation and to form a better working alliance with both parents. I would read it to them when the *right moment* arose.

At the next family therapy session, the dad said (in a fairly stern voice) about the now 5-year-old boy,

> I understand he had a hard life before he came to us. But now he knows how to get one over on us. He manipulates us. He is narcissistic. He wants to be the center of the universe. He wants his way and won't stop bugging us when we say no. He thinks his needs are more important than anyone else's. He needs to stop taking things that don't belong to him. He needs to look at me when I talk to him. Sometimes when I talk to him he just stares at me as if nothing is going in.

The boy, hearing his dad talk about him this way, shrunk down in the sofa and tuned out. The mom put her hand on his knee, and he moved a little closer to her.

I said, "Hey, let's take a break and read a story." I handed him a squirrel puppet and said, "You can be the squirrel, and your mom can be the owl." The boy gave his dad a puppet and said, "You can be a friend." The parents looked a little sheepish and uncomfortable, but therapists will find that most family members participate as requested.

The boy cuddled into his mom with the squirrel puppet.

I had written *The Hungry Heart* (Pernicano, unpublished) for this child and his caregivers when the appropriate moment arose. It is an excellent choice for child or family play therapy with abused or neglected children and their parents/foster parents/guardians. This boy's caregiver was expecting too much given his developmental delays and trauma history. I wanted to help the father empathize with and better understand the "meaning" of the boy's behaviors and emotional responses.

The story is especially useful for educating parents about the *nurture needs* of children placed in out-of-home care who may be engaging in obsessive compulsive rituals, stealing, hoarding or rejecting the care of the caregivers. For the child who is isolated, withdrawn or attachment disrupted, the story *reframes* behaviors that can lead to shame and low self-efficacy. This is a great story to help overly critical parents understand the roots of child trauma responses and to increase attunement with and empathy for the child.

I read *the story to them* while the child pretended to be the squirrel, moving his hand around and making squirrel noises. In this story, an owl helps a young squirrel who lost his mom at a very young age. The squirrel hoards nuts and tries to survive on his own. Owl tells squirrel that he really has a hungry heart, not a hungry tummy. The owl and other forest animals offer kindness and nurture to fill the hungry heart.

The Hungry Heart

Pernicano, Unpublished Story

"What are you **doing?**" said Owl to Sammy Squirrel. "Your nest is overflowing with nuts and you are trying to stuff more nuts in there?"

It was true. Sammy's nest, a large hole in a comfortable oak tree, was overflowing with nuts. They were crammed in there tight, like sardines in a sardine can.

Owl added, "In fact, there are so many nuts in your nest that there is no room for **you.**"

"Yes," said Sammy, "that's true. I sleep outside under the tree."

"It's not safe to sleep outside under the tree," said Owl. "There are dangerous animals that might hurt you, not to mention thunderstorms and hunters!"

Owl continued, "There are enough nuts in there for TEN squirrels, and you are only feeding yourself."

Sammy looked at Owl with a slight smile and rolled his eyes as if to say, "Silly Owl, you don't know what you're talking about." He insisted, "I need them when I get hungry and I am hungry all the time. I need them to survive the winter. And I need them just in case."

Case Examples and Applications

"Just in case what?" asked Owl.

"Just in case someone steals the ones I have collected. Just in case I run out. And just in case my mom comes back."

Ah . . . There was more to squirrel's story. Owl prompted, "In case your mom comes back?"

Sammy had not really meant to say that, but it was on his mind and just popped out. He looked down and was very quiet for a moment. He did not like to think or talk about his mom. It made him really sad.

But Owl was his friend and Sammy trusted him, so he decided to tell Owl about his mom. "When I was a really little squirrel, before I knew how to take care of myself, my mom went away. I don't know where she went. But she never came back."

Sammy went on. "Sometimes I dream about her. In one dream I see her playing with a handsome squirrel and running across a telephone wire. In my favorite dream she cuddles with me in the nest, and I fall asleep with her warm fur wrapped around me."

"Maybe that's not a dream," said Owl. "Maybe that's a happy memory of your mom loving you."

"It could be a memory," said Squirrel. "That is a nice thought."

He looked down. "In my bad dreams a hunter shoots her or she gets hit by a car. Maybe I'll never know." There was a long pause.

"How did you survive without your mom?" asked Owl.

"It was really hard that first winter," said Squirrel. "I was very lonely and cried a lot. I ran out of nuts and nearly starved. But somehow I survived. When spring came, I learned how to collect nuts by watching other squirrels."

Squirrel looked up at Owl, "I know it's silly but I sometimes dream about her coming back. In that dream I never run out of nuts and I am safe and happy again."

Owl gently wrapped one large wing around Sammy's shoulders and gave him a big hug. "It's not silly at all," he said. Sammy rested his head on Owl and sighed.

"Sammy," said Owl. "That is a very hard story to tell. Thank you for trusting me with your heart."

Owl asked, "I wonder if you could tell me where you got all these nuts. Surely they did not all come from this tree?"

Squirrel said, "I can't tell you—I'll get in trouble."

Owl commented, "Telling the truth is usually the best thing."

Sammy had a guilty look on his face. "I know it's wrong, but at night when everyone is sleeping, I go out and gather nuts under the largest trees where plenty of nuts fall. I doubt the other squirrels even miss them."

Owl replied, "Yes, those nuts do belong to other squirrels, even if you think they won't miss them."

"I know," said Sammy, "It is a bad habit and I can't seem to stop myself. I worry about going hungry or think about my mom, and I just HAVE to go out. 'Just in case,' you know."

"You know," said Owl, You do not have a hungry tummy. It might feel like that, but you have a different type of hunger. You have a HUNGRY HEART. Your heart is lonely for love and comfort.

Sammy had a sudden "aha" at what Owl said—his tail flipped up in excitement.

Sammy exclaimed. "Why didn't I see it before? I have plenty of food in my nest, but it never seems to be enough. That is because I have a hungry heart! My heart is hungry for love and comfort."

It made so much sense. At a very young age, Sammy had to take care of himself and survive in a sometimes dangerous world. He did not need more food. He needed more love and comfort.

"Sammy," said Owl, "Let's return the extra nuts to where they belong. We will keep enough nuts to get you through the winter and leave some space in your nest for you to sleep. And if you ever get low on nuts, tell me and I'll be sure you never go hungry."

Sammy agreed with Owl, and that night, while everyone else was sleeping, they returned the nuts to the other squirrels' trees. Then they returned to Sammy's nest.

At the foot of the tree was a great pile of things: there was a stuffed toy that looked and squeaked just like a squirrel, a nightlight, a chew toy, a machine that made a sound like the ocean when you pushed a button, and a large very soft, fuzzy blanket.

"Where did those things come from?" asked Sammy.

130

The Boy With a Hungry Heart

Owl replied with a smile, "Those are for your hungry heart. The other squirrels in the neighbor-hood didn't know you were living here alone, and they wanted to help. The sound machine can block out the scary nighttime noises. The nightlight helps when you are scared of the dark. The toy is to cuddle, and the blanket is from me."

"Also," said Owl, "There is a grandmother squirrel down the street who just lost her husband. She is feeling sad and lonely. She did not like the thought of you being alone in your nest, especially at bedtime. She has offered to come tuck you in and sit with you until you fall asleep."

Sammy agreed to let the grandmother come tuck him in. After all, she was going through a sad and lonely time, and Sammy knew what that was like.

Sammy's adopted grandmother as well as neighbors and friends like Owl helped him fill the spaces in his hungry heart. He found out that a hungry heart is a lot like a broken heart. You have to be patient, because healing takes time.

The urge to take nuts did not go away—it came back now and then, as every bad habit does, but Sammy usually resisted it by seeing the nuts in his nest and knowing he had enough. Sammy learned he would never go hungry as long as he paid close attention to the needs of his heart.

THE BOTTOM LINE: Feed your hungry heart.

The dad silently looked down while I read and his face flushed. As the story ended, there was a long silence. He looked at the boy, then looked at me and raised an eyebrow.

In a gruff voice, with a small smile (while listening to the story, he had figured out exactly what I was doing and why), he said, "Well, that isn't *exactly* where *I* was going, but it'll do." With that, the child went to his dad and climbed into his lap as Dad wrapped his arms tightly around him. The boy sighed deeply then grinned and said that Sammy the squirrel probably found a new family, instead of living alone in the tree. I said maybe Sammy helped his new mommy cook and used his nuts to bake with her. The child agreed.

The dad was softer and more nurturing during the rest of the session. I observed that it was clear he loved the child and was a good protector. I told him I could see that he was upset over how the boy had been treated in the past. I commented that the family's love and patience had brought much developmental change in the past year. Both parents nodded. The dad then reminded the child that their home was the boy's too—no matter what.

THE PROGRESS AND OUTCOMES

For this family, a single story, tucked into the middle of a session, planted a "seed" and shifted things in a more positive direction. In subsequent sessions, this opened the door to discussing the harsh discipline the dad had experienced as a boy. Dad believed he had become tougher because of it but realized that this little boy had experienced far worse than he as a child, and the boy's behavior was not personally directed against him. The child was driven by developmental and attachment issues that would take a long time to heal, and the dad would be instrumental in that healing, through love and patience.

QUESTIONS FOR DISCUSSION

1. Conceptualize this child's functioning in terms of unmet attachment needs and developmental neglect.
2. How did the boy's play reflect his needs and desires?
3. How did the dad's upbringing color his view of childrearing? How did the story provide a new viewpoint?
4. Metaphor often communicates at two levels: the literal conscious and the symbolic (non-conscious). What were the levels of communication in this story?

14

THE WOUNDED ELEPHANT

A Case of Emotional Wounding

CASE INFORMATION AND BACKGROUND

On my first day of work at the group home, this 10-year-old little girl walked right into my office and introduced herself and asked if she could be my helper. I invited her to help me unpack my books into the book case. We visited as we worked side by side, and she was very talkative, a little "bossy" and had few boundaries. She was also a little physically clumsy and gawky, close to puberty and was outgrowing most of her clothes while going through a growth spurt. She was grouchy around other children and annoyed them with her chatter and interruptions. She had previously been diagnosed with ADHD and she met criteria for that condition.

"How old are you? Do you have kids? How long are you going to work here? Can you be my new therapist? Where do you live?" and so on. She asked about my dog and when I brought him in to meet the kids, she liked hearing about how I had "adopted" him and taken him home from a local park when he was lost.

Each day she came home from school, she made a beeline to my office to play with my things and draw on the dry erase board. Sometimes she told me how dusty my shelves and desk were, and she took it upon herself to wipe them clean. She liked to stay busy and was in motion most of the time. She talked about her day at school and upcoming visits home to her parents as well. She was hungry for adult attention, and we developed a good, but somewhat unconventional, therapeutic alliance.

PROBLEMS (AND RESPONSE TO THE PROBLEMS)

The previous therapist had already left the agency when I arrived, so many of her cases were transferred to me. This girl had been placed in the group home due to parental neglect. She had other siblings who also had been placed out of the home. She talked about her twin brother having a bad temper, and his placement in foster care two to three years prior. She was embarrassed to talk about how he had also been sexually inappropriate with her in the past.

Her teacher had called the CPS hotline due to concern about the child's lack of cleanliness, tiredness in class and unkempt appearance. CPS found that the house was not "fit" for living due to undisposed-of trash, animal refuse in the house and dirty dishes. Her parents were referred for therapy and parenting classes but had yet to follow through. They were offered some in-home services, but neither parent seemed motivated to do what was needed to have their daughter back in the home.

132

Her mother weighed over 400 pounds and spent the better part of the day in bed or sitting in a large overstuffed chair. She had COPD and struggled to engage in any physical activity. Her dad was simple and concrete, intellectually challenged, but a kind and nice man. Neither parent supervised their daughter or helped her with her homework, and she had fallen behind in school.

My client had been diagnosed with a learning disability and had an Individual Educational Plan, but teacher had trouble connecting with the parents. Meals were not regularly provided nor was personal hygiene attended to. Her parents allowed her to stay up late and to eat what she pleased. She had struggled with enuresis since she was quite young.

CONCEPTUALIZATION

This is a case where the sexual behavior by her twin was short-lived and, perhaps because they were same age and close, it proved to be more embarrassing than traumatizing, although it was possible that puberty would bring new adjustments. When her brother acted out with her, she was young, and it may have seemed more like a game. She was mad at him during our treatment and didn't like his temper, but her ADHD symptoms kept her from dwelling on it. She stated, "It is what it is" and accepted, as did her family, "for now" he had to live somewhere else.

The biggest problem focus of treatment was the severe neglect of her basic and emotional needs. She reversed roles with her mother and became a helper and caretaker, even during visits, getting meals for her mom, cleaning the kitchen, etc. She had never known an active mother who took care of her. Each time another child left the home, my client grieved and felt the abandonment, because sooner or later, it would be her turn. She was "stuck" in a "no-win" situation, because she loved her parents, but she found visits with them to be "boring" and stressful.

INTERVENTIONS

She met with me weekly; I planned hands-on activities, because she had an attention span of about 15 minutes and was easily distractible. We started with therapeutic games, like the Talking Feeling Doing Game, but her answers to questions were quite superficial. She avoided talking about feelings and her communication was simple in nature; at the same time, it was clear she was a lonely girl who yearned for her parents to "really want me." She was also sad and anxious, worried that "like the others" she would end up going to a new home.

I introduced her to the Dry Erase Squiggle Storytelling game and she really enjoyed the spontaneity and interaction. She started drawing things that communicated her discontent; the first drawing was a colorful volcano erupting. "Like me!" she said. "I get so mad that I can't go home." We talked about what gets her "hot" and what she could do to "cool off." We discussed the stages of volcanic eruption, from calm to blowing smoke to spitting hot embers and full eruption. "My brother was full eruption," she said. "You don't want to get in his way!" About that time, she talked about him touching her when she was "really little" and how that made her feel. She had told on him and felt guilty for his removal from the home.

She was spontaneous and unfiltered in her communication. My Squiggle turned into a huge dinosaur lying flat on his back on the ground with a stream of pee going straight up in the air, as if to say "piss on the world" (see Figure 14.1).

She giggled at this and said repeatedly in a playful manner, "He's peeing all over. He doesn't care!" I asked her how he was feeling. "Like a baby!" she said. "Peeing whenever he feels like it!"

"How are you like the dinosaur?" I asked. "Pee, pee, pee!" she grinned. She was right—she had many accidents at school, sometimes due to distraction but other times she was daydreaming and "off in her own world."

One week she came in after a visit home and announced, "They are the mom and dad, but I'm the only one that does anything. My mom never gets out of her chair. She's diabetic and she still eats the wrong things. We never do anything on my visits. We sit around and watch TV. It's boring!" She was close to tears.

133

Case Examples and Applications

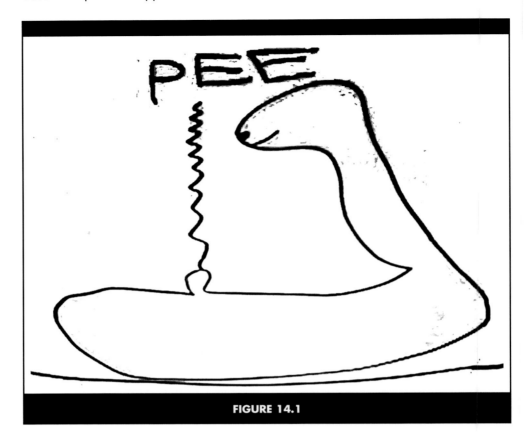

FIGURE 14.1

"You seem really sad," I said. "Yup," she replied. She missed her brother, missed her parents, and she could see that they were not following through. She was so frustrated and hurt that they could not get their priorities straight.

Not long after this, my client was on a weekend home visit when a frantic call came in from her father. He had noticed that his wife had not come downstairs yet and went upstairs to check on her. Only in her mid-30s, she had died in her sleep of diabetes and cardiac failure. He explained to his daughter that her mother had died and asked the group home staff to come pick her up.

"I don't want her to see her mom like that," he said. The group home manager went to pick her up and plans were made for the funeral later that week. We went with her to the viewing, and she flitted in and out like a butterfly. She dressed up and sat with her dad and brother at the funeral, then everyone had a meal at the church.

For the next few weeks she shut down emotionally. The other children in the group home were kind to her, as they had all "lost" their parents and understood that she would never see her mother again. She continued to visit my office daily, but she sat quietly, held stuffed animals and rocked in the rocking chair. She talked about her mother and shared regret that her mom had not lost weight or cared for her health. She grieved at several levels, including a deep grief at being separated from her twin brother. She felt disconnected from her father, who was dealing with his own grief, and for several weeks after her mother's death they did not have a visit.

Her dad stayed in close touch with the group home, and he told child welfare that with his job, he could not bring his daughter back home or raise her by himself. They made plans to find her a foster-to-adopt home in a rural area, somewhere she could be with animals and get the attention and nurture she needed.

Treatment became challenging because she had lost her mom, her dad had decided not to bring her home, and she was probably moving to a new home. I let her take the lead, gave her space and at the same time, normalized a wide variety of feelings she might be having. It was clear she was still angry at her mother, for dying and neglecting her self-care, but she also was thinking about having a mother who birthed so many children without making them a priority.

The Wounded Elephant

I recommended to the authorities that she have weekend visits with any identified new family before making a permanent move, so that we could help her grieve and stabilize, thus optimizing success in the new placement. I also asked if we could have phone contact with her after her move, until she felt connected to the new family. I pointed out that she had been angry at her mom at the time she died and that some residual guilt might complicate the process of her grieving.

I wrote a story for her, titled *A Little at a Time* (see Pernicano, 2012, 2014a), about an elephant who gives up and becomes immobile by the zoo pool. A long time ago, bad things happened to the elephant and she kept all her feelings, and poop, inside. She kept everything in for so long that now she can't move around like other elephants. She lays helpless by the pool of water and feels sad. She is afraid to let out her feelings and poop, because she believes they will all come out at once and overwhelm her. In the story, an elephant friend tells her she can let it all out, the feelings and the poop, a little at a time. The friend says that feelings and poop don't have to come out all at once. She agrees to try this and begins to share her feelings. As she gets up on her feet, with great encouragement from the other elephants, she begins to drop poop and make farts, then she starts to talk about her feelings as she walks around. She is proud of her success, a little at a time.

SHIFT

Soon after we read that story, the client came into my office with a feisty spirit, flopped down in my chair and grabbed the dry erase board. "Let's do Squiggles!" she announced. I gave her a Squiggle to complete, and she turned it into the colorful elephant below. See 'The *Meaning* of Color' from page 202 for full-color version of this picture.

The colors (bright pink, green, orange, purple) were in contrast to the story's theme, she said, "This elephant is very hurt. No one cares. He is covered with scratches. See his face and trunk? Scratches, scratches and scratches!" She announced as she added more scratches, with some

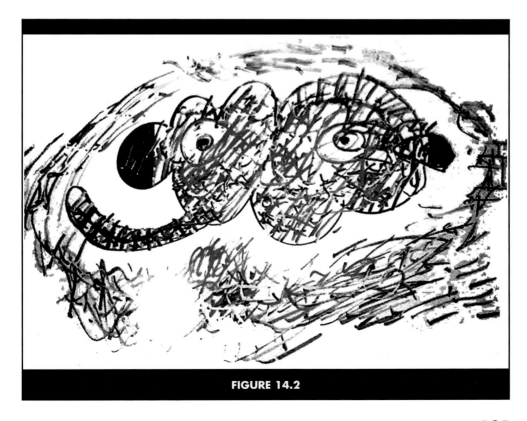

FIGURE 14.2

Case Examples and Applications

intensity. "He wants to get better. He goes to the doctor, and the doctor takes good care of him. The doctor gives him medicine to put on all his wounds. The End."

I asked, "How is he feeling?"

"Sad and mad!" she replied.

I empathized, "That's terrible! Poor elephant. . . . He needs some tender loving care (TLC) to get better."

Then I asked, "You know, they say an elephant never forgets. Is that true for him?"

"Absolutely!" she said. "He remembers everything. He just doesn't talk about it."

"What bothers him the most?" I asked.

"No one paid attention to him. They hurt him, and no one cared."

She suggested that the elephant on the dry erase board would let out his feelings and his poop a little at a time. She lumbered around the office, stuck out her bottom and made fart noises, which sent her into giggles and hearty laughter. She farted, trumpeted with her "trunk" and laughed until she had tears in her eyes. I joined her in the play and then I asked, "How does the story end? Does he get the TLC? Does he talk about his feelings? Does he get better?"

She sat quietly and then responded.

"His scratches heal. He talks about it. He gets to a happier place in his life. You know, Pat, there really isn't happy ever after. That's just in fairy tales."

I said, "Hmmm. You have a point. I think there is *good enough* ever after. And maybe that's good enough."

She gave me a hug and bounded out of my office as quickly as she had bounded in, but this Squiggles session became a shift in her recovery. She found herself able to communicate in a more personalized manner through "the elephant." First person disclosure was a struggle for her, perhaps because of her learning disability, and the drawing activities freed up emotions and spontaneous expression.

This shift in her treatment progress was reflected at school and home. Her "accidents" were less frequent, and she engaged in more self-care regarding her personal hygiene. Puberty arrived without any significant hiccups, and she argued less with the group home staff. She talked more openly about her anger, her childhood sadness and regrets as well as her happiest memories; best of all, she started talking about her imagined "new family."

PROGRESS AND OUTCOMES

Child welfare found a foster-to-adopt family that sounded like a good fit for her, an older couple who had raised and launched their children and found their lives too empty. They lived close enough that she could still have visits with her dad, and they agreed that we could have phone contacts at her initiation.

She went for her first visit, and came back in a good mood, eager to share. "They have a farm!" she told me, with a smile. "Dogs, cats, horses and a swimming pool in the back yard."

The family took a liking to her as they had regular visits, and she would be the only child. They had grown children who visited at holidays, but she would not have to share their affection or attention at other times.

We had a good termination process and the day she "left for good" was a happy-sad day. She drew a picture, ½ of the butterfly in blue and the other half in lavender, her way of saying goodbye. See 'The *Meaning* of Color' from page 202 for full-color version of this picture.

She finished drawing, then entwined her fingers with mine and said she would miss me. I told her that I would miss her too, but like the purple and blue colors on the halves of the butterfly, we would always be part of each other. After she left, over the next few months, she called me out of the blue two to three times, and seemed happy in the new home. From what we heard, she made a good adjustment.

Child welfare decisions are not always made in the best interest of the child, but for those of us who have worked in residential settings, we work with what we are given. We have all seen children precipitously removed without notice and placed in homes that later abused or neglected them. We should all work together systemically to continue to reduce such disruptions and base

The Wounded Elephant

FIGURE 14.3

agency or child welfare decisions on the child's attachments and needs rather than on "fiscal" or other barriers. I am grateful to have been part of an optimally stable, collaborative transition.

QUESTIONS FOR DISCUSSION

1. How did this child's ADHD get in the way of her expressing her thoughts and feelings?
2. When she talked about the elephant, what was she saying about herself?
3. How did the group home meet the child's needs in a way that her parents could not?
4. This client had ambivalent feelings complicated by her mother's death. Please discuss.

ADOLESCENT CASES USING STORIES, ART AND PLAY

15

"TELL ME WHO I AM"

A Case of Grief and Identity

CASE INFORMATION AND BACKGROUND

A high school student and her mother presented for intake. The girl's grades had fallen the prior school year (she was failing most subjects), and she had lingering symptoms of depression. She had been suicidal at one point; although she was no longer suicidal, she remained lethargic, slept too much, engaged in binge eating, gained weight and was not spending time with friends. Her grades had suffered through middle school, and she and her family had gone through a painful situation at their church. Although she wore artsy, colorful attire and presented as a "free spirit," this client's mood remained dysphoric. Her superficial, glib, happy face hid a darker side—she had "hibernated" and "cocooned" in her depression and avoided connection with others.

The family had moved from another state for her dad's teaching job not long before he became terminally ill, and he died four days before her 10th birthday. Her mother worked two jobs to support the family after her husband's death, and they had to move to a new house. She and her mother mutually depended on each other after the father's death, and both wanted the girl to get "back on track" so that she could apply for college the next year. Her mother immersed herself in her work and at the same time was very supportive of her daughter's therapy. We agreed to meet twice a month to address the teen's depression and grief.

THE PROBLEMS (AND REACTIONS TO THE PROBLEMS)

In the first few sessions, her lack of energy, lethargy and anhedonia were palpable. Since she had been depressed for nearly a year, I referred her to her PCP for SSRI medication, to "jump start" her mood and energy and potentiate her response to therapy.

She was a smart and verbal teen but somewhat insecure, young and childlike in her presentation. She was dependent on her mother and had not gone through any period of "rebellion" while growing up. In some ways, she seemed afraid to grow up and she planned to live at home while starting college the next year. The parents had been happily married for a long time, and her mother had not been prepared to be left "on her own" emotionally and otherwise. The teen had become her mother's "emotional partner" in some respects, and her mother realized she needed help to "launch" her daughter into young adulthood.

Case Examples and Applications

THE CONCEPTUALIZATION

This teen did not have any stigma about psychotherapy and was a wonderful client. Our conversations revealed layered concerns such as identity, sexuality, separation-individuation, emotional intimacy, depression as well as grief and loss. She communicated best in artwork and through that medium I came to better understand her. The loss of her father, with whom she identified, and her failure at school left her floating in the ocean without a paddle, in danger of drowning. She was close to her mother, but she didn't want to impose her own sadness. Her social isolation and sexual issues arose from a different source, not solely due to depression. She was an "old soul" in some ways, not able to appreciate and enjoy the superficial interactions of many of her peers. Again, through her art, she found others who "saw" her clearly and accepted her as the person she was. She had diverse friends who served as a strong support system, but there were past issues she had not yet dealt with. Given her age, openness and stage of development, our work together became relational and focused on her growth as a person, both a bridge to the future and a link to the past.

INTERVENTIONS AND TRAUMA NARRATIVE

Initially, we did grief work, using *The Cracked Glass Bowl* story, and she processed the *present and future losses* related to her dad, including things only they did together, the dreams she had of him seeing her graduate, him walking her down the aisle at a wedding and all future envisioned hopes. "I do feel broken," she said, and "as if my life will never again be the same." She drew the main cracks on her glass bowl, and she was articulate in her description.

"This one," she said, "is being cheated of him knowing me as an adult and me knowing him as a person. When he died he was my daddy, but when you get older you get to know someone as they are as a human being. As adults you can share things you don't share with little kids. We did things together, we had such good times."

They had enjoyed so many of the same things that were unique and special to their relationship.

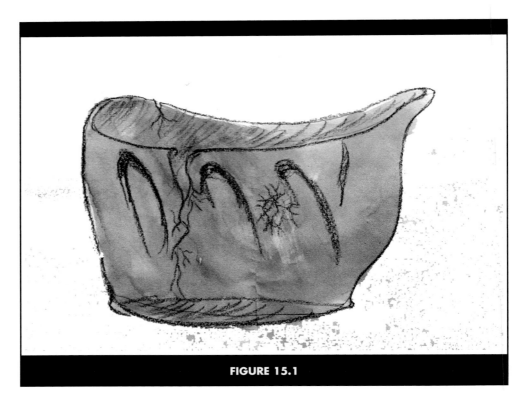

FIGURE 15.1

"This one is for the crack in my mom's heart. He is all she had, since they were both very young. Now there is an empty hole in that place."

She pointed to a chip and said, "That one is missing him in the future, my college graduation, all the important things you want to have your dad at. There will be no HIM in my future."

She said about the bowl, "That's pretty much me and my family—cracked and broken. Some of the other cracks and chunks, I'm not even sure what they are or how to fix them."

In talking about her grief and loss, she shared many happy memories of family times, moves, her parents and her dad. Her dad had *anchored the family* in many ways, and without him in her life, she felt adrift. The reader will notice that she grieved *ahead*, because she anticipated the future without him and judged it to be bleak and less meaningful. Over time, her urge to die dissipated, and her grief became less acute, gradually morphing into acceptance and the decision to live her life in ways that her dad would be proud of her.

She identified with the main character in one of my stories *The Black Cloud*—the basset hound character with a black cloud over his head. The black cloud blocks his view of the sun, so his world is gray and dark, and his mood and thinking reflect that "negative reality." The black cloud prevents him seeing and experiencing the sunshine. The black cloud had arrived following some negative life events; now he lacks energy, sleeps too much and is very irritable. He doesn't realize that his thoughts and feelings affect the color of the cloud, until his friend points it out. Eventually he takes charge of his thoughts, feelings and the cloud, and this brightens his perspective.

My client needed behavioral activation, to engage more with others her own age; we talked about the nature of depression and how action must precede energy and motivation. She started reaching out to friends and engaged with people at school around her artwork. We often talked about the self-representation in her artwork, even when she said it didn't really "mean" anything. I wondered aloud about possible meaning connections. Initially, she had little insight as to the degree to which her art paralleled her development and view of self. We explored *her* meaning of the art; I gained a deeper and more personal understanding of her views, her emotions and unmet needs. She discovered that she could speak about someone or something depicted in her artwork in the first person, and thus expand her view of herself. I am grateful for her permission to share some of her work in this book, and I have selected pieces that served as her personal metaphors.

We did some CBT type work after reading *The Black Cloud*, and I invited her to draw a cartoon that was a self-representation. The cartoon on the next page was the first indication for me of the extent of her "dark side." The reader will see that the cartoon depicts the dark, self-critical inner dialog that floods and overwhelms her, leaving her with a feeling of powerlessness. There is a dark sense of futility and hopelessness. The *negative chatter* within her is portrayed powerfully, and the turmoil depicted in the dark lines is weighty and mind-boggling. It is easy to see how she surrendered to such darkness.

As we talked about the cartoon, she considered what further panels might portray, such as giving in, giving up or fighting back. We spent several sessions processing this cartoon, and I encouraged her to strengthen the voice of the main character. With some guidance, she talked back to the darkness and argued with the assumptions, providing alternative views and exceptions. This client's presentation did not reflect the dark intensity of her inner world, and only through the cartoon did I capture specific critical, hopeless thoughts and negative self-perception. The cartoon also prodded me to make a referral for anti-depressant medication, and the addition of an SSRI contributed to her subsequent progress. The cartoon provided the opportunity to engage in CBT techniques to help her challenge her negative self-talk and develop a more positive view of self. See 'The *Meaning* of Color' from page 202 for full-color version of this picture.

THE SHIFT

The first shift in the client's mood was after starting an SSRI medication that provided a jump start in energy and clearer cognitive focus. She had been very lethargic, with loss of interest in doing things and over sleeping. She had gained a great deal of weight and found it hard to focus and concentrate. On the SSRI, her grades came up, dramatically, and her motivation to change

Case Examples and Applications

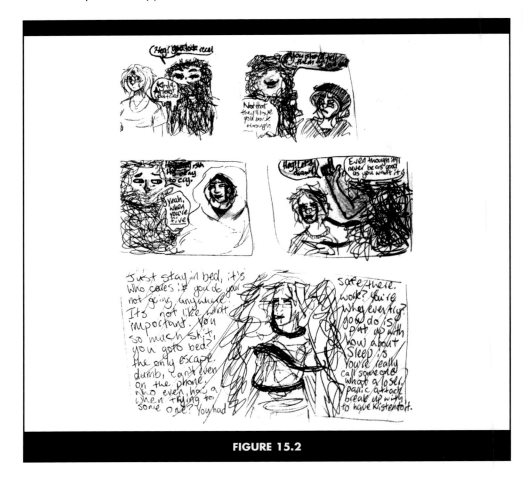

FIGURE 15.2

was activated. From the time this client started her senior art portfolio, there was a shift in her treatment, presentation and self-representation.

She titled the portfolio, "Tell Me Who I Am," and that title suggested a number of different possibilities. The first was like playing a game called Pictionary, where you draw something, with intent to communicate, and then you say, "Tell me what I'm drawing." In that case, you know what you are drawing and you rely on the others to figure it out. The other possibility was that she was asking for help in defining her Self. I think that perhaps it was a little of both.

I remember a discussion we had where I encouraged her to define herself and to answer some questions about herself. She struggled to answer personal questions and sometimes changed the subject. In time, she realized that only she could figure out who she was and who she would be when she was less depressed and more self-accepting. One piece of artwork at a time, and therapy discussions with stories, she explored her self-concept and deep sense of loss. We reminisced about her family's past and the closeness they had experienced. She had enjoyed doing things with her father and now there was a "hole" in her heart.

She sent the portfolio by email when I asked permission to include her art with her case study, and the labels for some of the pieces are telling, as you will see below. Certainly her artwork conveys that she has *much to say but had not yet found the words to say it*. The reader will notice that she was in the process of clarifying and questioning her sexual identity and seeking to be more "visible" to others at her school, as well as dealing with the loss of her dad and seeking a way to move on. For full-color examples of her artwork, see the 'The *Meaning* of Color' from page 202.

The cover artwork, labeled "Poopy Hair" in the file she sent me, and titled *Pretty Lies* in the portfolio, depicts an individual shutting out all sensory cues, sight, sound, taste, etc. The self-imposed muteness with closed ears speaks to avoidance. This teen talked in therapy about how difficult it was for her to be genuine with others. She had a "little girl" superficial sweetness that

144

hid deeper thoughts and concerns as well as strong feelings about herself and others. She recently wrote, "*Pretty Lies* is about anxiety and depression, but (during) the beginning stages when you deny it and tell yourself and others that all is well." The words around the flower petals speak poignantly to the loss of her father. They refer to someone who says she is "fine" but is not, and an awareness that she has to "let him go" and say "goodbye."

This next piece of artwork was labeled "Poop Nose" in the file she sent me. This art piece depicts well the tendency she had to entertain others on a surface level and hide her feelings beneath a "clownlike" facade. She found it difficult to face things "head on" and presented a caricature rather than a whole person. The look in the eyes of this individual is defiant and questioning, perhaps sarcastic. See 'The *Meaning* of Color' from page 202 for full-color version of this picture.

The piece after that, titled People Face Poop in the file, shows a prism being held up to the girl's face. Colors to white light, two aspects of self, one dark and one multi-dimensioned, a search for self and integration. See 'The *Meaning* of Color' from page 202 for full-color version of this picture.

FIGURE 15.3

FIGURE 15.4

Case Examples and Applications

This piece below is haunting and expressive and shows the depth of her inner struggle, as well as a rich sensuality that had not yet been realized in this girl's day to day life. She labeled it, Poop Chalk Monkey Bars in the emailed file. It depicts two sides of herself; one closed and depressed and the other clearly more "out" and seductive. "Love" and "please" are written in the background. The rainbow self is urging her monochrome self to "open" to the affection. It is a sad depiction of her split self perception- and the ambivalence she experienced in loving self and others. Her drawing also conveys a sense of ghostlike emptiness and the darkness that absorbed her after her dad died.

She wrote to me recently, "The girls in the embrace, the one kissing the other on the cheek, is about loving yourself. Part of recovery is finding love in your body and who you are. This was something I found very important in my self-recovery." See 'The *Meaning* of Color' from page 202 for full-color version of this picture.

FIGURE 15.5

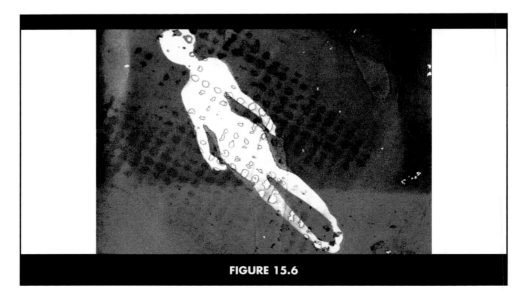

FIGURE 15.6

"Tell Me Who I Am"

FIGURE 15.7

We talked of many things in therapy, such as her relationship with her mother, spirituality, hurts, sexuality, rejection, missing her dad, developing new relationships and what to do about college. Without her art, I would not have known the depths of her struggles nor the many facets of her self-perception. The picture below shows a figure sinking, drowning, motionless, a good depiction of depression, nothingness or death. See 'The *Meaning* of Color' from page 202 for full-color version of this picture.

I recently asked her to provide her personal meaning for the picture labeled Figure 15.6, and she replied, "The girl with the butterflies flying out of her mouth (Figure 15.7) is about letting go of anxiety. Anxiety is something every person deals with, some more than others, and when you are able to let it go, it is an incredible feeling." See from page 202 for full-color version of this picture.

PROGRESS AND OUTCOMES

My client developed a more colorful, positive self-representation during her senior year of high school. Figure 15.8 is a picture of an open flower, with its rainbow colors, held gently and with pride, paralleled her emerging sense of self toward the end of treatment. She had become capable of self-affirmation and responded well to the encouraging feedback from her teachers at school regarding her career goals and artistic talent. Comparing this to her depression cartoon, the reader will see that her mood was much less constricted and depressed as she started planning for college and forming new relationships. See from page 202 for full-color version of this picture.

She was ready to end therapy, at least for the time being, as she finished high school, interviewed for her first job and planned to start college the next year while living at home with her mom. She was comfortable with her sexuality and spirituality. She maintained a protective barrier around her heart, but said recently that there were things in her past that she still needed to deal with. I was proud of her courage in seeking therapy on her own, and through an unencumbered relationship with a caring adult, she began to accept the confusing, contradictory views of herself.

We finished our treatment in 2015; I wrote to her in early 2018 to request permission to include her case and artwork in my book. I asked her to include any comments she wanted to make about what was memorable or helpful to her in therapy. She said she had finished three years of college

Case Examples and Applications

FIGURE 15.8

and was taking a semester off before returning to study social work. She is working full time for a social service agency and has found her "calling." She shared the following:

> My portfolio was about the color and darkness in life, as well as the hidden psychosis and emotions we feel every day. Dr. P was key in pulling me out of the hole I was in. I was numb and severely depressed to the point of giving up on life. Dr. P., with her hands on activities, and attention to my strengths (art), gave me methods to redirect my feelings into positive actions. I went from barely living to a person who was top of her math class and made an entire art portfolio in one year.

I wrote back to say that I was grateful to have worked with her and reminded her that she was the one who did the work, with me as only a catalyst.

QUESTIONS FOR CASE DISCUSSION

1. Pick one drawing and describe what the symbolism means or suggests to you.
2. How did the girl's artwork reflect depression and gradual healing from depression?
3. What were some of her inner struggles, and how might those affect her separation/individuation and self-esteem?
4. How might her relationship with her mother need to change to allow her to move forward?

16

THE ZODIAC QUEEN

A Case of Adolescent Dissociation

CASE INFORMATION AND BACKGROUND

I selected this case because it is a fascinating example of a teen's metaphorical depiction of her dissociation, a condition that arose due to vulnerability and need for protection at a very young age. I title it The Zodiac Queen, because for most of the nearly three-year period in which I worked with her, from middle school into early high school, she lived a parallel life within a complex alternate universe (Celestia) where she was "identified" as the chosen *Queen*. She had been *told* that she was *destined* to lead them in defense of an attack on their world, a world that existed within her mind. Her dissociation had arisen in childhood to protect her from an *attack* on her safety and security; a parallel attack threatened the universe within. She and her parents have permitted me to share the case so that others might understand the unique ways in which dissociation presents.

She was the only daughter in a middle class, two-working-parent family. They attended church regularly, the college-age son helped with the youth, and the daughter was active in the music ministry. The parents were in a conventional, somewhat non-intimate relationship. Family roles were traditional, where the mother cooked and cleaned and the dad "hung out" after work in what the family called his Batman-cave, a spot in the basement filled with Batman memorabilia. As a family, they spent time with Mom's parents who lived nearby, and they had a circle of friends. The client's maternal grandparents had taken care of her when she was in preschool, until (per client) "my dad thought we talked too much and pulled me back."

Early on in treatment, my client's dad was described by wife and daughter as rigid, angry and punitive. Per the girl and her mother, he had always been controlling and judgmental, with an all-or-nothing view of child obedience; when my client would not comply he sometimes grabbed her to "make her" do what he wanted or became emotionally reactive. As my client moved toward puberty, she was angry at her dad and wanted to debate his arbitrary decisions. There had been similar problems when the older son had entered his teens, and when he came home, they still tended to "get into it" over the dad's top-down parenting. My client's brother and she had always been close; he played video games with her, sometimes ones that were designed for older teens and adults.

PROBLEMS (AND RESPONSE TO THE PROBLEMS)

When she first came in for therapy with her parents, my client was in late middle school and had no prior mental health involvement. She had *attacked* her father late that summer in an unusual display of aggression, and her parents were very concerned. She had been "sweet" and "well

149

behaved" until that year, but had assaulted her father over his giving her "unfair punishment" for what was described as a "misunderstanding." She did not seem to recall all the details afterward, saying it was like she was "in a dream." The attack scared her dad, and it threw the family into crisis.

When we first talked, the teen was somewhat defiant in justifying her behavior, but could not explain the intensity of her response. She shared bits and pieces of the event as we created a sequenced time line for the event. After an argument over laundry, her dad had walked away from her down the hall, and "something came over me and I jumped on his back" in anger. She "pursued" him into his bedroom, was briefly pinned down on the bed, and then ran to the kitchen to get a knife (supposedly for protection). After this incident, her parents brought her in for treatment, and the first thing we did was safety planning. She did not present as being a danger to her dad or herself by the time of intake, so I obtained background information to try to make sense of the sudden attack.

CONCEPTUALIZATION

This case is conceptualized as trauma based, but there is not yet a clear picture as to the source of her problems that began around age 3–4-years-old and culminated in the attack on her father. At age 3–4, an age at which she had only been around grandparents and family members, she started taking things from her father and brother, but not from her mother. She was very close to her older brother and sometimes hung around him and his friends. When she was 5–6, and he was pre-puberty, she viewed his porn that he had found online. From what we know now, the client began to dissociate sometime around age 4–5. The first *alter*, Mystery, was reported to have *appeared* from kindergarten through 1st grade, with his mouth sewn shut. He was a protector but he could not tell what he knew, at least not at that point in time. The first helpful alter, Cas, came in elementary school when she was bullied for her weight, pushed downstairs and into lockers. In middle school, one of the "others" apparently told people at school that she had a sister who had died because my client did not recall doing so. At the time I met her, my client was exploring her sexual identity. She had no sexual experience, other than exposure to pornography from her brother's downloads when she was very young, and she reported no interest in sexual experimentation. Given the time line and symptoms in a girl raised in a very conservative family, it seemed likely that her recent aggressive outburst was triggered by more than an argument over laundry.

MORE BACKGROUND

My client had a wide-eyed look of naiveté and reported having no close friends, preferring to spend time alone, with her parents or with her much older brother. She seemed "confused" by events in her life that she could not easily explain. She was short, stocky and overweight, and she dressed in flannel shirts and slacks. She was also musical and artistic, but her favorite activity was gaming with her older brother. When she was younger, she had helped her dad work in the garage on projects and seemed to enjoy the hands-on time together, but they were no longer close. Soon after starting therapy (and each autumn after that), she began acting out in ways that were not consistent with her beliefs or values; she reported significant lapses in memory at times that she clearly (by parent report and my observation) was not behaving "like her typical self."

INTERVENTIONS

Initially, I worked with her and her parents to determine the rationale for the attack, reduce risk of another attack, increase non-controlling parenting and improve communication. Her dad signed up for parenting classes at his church and my client's parents agreed that they would make parenting and discipline decisions together. Generally the parents made decisions together, and both attended therapy regularly. Over time, I helped her parents understand and accept that her dissociation was not a short-term problem and that the roots were most likely in early childhood.

Over time, more information emerged about the attack on her father. It became clear that my client had not been "fully present" during parts of the attack, as she could only describe the beginning and ending of the episode, with spotty memories of what happened between those points in time. During individual therapy, she began to describe an extensive inner system with protectors and "friends" that she could see and hear that had been part of her life since elementary school, perhaps around kindergarten. Each "other" had a distinct personality and role in the inner system, and most of them were gay. The inner world, referred to as Celestia, sounded like an elaborate video game, and she was "destined" to become their leader in battle. At times, the "others" in the system "took over" and engaged in behaviors outside her awareness that got her into trouble (porn, graffiti on a church bathroom wall, not turning in homework).

Our therapy goals included discovering why each had come, reducing "switching" with time loss and improving co-consciousness. The "others" appeared to be protectors and helpers for the most part. Although there was no history of command hallucinations, she reported seeing the "others" and having conversations with them. Her childhood attitude toward them had been one of curiosity rather than fear, and she maintained that attitude as a teen.

Initial psychological testing showed no psychosis, she had above average intelligence, excellent reasoning ability, no learning disability and significant depression. She had no elevation on a scale that measures oppositional behavior, and her IQ was well above her current level of academic achievement. There was some suggestion of inattention and problems with insight and memory. Throughout treatment, my client "cycled" in and out of mood and behavior changes, with periods of decompensation each fall, two to three months after school started, for three consecutive years. This period coincided with the time during which she and her parents first sought treatment. She had a habit of *lying* about doing and turning in her schoolwork. She took her sketchbook everywhere she went, and she doodled and drew in it in lieu of taking notes at school. At times drawings would appear in her sketchbook that were *new* to her as well, by her report. The client was confused by these lapses, and later in treatment, expressed tearfully with anger and frustration that they had "taken over" her life and made it very burdensome.

SHIFTS

Soon after I began working with her, my client had a bout of serious depression with suicidal ideation. That first year, I became concerned about her obsessive interest in a website that posted a story of "Jeff the Killer," a boy who seemed possessed and "lost his mind." When his parents did not understand him and disregarded what he said, he then killed them with a knife. She was not anxious or worried at telling me this story and found it fascinating. "He didn't know what he was doing," she said, and she didn't directly relate his story to her life. I was concerned about her identification with this website, and we increased home monitoring. I also began talking with her more about how she felt misunderstood and disregarded, especially by her father. Around the same time, her taste in music changed, and she started listening to violent and sexual song lyrics, not appropriate for someone her age. It is not unusual for young teens to engage in behavioral experimentation, but her day-to-day presentation and moods did not align with her behavioral changes.

About a year to the date of our first session, the following September, a very sexually explicit picture appeared in her sketchbook showing a defiant-looking adult male character (standing with an accurately drawn erect penis) and another character, on his/her knees. She was not sure where the drawing came from; the details suggested some sort of coerced sexual experience. My client reported having had no sexual experience, "gagged" when she saw the picture and said she was "grossed out" by the penis. Porn started showing up on her phone, and she was confused and frustrated as to the origins; her parents and I wondered about sexual victimization.

In our second year of therapy, she developed better understanding of the inner world and we talked about the protective nature of the dissociative system, because she had some awareness that the "others" kept information from her about herself. She pieced together information from

Case Examples and Applications

the "others" and reported, "They are keeping seven keys to my knowing myself and having my own information." She added, "They have taken my memories and locked them up—they have the only keys to the vaults in Celestia." She was aware of memory problems and dissociation, but she understood her symptoms in the context of the complicated inner world of the Zodiac.

That fall, her parents discovered she had skipped band and left the school campus a couple of times to smoke, although she was vehemently opposed to smoking. My client struggled with suicidal and homicidal ideation the fall of our second year of treatment, a time during which her parents noticed increased dissociation at home. My concern grew when she took her dad's pocket knife, insulin syringes and razor-blade knife, and she was not clear how these things came to be in her possession when they were found in her backpack. She threatened to kill a girl on her bus and did not fully understand why she was later questioned. We admitted her to an intensive outpatient program at that time, to ensure safety for her and her family. She stabilized and was discharged four weeks later.

Soon after, she relayed to me some important new information she "learned" during IOP, that one of the "others" had been the one to cut her body, and another, who was interested in pornography, had drawn the sexual picture. It was also revealed that the "angry one" that attacked the dad had been a protector. Her mother and I talked with the "others" and communicated the importance of working together as a team and not acting outside the client's awareness, even though there was no clear indication of "why" the "others" were engaging in such behaviors.

Dissociation like this is most common when there has been repeated or severe abuse at an early age; my hypothesis was that my client had experienced sexual activity of a traumatic nature sometime before the arrival of the first protector. I asked about her early relationships, including the "very close" relationship she had with her older brother, but she denied maltreatment and had always "adored" him. He had, however, drawn and viewed nudity and porn since he was in the 3rd grade; my client had seen porn on his tablet when she was 5 or 6 and he was 12. She was annoyed that her brother still teased her, saying, "he tickles me on my chest" (pointed to her belly area) and "he uses touch more than talk to communicate," so I talked with her about establishing protective boundaries with her brother; we had a family session with the brother. I wondered about neighborhood or church friends and about extended family relationships. She was close to her grandparents and had spent much time with them in her early years, but again denied anything inappropriate. Her hostility toward her dad raised a flag, but it is not unusual for adolescents to rebel against authoritarian parenting practices.

INTERVENTION: THE ZODIAC QUEEN

Zodiac refers to the organization and arrangement of my client's alternative universe, a metaphor for dissociation. That world had different levels and roles, and there was one or more "persons" (all males) eventually tied to each Zodiac sign. It is a fascinating depiction, with different functions/ roles for each character. The first one to arrive in her world was "Mystery" (1st grade) and his mouth was sewn shut, because Mystery had secrets he was not supposed to tell. I tried to cut his threads in session, but she reported that they grew back, so he communicated with me in drawing, nodding and writing. Based on this information, I suspected that some sort of "unspeakable" traumatic event had occurred prior to 1st grade and that the dissociation began as an adaptive and protective process.

The universe she mapped and described had a "portal" into her world through her brain, and in that universe, years might represent minutes or hours in her earth world. She drew the portal to help me understand "how things work in my brain." This is a very modern-day depiction of dissociation by someone with interest in technology, and her inner world parallels the "battles" in her own life, in the context of video games, internet themes and fantasy.

My client had heard the voices of the "others" since 3rd–4th grade, when these protectors and "friends" started coming "through the portal" into her earthly life. A "protector" was apparently present from kindergarten forward. Certainly, in a case such as this, I needed to assess for fantasy, psychosis and dissociation. My client could see and draw the *others* (pointed to them in the room during therapy when they were present and told me what they were saying), and eventually

I was able to talk with some of them directly. Each presented differently in terms of stance, eye contact and style of communication. She does not present as psychotic in her eye contact, affect or language, rather, she has been very rational and detailed if not obsessive in her depiction of her inner world. She has never feared the "others," almost blandly accepting their presence; she "knew" they were there to help. For the most part she is non-aggressive, because her anger and the aggressive side are well-contained. In 2017, a new and unknown dangerous "evil" entity arrived unbeknownst to the system. This individual went back through the portal before revealing him/herself, and this "threat" to the system will probably return.

I worked with the client to better understand the inner world and evaluate why each helper might have come into her mind and world. One who arrived in 3rd–4th grade, named Cas, has presented himself as a peacekeeper and has kept her mother informed of risk. I pieced together that Cas arrived when my client was being badly bullied in elementary school (pushed downstairs, shoved into a locker, taunted). She remembered landing at the foot of the stairs and having Cas with her, but she did not recall being pushed, because Cas had that memory. She has had many periods of lost time, when one went to school, several played video games with her brother, one came out in a church bathroom, and one doodled inappropriate things on her sketch pad.

Her father struggled to believe his daughter and thought at first that she "lied" about dissociation, to have an "excuse" for behavior that was "immoral" or disallowed. Her mother, however, had "met" some of the others, and in time her dad noticed when she would "switch." We recognized reliable changes in facial expression, body language, tone of voice, content of discussion and interests when the different "others" were present. Her mother sought to form relationships with some of the others, and others have consistently trusted her mother and disliked her father, because of his anger and suspiciousness.

This young teen was extraordinarily creative throughout treatment, providing much material in art, music and writing so that I might better understand her. At first, her parents and I wondered if she was living in a fantasy world, as opposed to dissociating; her memory and time lapses, and observable/consistent changes in her verbal and non-verbal behavior/functioning (unique personality differences in stance, interests, values, eye contact, tone, mood, facial expression) suggested the latter. Her parents and I do believe that she has "added" to the system more recently, as there are many new players and plots, and these seem to be more the substance of fantasy than dissociation.

The Zodiac Harbingers

What she refers to as the "Harbingers" (the original Zodiac "alters" who came to her during childhood, occupied her body/mind, resulted in loss of time/awareness) have become part of a complex inner world. Eventually, without prompting, my client mapped the system, and used the dry erase board to write and talk about each Zodiac; the *others* also used the dry erase board to tell me things they could not voice. See Figures 16.2 and 16.3 as examples. Therapeutically, it is likely that the degree of complexity is protective and a form of obsessive, systemic avoidance, because when she spends so much time and energy dealing with the story line, she can avoid seeking and finding answers to the original purpose of the system.

The Harbingers serve a protective function, to reduce her stress and to hold her memories of trauma. Each arrived at a different age, hypothetically to help her deal with life events of which she is not yet fully aware. As she mapped her system, I addressed the following:

- We established an inner meeting place where we could gather and talk. The others agreed to work with me, except for a very angry, aggressive *other* that emerged about the time we were terminating treatment due to my pending move.
- Since she would be queen in the inner world, they needed to let me help her so that she could "drive the bus" of the system. I relayed to them that they were helpful to her when she was much younger, but that their over-protection prevented her from being age-appropriate. At her current age, I needed to teach her the skills to protect herself.
- The whole system needed to support stabilization i.e., no cutting or self-harm; no physical aggression toward others.

Case Examples and Applications

- I obtained inner consent that they would not do things in her world that she could do for herself, especially things that would get her into trouble at school/church and that were not appropriate for her age in this world.
- We agreed they would not "take over," i.e., take her eyes, mind and hands. They would work toward co-consciousness and I would "meet" the others to assess protective function, purpose, age at which they came into her life (usually by school grade). This is a very slow process, because some of them still believed she was "not ready to know" things that happened to her at earlier ages. At the time we stopped treatment, she was still not "aware of" what traumatic event resulted in the first episode of dissociation. "Mystery" came in 1st grade, and his lips were sealed (sewn shut). There was clearly an onset before "Mystery."
- We would identify what was going on in her life at each point in time, to identify possible risk factors, coping and source of dissociation.

I have a concern based on her recent list, i.e., that the 10th Harbingers are said to have *absolute and total control* over her, which is a new development that must be addressed in treatment. Previously, there was an agreement to let her "drive the bus" in her own day to day world, and now the 10th Harbingers could hijack the bus. With DID, it is important for the players to develop and practice co-consciousness, as well as to balance out and share power and control more cooperatively. The others have worked hard to "protect" my client from knowing her whole story/history, and some of them continue to block early memories. There is some protective purpose, as yet unidentified, for the system, in maintaining such control.

I have listed the original Zodiac characters below, referred to by my client as *The Harbingers*. The client drew and described each of the Zodiac persona as she was "given" awareness and information from within. Cas, who was the first to "come out" to this therapist and to the client's mother, is depicted in Figure 16.1 and he shares some of the qualities, abilities and talents of my client. He presents as older and wiser than this young teen, and he has excellent communication skills, both with the others and with the client's mother.

First Harbinger: *Castiel Leandros (Cas)—Capricorn, 23 (460 by Celestial calendar), Former Royalty, in a relationship with Jake. Cas was the first of the others to present himself, in the 3rd or 4th grade. He is a helper and had a great deal of information about the inner world. Cas had entered in elementary school at a time my client was being bullied by other children, pushed downstairs, shoved in locker, etc. Cas said he held memories that my client was not ready to have.

Second Harbinger: *General Shakran Leonidus (Shanks)—Leo, 24 (480), astute warrior. Shanks "came" into her world when she was in the 3rd and 4th grades, after Cas. At that point in time, her older brother was in the 9th grade and played in the HS band. While in the 3rd grade, client started gaining weight but didn't know why. This would suggest that some sort of trauma was going on during elementary school. In exploring this arrival, it seems that she was being bullied at school, and it is not clear what else might have been going on. She had few friends and was heavy for her age.

Third Harbinger: *Sir Grayson of Aquarius (Gray)—Aquarius, 25 (512), twin brother to Danté.

Third Harbinger: *Sir Danté of Aquarius (Danté)—Aquarius, 25 (512), scholar, twin brother to Gray.

Fourth Harbinger: *Jakorian Renos (Jake)—Libra, 20 (416), Royal Advisor, in a relationship with Cas. Jake was reported at one point to have drawn the sexual pictures in her sketchbook.

Fifth Harbinger: *Lieutenant Dirkonora Markos (Dirk)—Aries, 26 (524), former gladiator.

Sixth Harbinger: *Archean Arete Adonis Vasilios (Arch)—Gemini, 24 (487), formerly known as "Mystery." Mystery came to her world to protect and defend her in the 1st grade. He reportedly "had something bad happen to him at age 5" (as did my client most likely). His lips were sewn shut and he learned to communicate by writing with his left hand. He keeps secrets and was very angry with my client's parents "for something they did or did not do." He stated that he drew sexual things on her pad as a "clue, to let her know some things." Her brother ("when he was 12, the same age I am now") had shown her porn ("I was 5–6"), the time when Gemini/Mystery had come. Early in 2017, client reported that Mystery was "ready and has a right to know his history, but not all at once, he would go bonkers." She added, "He forgot his history, lost his memory and perhaps we will all have to reboot his memory." Her description of Mystery, and clear identification with his plight, shows that to some degree she is aware of her own lost memories and the need to "reboot." Mystery will be key to discovering some of the roots of her dissociation, given the age at which *his* trauma occurred.

Seventh Harbinger: *Kairon Matthias—Taurus, 21 (213), bladesmith, married to Shanks.

The Zodiac Queen

FIGURE 16.1

Eighth Harbinger: *Captain Paraklesis—Cancer, 20 (417), Captain of the City Guard.
Ninth Harbinger: *Jaidorious Nannos (Jaiden)—Sagittarius, 21 (426), Royal Knight, knows every constellation by heart.

She lists the following 10th Harbinger as three individuals, who are said to be "the same person." It is not clear why the client depicts the 10th Harbinger in this way; it was a more recent development.

Tenth Harbinger: *Istvan Alekos Thanos Vasilios (Istvan)—New King of Celestia, God of War, same person as Ilkay and Iris, Savior of Celestia, **has full control over one XXX**, Gods' Beast Arte.

155

Case Examples and Applications

Tenth Harbinger: *Ilkay Alexias Thanisis Vasilios (Ilkay)—New Queen of Celestia, Goddess of War, same person as Istvan and Iris, Savior of Celestia, **has full control over one XXX**.

Tenth Harbinger: *Iris Aleka Thanosa Vasilios (Iris)—(agender) New Ruler of Celestia, same person as Istvan and Ilkay, Savior of Celestia, **has full control over one XXX**.

Eleventh Harbinger: *Avion Calla Vasilios—Scorpio, 26 (527), Princess of Celestia.

Twelfth Harbinger: *Alena Adonia—Pisces, 22 (247), health worker, engaged to Dirk.

XXX = Client's Name

During early treatment with this client, one goal was to help her develop co-consciousness, so that the system could live and work "as a team," with her "driving the bus," instead of the others doing things "behind her back." She was not open to the idea that they were all part of her, but she was aware that they lived in her brain and sometimes occupied her body. She would be held "responsible" and "accountable" for the things *they* would say and do, which was why she had to be kept in the loop. She was open to the idea of "sharing" her world and we addressed the fear some of them had that I was "trying to kill them." It turned out that one of them really liked school and went sometimes without telling her, so we agreed that only the client would attend school and do her own work. A few of the others popped out or asked to meet with me as the system became more open, so we did that while she "listened in" from the "inside." At times, she "switched" unexpectedly during session or we (her parents and I) saw a glare in her eye that was not "her," such as when one of them was angry with her father during family session. Between sessions, the others communicated fairly well with my client's mother, and her mother became adept at noticing dissociative shifts at home. We discussed when and how the Celestians were permitted to "come out" in her world to play video games. We clarified "risk" and "threat" of them "taking over" (with regard to sexual behaviors and violence) and communicated that she needed to learn to fight her own battles. After all, if she was queen in their world, they had to let her learn to defend herself in the earth world.

As we worked together in treatment it was clear that most, if not all, of the Zodiac friends "hated" her father, "loved" her mother and "got along with" her older brother. I asked some about their reasons for coming through the portal into her world, in her mind. They provided information that pointed to their protective role in her life and gave me permission to share things with her that they had not yet shared. The system believes that she is not ready to have the keys to her memory and past experiences that brought them into her world. My client wanted me to understand her inner world and how the system worked; at the same time, she has not yet been "permitted" to have information about why her memories were "taken" by the system and "locked in a vault."

After completing the drawings in Figure 16.2, she stated, "This is how the Celestians appear to me." She keeps a detailed list in her notebook of their individual characteristics, and most of them share her interest in music (see Figure 16.3).

She described the roles and caste system of Celestia in Figure 16.4, and the roles suggest the function each might have in her life. Some have protective roles such as "advisor," "warrior" and "gladiator."

See Figure 16.5 for an early depiction of the portal into Celestia.

Figure 16.6 is client's depiction of the Zodiac town, set around a central town hall.

In Figure 16.7 the client depicts the process of dissociation as she experiences it. She was trying to explain how a "new one" (not friendly, the others were not aware of his presence) had come into her brain from Celestia (upper right) without her awareness and then was aggressive toward her brother in 2017. This "new one" was angry and "unknown to all the others." Her drawing and description shows an awareness that the process takes place in her brain. The concept of "portal" is fascinating, as it is an access point that opens and closes, akin to neural connectivity, and the others can't choose to come through randomly. Usually, they are *shoved out* to enter her brain when something happens in their world that parallels an event in her world. It is not yet fully clear to her that they represent aspects of her and her experiences, nor that they came as "real" protectors in her brain. She accepts that they have some of her memories from preschool and school age years, and she believes that when they are ready they will give her those memories back. She indicated that someone usually "guards" the portal at a computer that is "in

The Zodiac Queen

FIGURE 16.2

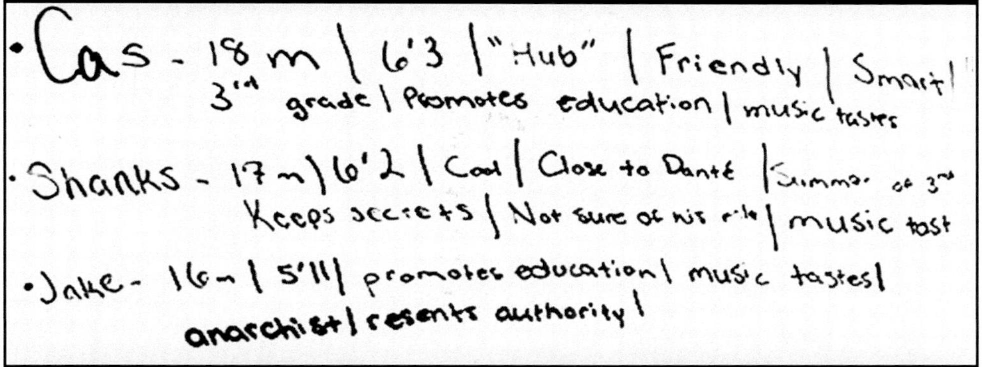

FIGURE 16.3

charge of my brain." This lapse reportedly happened at night, when she was sleeping, and there was no one "guarding the portal" at the "computer" in charge of her brain. The table depicts a gathering place inside her brain where they conference and talk. This is a fascinating computer-age depiction of dissociation.

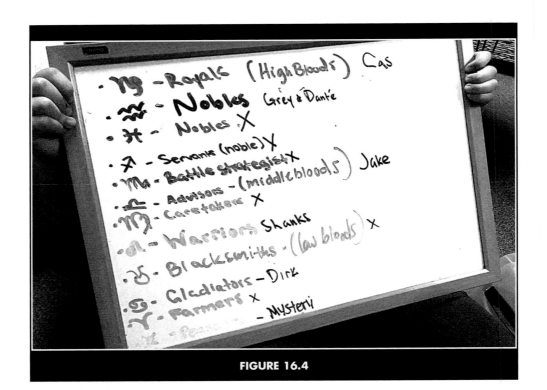

FIGURE 16.4

FIGURE 16.5

The Zodiac Queen

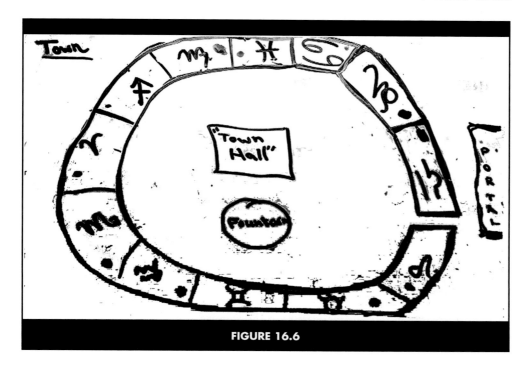

FIGURE 16.6

FIGURE 16.7

PROGRESS AND OUTCOMES

I present this case as a fascinating example of a teen's conceptualization of dissociation. Her compartmentalized mind is depicted as a Zodiac fantasy with a portal and characters, each of whom has a symbolic protective function. We are not yet "to the bottom of" whatever may have happened in her early life that resulted in dissociation nor what really triggered the first crisis,

159

Case Examples and Applications

even after several years of fairly regular therapy, both individual and family. She has stabilized through the therapy, with her parents' involvement and consistent sessions, but it is not clear what destabilizes her periodically other than the time of year, perhaps due to an anniversary date and other triggers that result in right brain activation of trauma symptoms. She may have experienced trauma of some kind when very young, because her behavioral symptoms began at age 3 or 4 (stealing from dad and brother) and dissociation became evident during a rage attack toward her father. During the time I treated her, she would stabilize for three to six months at a time, with a few small "blips" on the radar screen, and then have brief periods of crisis. The dissociative process seems to have gone *underground* at times but is still present, and I have concerns that she perceives herself as totally controlled by the dissociative system at this time. Her family made the decision to give her a therapy vacation when I moved away, because she seemed stable and the crises were fewer; also, her coping skills for mood regulation had greatly improved. It was good news that they are in the process of starting therapy again, so that there will be ongoing monitoring of her psychological and family functioning.

I fully expect the symptoms to recur and become problematic when she is triggered or stressed, because that is her pattern; dissociation is a complicated disorder, likely to re-emerge when the individual is triggered by stress, relationship conflict or activation of the original source of her problems. Her parents are pleased with her progress and current functional status (good grades, moods stable), but their own relationship is emotionally disengaged, and her previous history suggests that identity and mood issues are far from resolved.

Perhaps in time "Mystery" will be able to tell her what he knows, or the new one that "went back through the portal" will re-emerge and explain his rage. I hope that eventually she is given access to the memories the others still hold, locked in their *vaults*. An interesting change is that she told her mother she had fought in battle as the Queen, and during the battle she was "killed." We wondered about the symbolism in this and watched for signs of suicidality, but instead, she became more stable, freed of feeling the burden of responsibility for both her world and theirs. It is not clear what her role is in the system.

I am grateful to her and her parents for allowing me to share the case. I could not have worked with her effectively without utilizing her unique metaphor and symbolism, art and stories.

QUESTIONS FOR DISCUSSION

1. What were signs and symptoms that pointed to a dissociative process?
2. Why does the author suspect that the client may have experienced sexual abuse? Please comment.
3. In what ways has this client become the "identified patient" in her family? What are some systemic factors that need to be addressed in this case?
4. How does technology play a role in this client's conceptual understanding of her dissociation?

ADULT CASES USING STORIES, ART AND PLAY

17

THE GIRL BEHIND THE BRICK WALL

A Case of Anxious Avoidant Attachment

CASE INFORMATION AND BACKGROUND

A bright, Ivy-league educated middle-aged woman was referred for therapy to deal with her adult son's drug abuse, to increase self-care and to cope with aging parents who lived out of town. She reported symptoms of high anxiety, nighttime awakenings and depressed mood. I initially attributed her current mood vacillations to situational stress, adjustment issues and possible peri-menopause changes. Our initial treatment plan focused on anxiety reduction, achieving some emotional separation from her son and setting limits with her son to reduce co-dependence. Her psyche reminded me of an iceberg, where the bulk of the iceberg is below the surface of the ocean; looking below the surface, she had experienced extensive abuse growing up. Over time, her needs became clearer and her therapy shifted to trauma resolution, unmet attachment needs, co-dependency, mood regulation, anxiety reduction and self-care.

She was not close to either parent or her much older sister with whom she had a conflictual relationship; a much older brother had been "disowned" by her parents some years back. The household had been tumultuous, with everyone walking on eggshells around my client's father. He was, by her description, self-centered and had been emotionally and physically abusive to the children. Her father had frequent, unpredictable rage outbursts, and when the father was angry, her mother (who was described as critical and disengaged) tended to blame the children for triggering him, instead of being protective.

CONCEPTUALIZATION

My client had never felt "good enough" for her parents and had unsuccessfully spent years of her life vacillating between trying to please them and shutting them out. Her emotional states were poorly regulated, nearly manic at times with extreme agitation and anxiety/fear, then calm and very focused. She was childlike when reacting in panic (to feared loss/abandonment). During limbic rages, she would verbally attack her husband and threatened to end their marriage; then when rational and calm, she was centered and focused, grateful for his love.

She was not initially aware that many of her symptoms fell along the freeze-flight-fight continuum, the result of complex trauma from childhood that had been re-activated by her son's angry volatility and high-risk behaviors. She had been referred by a psychologist who worked with my client's son and realized that his high-risk behaviors might bring dire consequences. With her son, my client volleyed between "all or nothing ultimatums" and codependent caretaking. Growing up, her parents had not responded to her pleas for attention and nurture; my client had

163

Case Examples and Applications

developed an anxious-avoidant attachment with guilt attached to needing anything from anybody. She became an extension of others in lieu of establishing her own identity.

PROBLEMS

My client's traumatic childhood left her ill-equipped to cope with life events that threatened loss and abandonment. Her past and present anxiety, sleep difficulties, worry and mood dysregulation she experienced were intertwined. Frequent interpersonal triggers in the present pulled her back to core, unresolved trauma and attachment issues.

INTERVENTION AND FURTHER CONCEPTUALIZATION

The initial focus of treatment was her anxiety and her codependent role as the mother of a substance abusing adult son who had been in and out of rehab since his teens; I suspected that drug abuse was the source of his mood and behavior difficulties. He borrowed money, was verbally abusive and threatening toward his mother and was often "out" late at night. I hypothesized that what had been diagnosed as "bipolarity" were drug-induced mood states superimposed on a "thrill-seeking personality" style. He seemed to thrive on activities that brought an adrenaline rush; from a young age, he exercised poor judgment and lacked the capacity to learn from his mistakes. He was attachment-challenged, lacked empathy and responded to his mother with entitlement. His high-risk lifestyle and eventual medical complications of drug use took a toll on him and, vicariously, on his mother. They were enmeshed and she was terrified of "failing" as a parent; she believed that his survival was in her hands and feared that he would die without her involvement.

Friedman's Story (1990) *The Bridge* was a metaphor that we used throughout treatment; it was a good representation of her struggles. The concept of "holding the rope" rang true and "letting go" was what she feared most. As a child, she often felt dangled at the end of a rope, but there was no assurance that her parents would protect or rescue her, so she was left hanging, on her own to find a way back up or to drop and die. Many elements in this story paralleled my client's present struggles, and we have utilized the story repetitively as issues present. From my client's perspective, her son, family members and, to a certain extent, her husband represent the man with the rope, and she struggles to resist "helping" and coping with what she perceives to be their requests and expectations.

The story is about a traveler crossing a bridge on an intentional journey. A stranger approaches him and asks for his help. He unwittingly agrees to pause his journey and hold the rope that is handed to him. But without a word, the other man suddenly jumps off the bridge. Far below are rocks and a river. The stranger "expects" and even "demands" that he continue to hold the rope and take full responsibility for keeping him alive. The traveler holding the rope struggles with this dilemma, as all he wants to do is to continue his own journey.

I will describe some aspects of the story and their relevance for my client, since they parallel and symbolize my client's life circumstances:

> *The man has a clear goal and is moving in the right direction. The book indicates he is walking across a bridge and is interrupted by the other person. It is a nice depiction of past, present and future, with a bridge connecting them.*

My client's goals were initially those her parents wanted for her, and in her teens she engaged in many activities that they encouraged. After she finished college and graduate school, she became successful in her career but left to raise her child. Her goals were now subsumed within the roles of "good mother" and "supportive wife." She became all-consumed by her son's addictions during his teen and young adult years, doing whatever she could to access treatment and keep him alive. She volunteered to do things for her professionally trained spouse, and she was at the beck and call of her older, verbally abusive sister who controlled her and their parents. She took every rope that was offered to or thrown at her, in part to gain approval, and she stopped traveling her own road. She seemed unable to establish goals for herself in her own right and had stopped

The Girl Behind the Brick Wall

moving forward with no clear goals when she entered treatment. She had taken her eyes off her own road because her energy, time and emotions had been so caught up in her husband's and son's life (hoping her husband would change, hoping her son would recover from his drug use, "helping" both out of guilt, worry and hope overall but enabling both in many ways).

In talking further, we realized that perhaps she never had her own journey on her own road. She lived as if she existed for others and tried hard to avoid Dad's anger, reduce fear/anxiety and to please her mother without questioning. She found herself unable to enjoy her achievements, talents and activities, because her goal had been to please others rather than focus on her own talents and needs.

The concept of walking a road and of moving forward became important for her treatment. She is a spiritually minded individual so we talked about a Thomas Merton prayer that refers to not knowing what road he/she is on, or where it is going. She and I discussed the concept of moving forward, one step at a time, without "knowing" the end. She also relied on a Jeremiah verse that speaks to "hope and a future" without harm (Jeremiah 29:11). The first part of this story reinforced that my client's life was a journey, and that she could walk forward while not knowing where her road is heading at this point in time.

The person hands the main character a rope, and he takes it to be helpful. He believes it will be a brief interruption and then he will get on his way.

My client tried to be helpful in every way she could, at the expense of moving forward in her own life.

The person jumps off the bridge and leaves the main character left holding the rope. The main character feels burdened and scared. He feels responsibility for something he did not choose. He feels confused and wonders why the other man has done this.

This part of the story became important when she saw how her son left her holding the rope: financially (he chose to work only part-time, she covered his health insurance), when his car "broke down" or he wrecked (while high), when he needed a place to live (parents got him a condo), when he brought drugs home in his car (she disposed of them) and when he repeatedly called her in crisis in the middle of the night, even when she was on vacation. Repeatedly, she accepted the rope when he handed it to her. Her sister handed her the rope by holding her emotionally captive and through time demands, and her husband handed her the rope by asking her to write his letters, send his emails and deal with his office staff. She didn't yet realize that she could decline to take the rope and resist offering even when she saw areas where she might "help."

The person refuses to do what he could do to save himself, putting the full responsibility in the main character's hands. The main character feels trapped and believes he has no choice. He is frustrated and angry and starts bargaining with the man dangling from the rope. The dangling man does not cooperate and tells the main character that it will be his fault if the man dies (that he will fall to the river and the rocks below).

My client has felt hurt, abandoned and betrayed by her parents, sister and son. As a child, her mother gave her the rope of guilt, of being "not good enough" and a covert demand to fulfill the mother's unrealized dreams for herself. Her father gave her the rope of his anger when he blamed her and others for his volatility. Her sister threw her the rope of guilt and rebuked her suggestions. This pattern began when my client was a child with threats, sexual abuse, physical coercion and intimidation. Until recently, my client did not speak up about her hurt feelings, set limits when her time was interrupted or refuse when others made demands. She remained enmeshed in her son's treatment, ostensibly to prevent his self-destruction.

Until recently, she had lost sight of her choices, and now she has realized that, when said respectfully, there is power in the word "no." She has set firmer limits with her sister, even though she reportedly continues to blame and verbally abuse her, and she now knows she can't help her sister unless her sister decides to help herself first.

Her relationship with her parents has improved since she started being more open, nurturing them, speaking up and setting limits with love.

The main character realizes that the other man made his choice when he jumped off the bridge. He left the other man holding the rope and deliberately put a burden on the main character. Perhaps he was jealous, didn't want to see someone else moving forward. Perhaps he was so self-centered that he thought only of himself.

165

Case Examples and Applications

The main character realizes and accepts that the other man made a conscious choice. He does not have to "join" or bear the consequences of the other man's choice. He frees himself of the burden, guilt and self-blame as he lets go of the rope.

My client talked about "letting go of the rope" and what it would take for her to do that in her relationships with others. She began to set reasonable limits, for the sake of her own self-care, and she started to recognize that she was not responsible for the outcomes of others' lives. She let go of the rope emotionally when she started challenging what she had always been told by her parents and sister; she stopped believing what they said about her. She understood that her sister and parents had their own choices to make and that she did not have to join them nor agree with their choices.

By letting go, the main character acknowledges that it was not his burden to bear. It is sad and tragic, but not his fault. He thanks the other man for making his decision, acknowledging that man's choice, and releases the rope.

My client's new understanding about self-care has freed her to release her ropes and allowed her to meet her needs in different ways. Mostly, she stopped rescuing and caretaking her adult son and she began declining her husband's requests when he needed to do these for himself. She has buffered her heart from her sister's abuse and knows that she is not the source of her sister's emotional problems. Sometimes now, when she notices she has stepped back into an old role, she announces, "I picked up a rope again," and she sees more clearly when someone is handing her a rope that is not hers to take. Her desire to feel needed, wanted and respected was a liability, and she has learned to discern whether her desire to help is either a need or a choice. She has come to understand that there is no harm helping or supporting others, but there is a problem when "help" is at the expense of her own self-development.

I have worked flexibly with this client in order to match treatment to her unique strengths and needs. My client loves to read and has requested material to "help"; she is very verbal and analytical. Her reasoning and attribution, however, has not always been logical or rational. Early in treatment, I noticed that she would devour books with her left brain (cognitive understanding) but did not allow herself time to absorb the emotional nature of the material. This has improved as she learns how to regulate her moods, to pause before reacting and to stay on subjects even when they bring discomfort. At times she became agitated, we breathed and listened to the Tibetan singing bowl, and she was able to quickly move from frantic panic to calm reflection.

She benefited from Cognitive Behavioral Therapy (CBT) interventions such as thought-stopping, asking herself to "prove it" (when she ruminated excessively and engaged in "what if thinking") and learning to rely on facts more than feelings; she also did quite a bit of meaningful "mental processing" between sessions. Our best work together has been interpersonal, with a focus on attachment (myself as the secure base), internal family systems (roles and internal states) and experiential activities. We used stories and metaphors, some that came from her childhood and some that paralleled her current experiences and reactions. These provided the opportunity to move into emotional coping and healing so that trauma could be processed.

One week I diverged from our "planned" session to talk with her more in detail about her childhood. That week she revealed that she played, and sometimes hid, in the basement, behind her cardboard brick wall, when her father was really angry. He was "mean" to her older brother (physical and emotional abuse), and she felt "safe" in the basement. She had little interaction with her mother but had a strong loving bond with a nanny who cared for her from birth. The nanny ironed and cleaned in the basement and the two of them hung out together watching soap operas. On the nanny's day off, my client reported being anxious and fearful.

As she discussed her early family life, she said, "I have always wondered why my mother took a vacation when I was only two weeks old. My parents went off on a cruise 'to relax' and left me with my nanny. Most mothers would not do that." She was correct—most mothers would not do that.

New mothers have difficulty separating from their newborns, and the first "overnight" separation from your mother is not typical in the first few months of life. I wondered why they had not taken her with them, and a new hypothesis formed: perhaps her mother was not only depressed and critical in her older years, but had shown a life-long disengaged and poor attachment to her daughter. Perhaps the older sister also had mental health or attachment problems that began in childhood.

She continued, "I think the worst day of my life was when I was about 10 and my mother fired my nanny. It was my fault and I have never forgiven myself." She had told her mother that they watched her nanny's soap operas downstairs while she cleaned and ironed. Her mother used that as an excuse to fire the beloved caregiver, but in hindsight it was more likely that the mother resented and was jealous of the close bond between the nanny and her child. My client's view was that she had betrayed her nanny by "telling" and it left her feeling vulnerable and alone in the face of her father's anger and her mother's critical disregard.

I worked with her on these cognitive distortions and helped her come up with other interpretations of past events. Her mood dysregulation and anxiety had trauma and attachment-based roots that contributed to her reactions to recent life stress. Likely, recent stress had triggered "old" memories and experiences related to attachment loss and unmet needs. When she shared that significant piece of history, it provided a new systemic context and an updated conceptualization, within which we could more closely examine her childhood experiences that continued to impact her adult responses and functioning.

Nesting dolls were very helpful to this client in talking about stages of her childhood and events during her childhood that contributed to her self-perception. The dolls provide visual perspective and allow the therapist to establish a "time line" when discussing family interactions.

When I first offered the dolls, she took them apart, picked up the smallest, cradled it and said, "Poor little baby, left with the nanny." She said she remembered crying in a crib when she was a little older, standing and calling for parents that did not come. As mentioned above, her nanny cuddled, nurtured and praised her until about age 10, providing a secure attachment in an otherwise emotionally deprived home.

The client also described a wall, constructed of red, cardboard bricks, that she built in the basement, behind which she watched her nanny do chores and watch television. She spent many hours in the "safety" of her wall.

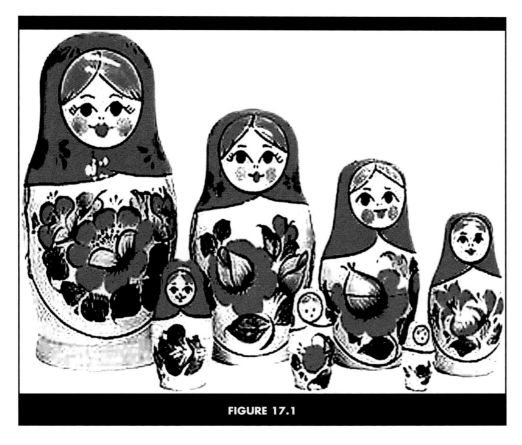

FIGURE 17.1

Case Examples and Applications

FIGURE 17.2

The blocks represented safety, security, a haven with nanny and a hiding place. One session I handed her the nesting dolls. "Show me you and nanny," I said. She selected a small nesting doll for herself, and a larger one for the nanny, who talked with her lovingly, calling her "baby girl." Her delight was palpable. She described special treats nanny made for her and stated, "When I feel sad, I still make that for myself." She teared up as she experienced the memories and interaction.

I asked why nanny left and she looked sad. "It was my fault," she said. "I told my mother we watched nanny's soaps together while she worked. My mother fired her. We didn't get to say goodbye." The mother told her daughter it was her fault for "telling." What my client didn't realize was how jealous her mother had become of her daughter's close relationship with the nanny, and as a result, she deliberately took it away. We talked about this in some detail, to address the cognitive distortion; she realized how cherished she had been by her nanny and that it was in no way her fault that the nanny had been fired and their relationship had ended.

The client described the little place behind the wall as her zone of comfort, a safe and happy place when nanny was there, and a place of hiding when nanny was not there. Once a week, when nanny was off, she played behind her wall in the basement, to hide from her parents. She also went down there to hide in fear when her father was angry, to escape his wrath. "I made him angry," she said.

SHIFT

I handed her the dolls. "Show me," I said, "how old you were when you first hid from your father's anger." She said she must have been about 3, and pointed out a small doll. She pointed at a large doll for her father, and commented how big the father doll was and that he should have controlled his temper.

I asked, "Is there anywhere else as a child that you spent hours alone?" She indicated she spent many long hours alone in her childhood bedroom, then she shared a memory from when she was also about 3.

I was mad at my parents, and I had a temper tantrum. I ran to my room and slammed the door. I dramatically threw my stuffed animals that I loved out in the hallway, one at a time in the direction of where my parents were. As if to say, "So there!" I threw them until they were all gone then I waited.

"Did you get their attention?" I asked. "No," she said.

They never came. I fell asleep in there without supper. When I woke up the next day, my mother sternly told me since I threw them out, I needed to retrieve them before I did anything else. Then she walked away.

"What had you wanted them to do?" I asked.
She thought and replied,

I was just a little girl. I wanted them to come, give me a hug, tell me they loved me, pick up the animals together, tuck me in or feed me supper. Even just check on me to be sure I was alright.

"What is your wall now?" I asked. Her eyes grew big. "I guess it is my bedroom. I go in there when I'm upset with my husband. I spend hours alone in there."

My client had reported a pattern of largely untriggered episodes of childlike *temper tantrums*, including moments of angry, critical derision when she threatened to leave her husband; at other times she was angry that he did not take care of his health and would become sick and die (leave her). She was misdirecting her anger, which was more about her parents, who were too old and frail for such an attack. When she *lost it*, the rage was "vomited on" her confused spouse. Following such an outburst, she went to the bedroom and hoped that he would come to check on her. It was her childhood pattern, all over again. I thought it might be helpful for her to realize the connection.

I asked, "What's going on when you are alone in your room now, upset with your husband after an argument?"

"OMG!" she said. "I'm throwing the animals. I want him to come comfort me. But he never does."

Her spouse had been described as a non-threatening and somewhat introverted, self-absorbed man. He had adored her in a way that her parents and first husband had not. He was usually confused by her outbursts and left her alone to calm down; she perceived this as rejection, a lack of caring. His intended kindness was *felt* as *parental disregard*. After these incidents, she typically felt guilt and embarrassment, re-enacting her childhood experience of non-validation. Like her and her parents, they rarely spoke of these episodes and went on as if they never happened.

TRAUMA NARRATIVE

My client noted that when they were first married, he had *taken care of* her. They had worked together professionally for some time, and she enjoyed her work as an office manager. At the time she entered treatment, she was experiencing some ambivalence about her role as wife and professional, because the two were bound together. It was clear that my client's anxious/avoidant attachment prevented her asking for help or letting others take care of her. As a child her mother had resisted taking the children for needed medical care, expecting them to tolerate their symptoms and not complain. She grew up not wanting to be "a whiner," and she demeaned herself when she could not tolerate legitimate pain. On one occasion while in the hospital and very ill, she offered her husband her food and beverage when he indicated he was hungry and thirsty. He did not refuse, and later, she had a feeling of sadness and even resentment; she had wanted him to *notice* her needs and take care of her, without her telling him. She wanted him to care for her but was reluctant to ask; ultimately she expected others to belittle her needs and expect her to deal with it alone. When she left the hospital and returned home, she tried to get better quickly so that they could resume their normal routine, with weekly dinners out and her back in charge of the household.

Case Examples and Applications

I noted how hard it was for her to ask for nurture, because her parents had put their needs first, inattentive to her needs and feelings. I suggested that those early experiences likely colored her adult perceptions and responses; perhaps she might communicate with her husband more about her thoughts and reactions to his behavior, rather than assume his intentions.

Another significant memory was from elementary school age, when her dad, in rage, smashed a glass table and cut his hand. It was the client's perception that he had been angry with her. She was terrified and ran to a nearby playground, where she hid inside a large culvert until it was dark. No one came looking for her, and she eventually went back home. No one knew she had been gone, and the incident was not addressed. She felt invisible.

When she married, what she most looked forward to was raising a child. She loved being a mother and threw herself into parenting, wanting to love and nurture her son in ways her parents had not. As her son delved into drugs, his volatile, unpredictable, angry behavior re-victimized and paralyzed her. She enabled him in many ways, trying to be a "loving" mother, and became emotionally entangled. When she said "no" he threw blame in her direction and she caught it.

My client and I realized that her traumatic experiences in childhood were being re-activated by current relational stress and impacting her adult attachments; we engaged in therapy focused on self-care and how to manage her emotional triggers. She was insightful and picked up quickly on connections. She recently reported she had been having unusually strong emotions about separating from her dog. She has often traveled but considered canceling an upcoming vacation due to her obsessive preoccupation with *abandoning* her pet at a place he enjoyed and where the staff lovingly cared for him. She cried and felt guilty at the thought of leaving him (although she had left him there before). She said that during her last trip, she could not "enjoy it" because she was worried about her *baby*. I am aware that pets are loved as family members and often treated like children, but the dramatic onset and intensity of her reaction caught my attention. Her language used in talking about her dog seemed layered and symbolic.

I asked her what she had been telling herself as she imagined the upcoming trip, and she identified some of the following:

> *What sort of owner are you to go away and leave your dog?*
> *You are selfish to put yourself first and leave him behind.*
> *If you really loved him, you wouldn't leave him.*
> *He probably pines away and wonders where you've gone and why you left him.*
> *I can't enjoy the trip because he's all alone at the kennel, sad and crying for me.*
> *I would never forgive myself if something happened to him while I was gone.*

The kennel owner had already reassured her that they enjoyed taking care of her sweet dog. The veterinarian knew her pet and although he was older, he was in decent and stable health. He liked the caregivers and showed good energy when my client brought him in for a stay.

"I shouldn't be so worried—he likes it there," she said. "When I dropped him off the last time, he jumped right into their arms, and looked back at me as if to say, 'Bye, you can leave now.'"

The not-so-happy look on her face made me think about her adult son who had moved away a little over a year ago. He had been out of touch lately and had not even acknowledged his holiday gifts, which my client selected and sent with loving care. His behavior had hurt her feelings and made her question the nature of their relationship.

"How did you feel?" I asked (about the dog).

She replied,

> Jealous . . . Abandoned . . . It doesn't make sense. He clearly is well cared for and he likes being with them. I should be grateful. Maybe I want him to miss me. I'm usually OK when I drop him off. But once I'm gone, I think I'm a horrible owner, and that I should never have left him. What is going on?

Her choice of words sounded as if she was speaking about a mother and child, not an owner and dog. The meaning of baby, guilt, loss, being needed, being wanted, bad mother and proving her love was clearly about something more than her dog. These words were intrinsic to attachment issues and concerns about abandonment.

A few thoughts came to mind as we spoke together. She had often spoken of her dog as her baby. Her real "baby," an adult son, lived far away and was now in recovery after years

170

of struggling with addiction. She had been over-involved with his life, yet he had not been in touch recently, which upset her. He only called her when he needed money and when he wanted approval for his poorly planned decisions. Also, her aging parents were in poor health, and the possibility of their death loomed in the not too distant future. They lived far away and although she talked to them regularly, she was not able to visit. In the course of her therapy, she had developed a more adult-to-adult relationship with her parents. As a baby, her mother had left her with a nanny as a newborn, and her childhood had been without strong parental emotional support or nurture. Now, over the past year, she had developed a closer relationship with her mother and feared losing that, anticipating the emotional loss in a bittersweet manner.

At this stage of her life, the "baby," "guilt" and "fear" went both ways, between her and her son (loving and resenting), and her and her parents (her as a child/ her as an adult), especially her mother. In this scenario, *she was the dog*, being left behind (by her mother and her son) and needing love and reassurance. She was *also the caregiver*, loving her son and parents, and feeling the bond threatened by absence and illness.

I asked, "This isn't really just about your dog, is it?"

"I know," she said. "It's about me, isn't it?"

We processed the layered feelings over the course of an hour, and she was able to zoom in on her choice of words and the symbolic nature of her feelings about her dog that were more about other relationships. As we finished our session, she said,

> Wow, this resonates. My feelings are more about my mother leaving *me* as a baby, my own *baby not needing me now*, being so far away from my aging parents who *are* at risk of dying and who need me, being separated from the ones I love. It's amazing how it's all connected.

Yes, it is.

PROGRESS AND OUTCOMES

My client has vacillated between guilt (not doing enough) and resentment (doing too much or being taken advantage of). She realizes now that she can live with uncertainty, over her son's recovery, her husband's choices and her parents' health; she is feeling more centered and realizes that these were not her ropes to hold in the first place. At times, she revisits Friedman's story, saying, "I'm holding the rope again," "I need to stop myself before I take the rope," she's trying to throw me the rope, etc. This metaphor has allowed us to talk about choice and responsibility; holding the rope has become her metaphor for doing things for her husband, enabling her son and previously acting as if "trapped" by her sister's emotional abuse. She is learning to refuse the burdens others try to hand to her and to pause before picking up a dangling rope, even when she wants to feel "needed" or "wanted." She has become aware when she seems to engage in repetition compulsion (engaging in triggered behavioral patterns) and is adept at using metaphor to succinctly describe her reactions. Recently, she found herself hiding in fear behind the adult wall of what-iffing and anxiety, and said, "There I go again, the little girl using those cardboard blocks to hide from my fears. I guess I better come out from behind the blocks and deal with it."

The stories I have told her have resonated and stimulated new ways of thinking, but for this very insightful client, discovering and using her own metaphors has proven beneficial. She has progressed far from where she started. She is still in treatment, and for the most part, she is actively avoiding ropes, making decisions that reflect improved self-validation, setting better limits with family members, regulating her moods and stepping outside the "walls" she has created since childhood.

QUESTIONS FOR CASE DISCUSSION

1. We speak of threads of emotion and beliefs that connect past to present. Give two examples of childhood experiences that shaped this client's adult beliefs and behaviors.

Case Examples and Applications

2. Childhood attachment (avoidant, anxious, disorganized, secure) impacts adult relationships and interactions. Which style of attachment do you believe is shown by this client? Give examples of ways in which her adult behaviors reflect that attachment.
3. How was hiding behind the wall adaptive and comforting for her as a child? How are her adult "hiding" and "avoidant" behaviors less adaptive?
4. Indicate childhood events you believe were traumatizing for this client and how those experiences impact her as an adult (behavior, thinking, emotion)?

18

THE GIRL WHO LOST HER VOICE

A Case of Sexual Trauma

CASE INFORMATION AND BACKGROUND

She resembled a scared rabbit, frozen, vigilant and ready to bolt. A timid, anxious, deferent middle-aged woman came in for counseling some years back, to better communicate with her teenage daughter after leaving the girl's father and to deal with unresolved feelings of betrayal after she discovered he was "cheating." She did not have any idea he was seeing other women and said that the relationship was "good" until she found emails of a personal nature from other women. In time, it became clear that he had seen other women for quite some time. He also had a substance abuse problem, but he had been a "good provider" and "he was there for our daughter; she thinks he hung the moon."

CONCEPTUALIZATION

This client had lost her "voice" and stopped developing emotionally at about age 14. She had married fairly young, and they had one child together. She depended on her husband financially and emotionally, and had been married for many years when she entered treatment. At that point in time, they were no longer together, because when she found out he was unfaithful to her, she left him and finished raising their daughter by herself. He had health and substance abuse problems, but he was not abusive to her, and she continued to take their daughter to visit him and to let him visit. They remained connected legally until their daughter was in her late teens. When she came to therapy, she felt weighed down by her bitterness over the past. She had kept letters and emails "proving" his infidelity and had not fully resolved the past. Once my client addressed his betrayal and processed childhood trauma, she was ready to move on and made the decision to file divorce papers. Her perceived guilt over childhood trauma, unresolved grief over losing her father early in life and her failed marriage were baggage she had carried for many years, and resolving these gave her new confidence and improved self-esteem, allowing her to release the past.

PROBLEMS (AND REACTIONS TO PROBLEMS)

After she separated from her husband, he had continued to financially support her and her daughter, but that would end when the daughter turned 18. The woman was petrified of the idea of going to work and supporting herself. She believed that she had no skills and that no one

Case Examples and Applications

would be interested in hiring her. She was intelligent, but with limited insight, and she had been emotionally paralyzed for some time.

INTERVENTIONS

This fairly reclusive woman had difficulty making eye contact and was socially awkward and very emotionally constricted when we began treatment. She was frank and open in therapy but had little insight into the threads that connected her childhood with her adult life. She did not talk much about herself but described herself as "very shy" growing up. As an adult, she had close relationships with her sisters whom she visited once a year in another state. She also had a close relationship with a stepdaughter whom she had raised. She had one or two friends with whom she occasionally had lunch. I began slowly with her, doing some motivational interviewing and collecting information about past social and work experiences.

She presented as self-depreciating, minimizing her own needs, with "frozen" emotions; additionally, she was unassertive and lacked conversation skills. She had high anxiety in crowds but did not report having panic attacks. She preferred to be alone (somewhat socially avoidant) but occasionally enjoyed the company of a few female friends.

She had not worked for 25 years, but in her 20s she had worked as a server in a restaurant. While raising her daughter, she had given up most of her own interests other than some photography. She enjoyed taking high quality nature photos on solitary walks and when taking her daughter to visit the girl's father, who lived in another state.

She never missed a session, but for a long time when she interacted, she displayed anxiety and caution in her eyes. We worked on reducing anxious and depressed symptoms through behavioral activation. She listed things she used to enjoy doing and friends she had not contacted in a while; she then started going out more on weekends to take pictures and reached out to her friends.

Early in treatment, we also talked about her former marriage, her unresolved anger and grief at the betrayal of her love, and her belief that she could not ask for much from others or her ex-husband. She had tolerated inappropriate behavior and, for many years, struggled to set clear boundaries. He had been a good financial provider, but she had found and kept emails and letters that were a testimony to his infidelity. I wondered why she had kept them, long after they split up, and perhaps it was her reminder of why she should not reconcile with him.

SHIFT TO EMPLOYMENT

When prompted, she began talking about her large family growing up without a father once he died. Resources had been limited, so "you kept to yourself and we never asked for much." Slowly but surely, she started setting some limits with her ex-husband, who tended to cross boundaries with her, and she finally made a decision to get rid of the old emails and letters, the clearest sign that she was ready to "move on" and focus more on self-care. She engaged in a ritual of *destruction* that cleansed her of much of her bitter regret.

Therapy went slowly, and at times I wondered if she was benefiting from the regular contact, but she was one of the most faithful and reliable clients I worked with. Finally, after quite a bit of avoidance, she knew she needed to consider employment, because the child support for her daughter would end in the next couple of years. She and I practiced assertive communication during sessions, especially around potential job interviews. The client continued to struggle with verbal communication and found it hard to put thoughts and feelings into words. I sat and listened through the long pauses and encouraged her to consider the experiences she had in life that might translate to work settings: organization, good planning, parenting, good listening skills, her responsibility and maturity, tolerance and acceptance of others, good computer skills and photography/art abilities. She had not thought of herself or her skills from that perspective, and she had greatly underestimated her own abilities. Even as a server many years before, the boss had relied on and trusted her and she created ideas to make the job more efficient. She was dependable and never called in at the last minute "like the young girls did." Together, we started translating her skills and experiences into a resume that

174

The Girl Who Lost Her Voice

could "sell" her strengths. This activity gave her confidence and after months of "what-iffing," coaching and practice, she wrote her resume using an online guide and began applying for jobs.

I began to wonder about past trauma but took my time to go there. She was very self-critical, and she made herself "invisible" around others in a way that seemed self-protective. It became clear that her childhood had been difficult, with poverty and lack of nurture. She grew comfortable with me, never missing a session, and she began to talk more about herself. The first sign of change was the humor that broke through when I described her ex-husband as a leech and read her a dark but humorous story about leeches that attached themselves to a vulnerable woman (Pernicano, 2012, 2014a). "She's a little like me," she said with a shy smile. We talked about the story and she noted that the woman's friend was a big help. I asked my client if she ever had a good friend like that.

She looked down, indicated she did as a young girl, but that the friendship suddenly ended when she was 14 after something bad happened. "We were disobedient," she said.

This was a shift, i.e., an open-door invitation to ask her about the loss of this significant friendship. I guided her through a narrative of what turned out to be a painful traumatic event. This event had been carried with her into adulthood and was the foundation of her self-judgment and low self-efficacy. She and her 14-year-old friend were spending the night together at her friend's house. They "snuck out" mid-evening to take a walk. That was the "disobedience." It was a small, usually safe, town and not much went on after dark. The girls enjoyed their walk until they came across a couple of older boys. The boys talked and flirted with the girls and suggested they all go together to the boys' apartment to watch a movie. In asking how old they might have been, she thought the boys might have been 17 or 18. Neither girl knew the boys, but they were flattered that the boys showed interest and agreed to go watch the movie.

The naïve girls walked with the boys to the apartment. Very quickly, they were separated when one of the boys took my client to his bedroom. She was scared to death and tried to leave. He was stronger than her, pushed her on the bed, pinned her down, roughly removed her clothes and proceeded to sexually assault her. She had no experience with boys and she "froze" in his room, crying silently through the assault. She blamed herself for not screaming or crying out, "but it was my own fault," she said. Afterward, he took her back to the living area, where her friend and the other boy were sitting.

She and her friend walked back to the other girl's house. I asked what they talked about, and she said, "Nothing." They walked back in silence and did not speak of it. I asked if she told her parents, and she said, "No, they would have killed me." She said she wondered if the other girl had sex with the other boy but did not ask. "I didn't speak of it then, and I never spoke of it since. This is the first time." She teared up and bowed her head. It is such a gift when our clients offer their trust and begin to share their deepest concerns.

Then I used the word "rape." I asked how the "rape" affected her afterward.

She looked up, met my eyes and said, in a confused and manner, "I never thought of it as rape. I thought it was my fault. We went to the house. We disobeyed our parents. We had it coming; it was our fault. Was it really rape?"

"Of course it was rape," I said. "You went with the boys to watch a movie. You didn't consent to sex. Disobeying your parents was a mistake, but forced sex is rape."

She teared up. "I never thought of it that way. We were too young to know any better . . ."

There was a shift over the next weeks and months as she started realizing that she had been raped and victimized, and she reframed her previous view of herself as "disobedient." We put her behavior in context of a curious, naïve 14-year-old who trusted everyone and never expected harm. She had never had a boyfriend, least of all any sexual experience. As we talked, she started to share other significant life events that continued to bother and impact her.

I decided to read/tell her the story of *The Cracked Glass Bowl* to help process the past, considering it might be easier to talk about things after she had the opportunity to write them down. She sat silently as I read the story, and when I came to the part "I am so damaged I will never again be the same," she began to cry.

"That story is how I felt all these years. Maybe there is still hope."

Her assignment was to draw herself as a cracked glass bowl and to label the cracks, gouges and chips as things that had caused her pain and left her feeling broken or damaged. Most clients put three or four events on the bowl. Figure 18.1 is what she presented the following week, a cracked green glass bowl and in Figure 18.2 a list of the painful things she had experienced

Case Examples and Applications

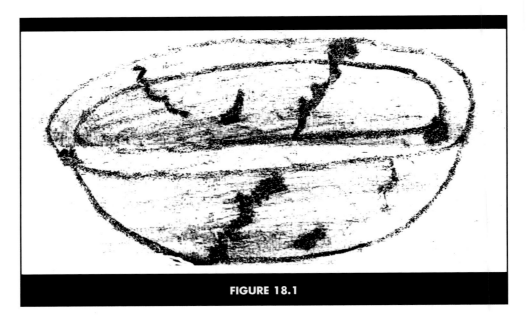

FIGURE 18.1

```
my Mom & Dad divorcing when I was 4.
not getting to see my Dad from age 4 - 10.
my step Dad whipping me so hard.
being scared of my step Dad.
my step Dad making me go outside at night by myself in a storm to feed
our chickens because I had forgotten to that day.
being so excruciatingly shy.
rape
my Dad dying in a wreck.
sexual harrassment at a job by a good friend's husband.
███'s affairs.
watching ████ suffer from depression.
having to give away my 2 cats (T.C. & Tiger)
my step Mom dying.
```

FIGURE 18.2

She had drawn the bowl and written a long list of negative life events, too many to write on the bowl. So ... much ... pain. She had not yet talked in detail about many of these things, so her bowl was her way of letting me know she was ready, an invitation to process trauma. I often use this activity to start the trauma narrative process, as it is a gentler, less abrupt process and usually results in less avoidance, less treatment dropout.

We began talking about her bowl, and one crack at a time, we processed what she had written. She started to be less emotionally constricted and showed a wider range of facial emotions as we worked together. Her voice became more expressive and less flat.

Her final assignment was to draw the new creation. Her finished bowl was lovely and mirrored the changes she perceived in herself. She left a few lines and said, "Those cracks are sealed now, part of me. Some things are so much a part of you, you never forget, but you can live with them."

PROGRESS AND OUTCOMES

Over the course of this therapy work, she started accepting her strengths (first through my eyes and then through her own). Then, another shift occurred; she had several job interviews and was hired at a local restaurant to do food prep. It was a significant life change, and after initial adjustment, she began to realize that she once again was a valued employee.

We ended our therapy after about a year, and I eventually left the area. She contacted me recently to let me know she was doing well and said, "You would be proud of me. My daughter has a baby and I'm a good grandma. I'm still working at that job and I've had two promotions." She wanted me to know that the therapy had "stuck" and that she was coping well. I know how hard it was for her to do all this, yet she knew I believed she could do it. I had to push a bit, and getting a job required several sessions working within the stages of change perspective. Now, as expected, she believes in herself, and she has a "life worth living."

QUESTIONS FOR DISCUSSION

1. Rape victims sometimes blame themselves for what happened. Describe this woman's reactions to her rape as a girl.
2. Learned helplessness is a term that refers to a passive acceptance that the individual is powerless to change. Self-efficacy is the belief that you can do something and that it will make a difference. Describe how this woman moved from learned helplessness to positive self-efficacy.
3. What does it mean to say that this client lost her voice at age 14?
4. How did her employment increase her self-efficacy and confidence?

19

GRIEF AND THE FOUR STONES

A Case of the Woman Who Chose To NOT Move on

CASE INFORMATION AND BACKGROUND

Early in treatment, this middle-aged mother and wife was preoccupied with guilt and soul-wrenching unresolved grief. She came to sessions ruminating about "what if" this and "what if" that. "What do I DO with ALL THIS?" she asked. She was referring to the "crushing sadness" and "darkness" she experienced daily. Like a worn, dirty sponge, she was too full of agitation and obsessive thinking to focus on anything else.

When she first came to see me, her son had been dead about a year, having died in his mid-20s of an accidental Fentanyl overdose. He had been a bright shining star and in an instant, his life had been snuffed out. From her description, he had been a lover-of-life with high energy and many friends. He was musical, athletic, friendly and outgoing. But starting in his early teens, he headed down what would turn out to be a deadly road of addiction.

PROBLEMS

The diminutive agitated woman in tennis shoes, sweatshirt and black pants came in one week and announced, "I hate the saying *move on*. That's what they say in movies and books. When someone dies, your friends and relatives say you should *move on*. I am never going to *move on*. I won't do it." This show of firm defiance was welcome—a spurt of energy, a feisty angry spirit, something different than the overwhelming sadness of the weeks past.

I asked, "What does that mean to you? To 'move on'?"

She paused, reflected and responded quite deliberately, "Move on to *where?* And what happens to what you leave behind? What do you do with it? Does it not count anymore? If I move on it would mean leaving him behind. How could I ever do that? I'm afraid I'll forget . . . his voice, what he looks like, how he was. I need to keep him with me. I can't forget." For this client, moving on (from her sadness, guilt, obsessing) meant she would be diminishing her son's value/meaning and would have "nothing left."

The night he died, he had called her to tell her he was going to meet her within the hour and was in good spirits. "See you soon," he said. When she tried to remind him of something he said, "Mom, I know what to do." But he didn't show up. For her son, that was not so unusual, and it was perhaps even typical of his drug-using behavior. For many years, she had experienced his getting high, missing appointments, not following through, promising things and forgetting

178

the promises. She was disappointed that he didn't show but didn't think too much of it in that moment. He didn't answer his cell, and she figured he had changed his mind.

She went to his apartment the next day and found him deceased, face down on the bathroom floor, his *works* a reminder of his last, deadly *high*. She often obsessed about why she had not gone there the night before, but the autopsy revealed he had likely died almost instantly given the dose ingested. As we worked together, my client started to realize that she could not have gotten there quickly enough to revive or save him.

CONCEPTUALIZATION

She felt like her marriage was empty, a shell, and she herself was empty. I pictured an empty hermit crab shell, no life within. She wore drab clothes and tennis shoes, and paid little attention to her own needs. All she could think about was losing her son, the light of her life.

I wondered aloud, "Eventually, you will be forced to focus on yourself and the marriage. You have no idea who you are without your son in the world."

She nodded. For years, her identity had been shaped by her son's problems—encouraging his participation in activities, trying to prevent relapse but also trying to not enable him, encouraging his treatments, buffering the rest of the family from his dishonesty and threats, now preserving her memories of her sweet boy and staying connected with his friends (many who also used drugs).

She had an excellent education and skills and had worked as a teacher in the past; she was not employed when I met her and had too much free time on her hands, without the energy to do anything. She had stopped exercising and socializing, and she was unsure of her future plans.

They had struggled as a family since the boy's teens, in response to his chronic lies and deception, his school behavior problems, treatments and relapses, and even aggressive behavior when they blocked his efforts. The dad traveled a lot for his job, and they had grown distant with one another; much of the home stress fell on my client's shoulders. They never talked about it, really, and when they did talk they often argued.

Their son had also struggled with gender issues since he was a very young child. The family sought help and was given poor advice, so her son had lived "closeted" until his teens. His mother often wondered, "If we had gone against the advice, let him be himself, would he have ended up like this?" She continued to blame herself for her son's death and obsessed about what *might have happened under different circumstances*. She did not know how to live in the present, with her family, without him, and she had little in her life to provide support and validation.

INTERVENTION

I validated her regret and sadness at having emotionally "hurt" her son; at the same time, they had encouraged his talents, provided him with a wonderful education and took interest in his friends and activities. His own choices and fun-loving personality had led him into drug culture.

I commented,

> It is not really fair to hold yourself accountable now for what you didn't know then. You followed the psychiatric advice you were given, and you didn't know what else to do. It is unfortunate, but it is what it is.

We talked about the time period during which they sought treatment for their son. Views were different then, and gender differences weren't affirmed or accepted. Many professionals believed gay persons could be *changed* to a straight lifestyle through behavioral therapy. This is mistaken, and her son hated the therapy. He had struggled with his identity between middle school and high school, but after he came out, he had a group of very inclusive friends; unlike the time in early childhood, his family accepted his gender preference as he was. He seemed well adjusted overall until drug use in his early teens began to impact his behavior and school performance.

For quite a while in her treatment, we processed her overwhelming grief, dark depression, heavy guilt and piles of "what if's." I thought about her disliking the term "move on." One week,

Case Examples and Applications

I said, "You don't have to move on and leave him behind. But perhaps you can find a way to keep flowing forward." I described a river, where his stream was part of and merged with hers until he died, then his stream ended, and she needed to keep flowing. His essence would flow with her. She had gotten dammed up and stopped flowing soon after he died.

This imagery resonated with her. "I like the visualization of the flowing. My son, my grief, we all flow together."

Her son had reminded her over and over that his turning to drugs had nothing to do with her. He was a thrill-seeking kind of boy, and early in his teens started using marijuana . . . then Xanax . . . then pain pills . . . then IV heroin (the beginning of his end) . . . the Fentanyl was his last, and fatal, high. He had picked the friends who introduced him to the heroin, and he never fully realized that relapse could one day be fatal. He had abundant numbers of friends who attended his funeral and a memorial ceremony on his birthday. They stayed in touch with the mom long after he passed away, and she found meaning in helping them. "If I can help even one, it is worth it." She drove kids to detox, to rehab. She offered to do research with them on treatment programs. His friends called and stopped by to visit her, and they continue to do so. I remind her that she is their rock, a secure loving base where they can remember her son together and find forgiveness for anything they might have done to contribute to his death.

Her son's drug use had changed the family in many ways, with family vigilance, anxiety about his drug use and high stress since his teens; now, each family member had residual traumatic baggage related to his anger, prior abuse toward them and the nature of his death. They grew apart as a family, each in his or her compartment, like eggs in a carton, separate and hard-shelled. My client struggled with ambivalent feelings as she remembered her son's last years.

She found some comfort in her religion and faith practices throughout treatment but continued for a long time to feel unforgiveable and was at times unable to regulate her strong waves of sadness, anxiety and lethargy. So often she said, "I still can't go in his room. I can't go through his things. And I keep thinking that this is all my fault."

"You know," I said, "it wasn't up to you to keep him alive. It was up to him." She raged at the helplessness of it all, at not being able to save him. He had not "meant" to die, as he had planned to meet her that night. The downward spiral began the moment he had said *yes* to heroin, then Fentanyl, the beginning of the end.

I affirmed,

> You will always love him, and at the same time it is OK to be angry and disappointed at decisions he made and what *you* lost as parents, as individuals and as a family. After all, in the end *he left you*—not on purpose and far too soon—but he took you through hell with him and it was not the life you would have chosen.

She acknowledged anger and disappointment, as well as great grief and longing. My client had gone through most of it alone, with her husband gone so much, and she started to share her frustration that he had left her holding the bag. She didn't know how to deal with her son's aggression and defiance in his late teens; she needed support and someone to talk to after her son's death. Her husband dealt with his grief through silence and avoidance, and her daughters who lived out of town had problems of their own. The family members were a fleet of ships traveling on the ocean—ships passing, and sometimes colliding, in the night.

I understood that this client would need to heal from the inside out, and metaphor became a vehicle through which she began to see new possibilities. We worked together for about a year doing a combination of trauma recovery with complicated grief and guilt work. Each session, she consumed a Kleenex box. Little by little, back and forth, she experienced and processed the stages of grief; for a long time she was unable to allow herself to be angry with her son, at the choices he had made and "leaving" her in such a dramatic and sudden way. She and her husband had funded rehab and treatment over the years, while their son was kicked out of private schools and "wasted" the opportunities. She was angry he had not taken recovery seriously, that he had mistreated family members, and angry that he had tried heroin. She was very upset that he had not done what he could to help himself, and that others wanted his recovery more than he.

The "what if's" lessened as we worked together in regular therapy. She realized that her son had come to grips with his gender issues and that he (and his friends) knew and accepted who he was. He had a wide circle of loving friends, and he made a difference in the world even though his time was short. The biggest realization was that he had thrown himself into drugs the way he did everything else. He liked getting high, experiencing altered states of consciousness and hanging out with friends. He saw himself as invulnerable and it was not until he first used heroin that his life took a downward spiral.

SHIFT (FOUR STONES)

At various points in therapy, my client had great difficulty managing her strong waves of guilt, regret and sadness. I decided to offer some tools for mindfulness and self-soothing. We used *Thich Nhat Hanh's* stone meditation described in the Appendix, and she found this uniquely helpful and memorable. This technique is centering, and the individual views the self as flower, mountain, clear water and air. When picturing and experiencing those attributes, the person becomes aware of self-dimensions. She is a very spiritual person, and her faith kept her flowing forward until we terminated our therapy.

I remember clearly the week she reported, "I finally went into his room. My friend helped me because I could not have done it alone. I gathered up some of his books." She had kept his door closed since he died and had been unable to touch or move any of his things. We had talked about "when" she would be ready to take a step to transform the room into a personal peaceful space for herself, something she desired. She took this step forward and began to conceive of a life without her son.

We talked about what it would mean to travel the river and "flow forward" so that her son's past would flow forward with her. She had been so afraid that in flowing forward, she would "lose" her son and for her, it also meant she would have to forgive herself for the many things she had done or neglected to do as an "imperfect" mother and human being. She would need to accept herself as "good enough" and stop using perfection as the standard against which she measured her parenting behavior. Self-forgiveness did not come easily; by being angry with herself, she avoided dealing with the anger she experienced toward her son. He had been addicted to drugs after all, and there had been years of broached trust and misdirected anger.

In time, she found a balance and her mood shifted in therapy. She did a number of things to help her honor her son's memory and move forward. She and her family took a trip together, in his honor, and visited a NYC shelter that served homeless LBGTQ youth. It was the first sign that the fractured family and marriage might one day recover. The trip was meaningful, and they talked about how much he would have liked them doing this; they made a donation in his name. She instituted rituals and kept in touch with his friends and they reciprocated.

PROGRESS AND OUTCOMES

It is never easy to lose a child, and in many ways that grief is unable to be fully resolved. Parents are "supposed to go first," and a child's death violates that expectation. However, it is possible to put the pieces back together, to find what we call a "new normal." Like *The Cracked Glass Bowl*, this woman's intense grief, love, faith and hope healed her from the inside out, as she softened her guilt toward herself with compassion, reformed and decided to live a life of value and meaning, even though her son was no longer alive. In the end, my client found purpose and meaning within her son's death in six ways: 1. by realizing that his life, although short, had meaning; 2. by allowing herself to be upset with *his decision* to try heroin; 3. by accepting that she could not protect him forever; 4. by telling others about her son's journey; 5. by educating others about opiate drug addiction; and 6. by sharing her grief with others quite courageously. She realized that her son's essence lives on in her memories and work. At the time we terminated treatment she had made significant progress, but there was work still to be done. Each family member had reacted differently to her son's death, and some healing needed to take place in the family relationships that were challenged by living too much in *crisis mode*. She began helping her daughters find their own resolution to their brother's death. My client had sacrificed her own interests and needs for many years, and she was contemplating creating a peaceful space at home for self-care.

Case Examples and Applications

FIGURE 19.1

She recently told me that she remembers something I said that really stayed with her. "You were not a perfect parent. There is no perfect parent. But you were good enough." That seems to be the bottom line; 20–20 hindsight is not helpful, nor is dwelling on the past. We simply can't hold ourselves accountable now for things we didn't know or see then. She did the best she could under the circumstances, with the knowledge, love and understanding she had at the time.

She has emailed me several times since we terminated treatment, notes of gratitude and sharing some pride about steps she had taken to share her son's story. A mass was held locally for survivors of drug/opiate death, and she became a local spokesperson to get the word out about addiction and things family members can do to help their loved ones during recovery and to heal after loss. I rejoiced in her growth and courage as she took these steps in her own grief and healing process. I contacted her recently for permission to use her story in this book, and here is her response, with a photo above that she took of her four stones (in the foreground in the small ceramic dish):

Dr. Pat,
I will be honored to have J and my story in your book. As you see, the stones are still with me. Just last week one of J's best friends was here and I told her how the stones came to be. Growth. Strength. Clarity. Spirit. That is what they are to me.

QUESTIONS FOR DISCUSSION

1. Discuss ways that this client responded to metaphor and how it helped her shift perception.
2. Discuss the systemic impact of drug abuse with regard to this family's functioning.
3. What turned this mother's grief into a complicated grieving process?
4. How did the metaphor of the flowing river help this mother not "move on" but, rather, to move forward?

20

THE MERMAID WHO FORGOT

A Case of Pending Loss

CASE INFORMATION AND BACKGROUND

She was a very bright middle-aged well-educated individual, with her PhD, excellent writing/ verbal skills and clear leadership ability. She was referred by a colleague and was very motivated for therapy, seeking help adjusting to significant family changes. My client and her husband were both competent professionals, and each had some history of depression and anxiety. They had gone through stressful (financially and personally) periods during their marriage, in part due to due to job changes and in part due to family stressors, but they remained close and committed.

My client and her husband had three sons, the oldest of whom had moved out a couple of years prior rather than attend college. The oldest son had a history of cannabis abuse and some behavior problems that started around middle school. Around the same time their son started having problems, the father had gone through a significant depression due to his own job situation, and he was less emotionally and physically available to the family. My client perceived that she had to deal with their son's issues on her own for the most part until he left home, because her husband had withdrawn emotionally. She and her husband agreed to allow their son to withdraw from school to work full time to support himself, and subsequently he left home. By his mother's description, he was emotionally disengaged and difficult to communicate with from his early teens, perhaps depressed and self-medicating. In the midst of this, my client was unexpectedly not granted tenure and chose to move on from her college teaching.

My client was very close to her parents, especially her dad, who had been a minister before his retirement. She herself had distanced from their conventional and traditional religious beliefs, but she enjoyed their visits and family time, especially family holidays. She wanted nothing more than to carry on the family holidays and traditions with her own children. My client's husband had "disowned" his family of origin, who were described as critical and disengaged, and had apparently never looked back. My client's husband got along well with his children, but sometimes my client felt he did not understand her emotions. He tended to be more understated and she more extraverted, but he was very committed to the family and faithful in the marriage. At the time my client entered treatment, her oldest son had a live-in partner with two young children and her middle son worked full time and seemed quite stable. The youngest son was very artistic, a bit of a loner and close to my client.

When her son and his partner moved in together, my client welcomed her as the daughter she never had. The young woman had been estranged from her biological mother because of her mother's overall instability and substance abuse issues that landed her in and out of jail. This had resulted in estrangement with her daughter, and the young woman left home in her teens to live with a grandmother. Now, she was a partner and mother, responsible for others and lacking

183

Case Examples and Applications

close family relationships. My client "entered the picture" as a mother-in-law figure and the two became quite close. They did things together, talked on the phone about the children, and she provided a great deal of emotional "mothering" to the younger woman. My client had a particularly loving, close relationship with her young grandson, this woman's child, who I will call "A." Her interactions with "A" provided much joy and meaning to her life. She provided much care and nurturing support for him (and later for his new sibling), and she took care of him during every-other-weekend visits.

PROBLEMS (AND REACTIONS TO PROBLEMS)

My client presented with an adjustment disorder with a mix of anxiety and depressed mood. Quite "suddenly" everything had changed for my client, and she felt in danger of "losing everything—my son, the kids . . . I don't think I could stand it if I lost them . . ."

Her oldest son had dramatically withdrawn from her, and he no longer allowed "A" to visit her every other weekend. His partner, in loyalty to him and his wishes, also pulled away from my client and her husband. The "regular" every other weekend visits were no longer "givens," nor were family holidays, and "permission" for gift giving was tightly controlled. She feared what that would mean to the child, to be pulled away without explanation, and to her own life without his regular presence.

Her son spoke to her less on the phone and seemed irritable and short tempered. Holidays changed, and it seemed that her son and his partner, in loyal support, wanted much less involvement. Around the same time, his partner reconnected with her extended family (sisters and grandmother) in order to be part of a family, something she had always wanted.

My client had adjusted very well to the loss of her college teaching position and landed on her feet in a new educator role, but she was not adjusting well to the potential "loss" of her grandchild and was panicking about living a life without that joy and warmth. My client reported anxiety attacks at bedtime, thoughts/fears about dying, and concerns that she would lose everything she valued. Her description of being tenuously tethered by ropes to her son, his family and her mother was a poignant metaphor. She feared that she and her son would remain estranged and that she would be "alone" later in life, without their love and support.

My client worried that her oldest son would totally alienate himself from the family, somewhat like her husband had with his; yet she found herself engaging more and more intensely with her son, trying to pull him back to her. She seemed desperate in her efforts and quickly realized that her fears, anxiety and tearfulness were out of proportion to the situation. They were also not likely to serve the intended purpose of reconciliation. As we worked together in therapy, she sought some balance in her interactions. She became aware that she might inadvertently be pushing him and his partner away by buying them things and *lovingly* communicating too much. She had become a ping pong ball, vacillating between "intruding" emotionally on her son's privacy (crossing boundaries) and backing off, emotionally "frozen." She felt as if her dreams and hopes were sliding through her fingers like a slippery greased pig at a rodeo.

CONCEPTUALIZATION

My client felt untethered, an excellent description of what happens during attachment disruptions, and the panic that can ensue at feeling unloved, abandoned or "alone." The potential loss of closeness with her grandson threatened my client because they shared a mutual unconditional love. She "worried ahead" to a future life without love and connectedness with the next generation of her family, especially at a time when she foresaw the loss of her parents and gained awareness that her spouse could not meet all her needs. She carried insecurities and unmet attachment needs from her own family of origin and from moving around so much as a child. There were some family secrets and financial stressors, both growing up and in her adult family. It was interesting that she picked a husband who had "disowned" his "toxic" family, yet she feared that her own son might do the same. Her emotional response was strong and somewhat

184

out of proportion to the recent change, because total abandonment and loss seemed unlikely, so I sought to help her regain some sense of security in her relationship with her son and his partner.

INITIAL INTERVENTIONS

My client recently wrote,

> One of the things I think you gave me in our early therapy was words—you named things for me that I couldn't name. I was telling you, tearfully, about the day I allowed (my son) to withdraw from school (husband and I finally accepted that we couldn't "make" him learn or value school) and then that I hadn't followed through with (other son's) IEP his sophomore year in high school, because it coincided with the time I didn't get tenure. I paused for a breath, and you said, gosh, it must be hard for you to breathe. I said, "What?" and you responded, "All that guilt, all that taking care of other people's children but feeling like you failed your own must make it hard for you to even breathe sometimes." I don't remember how I responded outwardly, but inwardly, I was all "Yes! Yes! Yes!" So one of the greatest things you ever did for me was to name something I couldn't admit I was feeling.

I encouraged her to find the words to communicate openly and directly with her son, to let him know that she understood he wanted to make his choices about his children and his life (without imposing a guilt trip on him); also, that she loved him and wanted to do things that would bring him close and not push him away. She apologized to both sons for ways in which her actions might have affected them. She recently wrote,

> I was sorry for missed opportunities, for failed connections, for sometimes just not knowing what to do. I asked them to forgive me. Now, maybe nobody in the world needed that but me, but for me, it took the weight of the world off my shoulders. It made me feel as if there was nothing unspoken between us. It gave me a sense of starting fresh—it let me forgive myself, which was huge.

We talked extensively about her "grief" and anticipated "loss" should her son and his family distance from her and no longer be connected. One session, I prompted her to tell me what she was feeling "through a story." In her story,

> I was falling toward the black void of space, tethered to the earth by two ropes. One of those ropes was "A," my grandson, who felt loved and needed me as much as I needed him. But (child's parents) were hacking away at that rope and it was strained almost to the breaking point. The other rope was my moms, and her deteriorating mental state was fraying that rope, so there were only a couple of threads left of it. When those ropes break, I said, I will be lost. I will float away from the earth and into the black void of space. I think this works well in describing the twin stressors that propelled me into therapy with you—I had a sense that I was losing everything, all the foundation that a strong sense of family has always provided for me.

The connection she had with her kids was not what she had hoped it would be at that point in time, and she had little else to fill her life other than work and her marriage. Without going too much into this, I will say that she greatly improved her boundaries and perceptions in her relationship with her sons and partner, by changing her thinking, behavior and expectations. She did not "lose" her grandchildren; rather, she developed richer adult-to-adult relationships with her adult children that continue to this day. She and her oldest son now have a more open, comfortable relationship, and she no longer expects her children or grandchildren to solely meet her emotional needs. As we worked on the nature of those relationships and how to shift her coping style, I began to see that other things were also contributing to stress.

NEW INTERVENTIONS AND SHIFT

The point came where we started talking about her high level of internal stress and worry, because she was having anxiety attacks at bedtime. I decided to create and tell her a story, to help her clarify and change her focus, i.e., see clearly that she was underestimating her value and abilities. Sometimes, spontaneously, I create a short story in the moment and strive to find parallels to the client and his/her situation. It was not written down at the time, but it is now titled *Dive Deep*. I had a mermaid statue in my office that portrays calm, quiet solid strength, in the stance

Case Examples and Applications

and materials. The story I told was about a mermaid who "forgot" her core identity. In the story, the mermaid is caught in a hurricane and tries desperately to swim to shore through the waves. I selected a mermaid because she can survive in water or above ground, giving her some options in the midst of a storm. Also, I could see dissonance between my client's interpersonal strengths and strong, loving commitment to her family and her perceived abandonment with out-of-control fear of horrific loss. She felt helpless, without self-efficacy, and I sought to help her reclaim a self-perception of competence and connectedness.

The following story resonated with my talented, competent, professional adult client who had "lost her way" in doubt and worry. She, like the mermaid, had many resources she was not using in the midst of her storms. I wanted her to shift her self-perception and draw on the resources within her that she was neglecting. The story "hit home" and has become one I use to help clients "dive deep" to get "out of the storm" (using mindfulness and breathing) rather than becoming exhausted trying to swim through the stress in their lives.

Dive Deep

Pat Pernicano (unpublished manuscript)

The mermaid had heard that a storm was brewing off the coast, but she thought she had plenty of time before it hit. She had ridden out many storms before, so the talk of a "big one" did not faze her. She was a strong swimmer and not afraid of a little wind and rain. Earlier that day, the sky had been blue and clear and the water had been calm and refreshing.

The mermaid hadn't been paying close attention as the storm approached, but now she could no longer ignore what was happening. The wind was picking up, and the clouds were turning dark. The waves grew choppy, and it became a real effort to keep her head above water. "I better head to shore," she said to herself a little reluctantly, and she began her swim.

"I wonder where everyone went?" she thought. Her friends, including four rainbow fish, an octopus, a starfish and a dolphin, had been swimming and playing with her earlier, and had urged her to get out of the water before the storm hit. Now they were nowhere to be seen.

The mermaid was still pretty far from shore when the storm hit. "Wow, that wind is very strong!" she thought as loud thunder boomed and lightning bolts lit up the now dark sky. "It's amazing how fast things can go from good to bad," she reflected. The mermaid got more and more tired as she swam through the large waves. She had a tight feeling in her chest and could hardly catch her breath. She redoubled her efforts and kept the shore in sight. "I have to keep going," she said, "It's me (alone) against the storm."

"Hey, Mermaid!" It was her friend the octopus, his voice rising above the sound of the howling wind. She swam over to him and exclaimed, "I'm sure glad to see you!"

He asked, "What are you doing? Why are you swimming in the storm?"

She replied, "I'm trying to get to shore, but it's really hard to swim in the storm. The waves are huge and there is so much wind and lightning."

Her friend paused. A long pause. And he asked, "Have you forgotten that you're a mermaid?" There was another long pause.

The mermaid looked confused, then answered, "I guess I did."

Octopus said, "You don't have to swim against the storm. When a storm comes up, be a mermaid. Use your tail, and dive deep. Get out of the storm."

"Follow me," he said.

Octopus headed into the depths of the ocean and Mermaid, with a flip of her powerful tail, followed. Deeper and deeper they went, until they reached a calm, quiet, peaceful place deep in the sea. No waves. No wind. No struggle. In no time at all.

"Now look around you," Octopus said.

Mermaid looked around and saw what lay beneath the ocean's surface. There was abundant life in the ocean depths, a colorful world under the sea. There were coral, plant life, all sorts of fish, sea creatures of every shape and type. Her panic ebbed and somewhere deep within, the calm and peace she discovered began to restore her.

The Mermaid Who Forgot

"I can hardly believe it," she said. "Just a moment ago, I was fighting the storm. I was so tired and discouraged. Now I feel calm in this beautiful place."

Octopus nodded his head in understanding and said, "It is because you forgot your very essence; you forgot who you were and lost yourself. Now look up." Mermaid looked up. Way up above their heads was the storm, still raging, the water churning.

Octopus noted, "Storms come and go. They are part of life. Some people say, 'Find the calm within the storm.' I say, get out of the $%*#!$ storm! No one needs to try to swim in a storm."

Mermaid commented, "When I was in the storm, all I could think about was keeping my head above water . . . to survive the storm . . ."

She added, "I forgot who I was. I needed to remember who I was to get out of the storm. Thanks for reminding me."

"Yes," replied Octopus. "You are a mermaid. When storms come up, remember who you are, and dive deep. Get out of the storm."

Like the Mermaid, we will each face storms in life. Don't forget who you are when you find yourself in the midst of a storm. Remember your very essence, and Dive Deep.

As I finished the story, I noticed that my client had teared up; she exclaimed, "Oh Pat, I am a mermaid. And I forgot that I am a mermaid." She was visibly shaken by the story and had experienced it very personally. Like the mermaid, she had forgotten her resources and had become somewhat helpless in swimming against recent stressors.

The friend in the story reminds the mermaid that when she is trying to swim "through" a storm, (problems, danger and stress) she sometimes tries too hard and loses perspective. Her goal becomes survival instead of growth, and swimming through a storm saps resources. My client, like the mermaid, needed to "dive deep" to gain a different perspective on the storm. My client identified both with "forgetting" her core self, and with not using resources with which she might restore her equilibrium. That week she took the story home and made it her own, and the metaphor of "dive deep" resulted in deeper therapeutic process in the months to come. The "aha" in the story resonated with her, she said, and she shared it with her friends and relatives, commenting that she wondered why she had not seen it before.

SHIFT

Soon after, there was a new shift. Our treatment shifted to discussing her unmet attachment needs. Some of her academic achievement and competence was at the neglect of her emotional needs. She was very close to her husband, but there had been long periods of time when he was depressed, during which they had been less connected. We talked about the desperate quality of interactions with those she loved. Her fear of loss was akin to that of a young toddler who panics when her parent leaves the room. She was like a dry sponge, trying to soak up love, validation and appreciation in every way she could, through her family, other people and her career, but it was never "enough." She was lacking a core sense of her own identity and she met too many of her needs through others. She had not invested in close friendships outside her marriage and family, likely fallout from moving around a lot as a girl and avoiding closeness to avoid loss. Her emotional needs had not always been promptly met while growing up.

In exploring her early relationships, her "ideal" family of origin turned out to have a few flaws. Her mother had been the "glue of the family" in carrying out family traditions and planning gatherings, but had not always been very nurturing, and the client had to reverse roles at times to meet her mother's emotional needs. Her mother also had problems with her spending, and earlier in life had spent church funds, getting her husband in trouble with the church and embarrassing the family. More recently, her mother had spent money without telling her dad, leaving them with budget crises.

Her dad had been gentle and kind as a father, but very passive and unable to deal easily with a wife who had been vocal that she never wanted to be a minister's wife. She always "seemed to want more," and what he provided was "never enough for her." My client may well have experienced similar feelings when her husband struggled with job continuity. The client also felt she

Case Examples and Applications

never had a "real home." They had moved around and lived in church parsonages, so "nothing was ours, not even the dishes or towels." When her parents retired, they had to get and pay for their own home and finances were further stretched.

Her fear of loss led me to wonder about her parents' current state of health and mind, since it is often memories from the past that are activated during stressful times in the present, and those memories become a filter through which the present is viewed. Her dad was in good health, but it slowly came out that there had been recent changes in her mother's mental and emotional functioning. To my trained ears, it sounded a lot like some sort of dementia. Her mom was hiding receipts from her dad and had gotten lost driving. She was not caring for her hygiene and needed help with daily living. One day, she sat alone all day watching TV while her husband sat in the other room, and neither of them ate because she had not fixed a meal. I told my client I was concerned that her father still let her drive, even if it was "only close to home," and that she still had keys to the house and car.

With my client, I broached the possibility of onset of Alzheimer's and suggested her dad take her mom for evaluation, but he was "not ready." It was clear that no one in the family was ready to move in that direction. It was also clear that my client was having strong feelings of sadness and irritability at the more and more obvious changes in her mom, and her father was feeling overwhelmed.

My client continued to try to plan visits and holidays, but her mother found that increasingly stressful, and their interactions during visits became more unpleasant. Her mother was short tempered, speaking rudely to others and behaving inappropriately in public. "That was never my mom," said my client. "She always was gracious and said the right thing, especially as the minister's wife." Now, her mother was not capable of filtering what she said, due to changes in her executive functioning, and she was easily frustrated. Her memory was clearly impaired and there was some risk in allowing her to drive, especially unaccompanied.

This was the other dimension of "potential loss," and my client felt it before she realized it. Loss of a parent almost always stirs up attachment issues, and with Alzheimer's, the loss greatly precedes the person's demise. At some level, my client was very aware that she was "losing" her mother. But she was fighting the need to reverse roles, still wanting the "mother I used to have, the person she used to be." She became short tempered and impatient with her mother's inability to be that person, because like most family members of Alzheimer disease patients, they see the "same person" on the outside and forget that it is not the same person on the inside. My client could accurately describe the changes in her mom but could not yet tolerate the idea that her mother might have a condition that would result in permanent loss.

Eventually, with my client's support, her father had the mother evaluated and Alzheimer's was diagnosed. I continued to do psychoeducation with my client, and in turn, she has tried to support her dad "from afar," since they live out of state. But he and his daughter continue to struggle and to hold unrealistic expectations.

We had ended treatment about eight months ago, but she recently contacted me for a "tune-up" session. "I think everything is OK, and I'm doing well, but it's been awhile and we're coming up on the holidays. It might be good to talk about my mother's condition and how things are going." We agreed to schedule a time to meet and soon connected for a telehealth session.

At our "tune-up," my client processed a recent interaction she had with her mother. During her parents' holiday visit, her mother became overwhelmed when they were wrapping Christmas gifts. Her mother became suddenly irritated when asked to make a choice (likely could not follow the flow) and said to my client, "You are being an asshole! An absolute asshole!" Her mother had never used that kind of language, and it was totally out of character.

My client was shocked, angry and hurt. She had experienced and "felt" her mother's behavior as "intentional" and "unloving." She did not *realize* or understand in the moment the neurological source of the behavior. She reacted back, "I won't let you talk to me like that. I am not going to tolerate that kind of language. We don't talk to one another like that!" Then she left the room.

My client had responded to her "old mother" and not to the "new" mother who had cognitive impairment.

I empathized with my client's feelings, then suggested that her "mother" did not realize what she was saying and was having a stress reaction due to feeling overwhelmed.

The Mermaid Who Forgot

"It's so hard to lose your mother," I said. "She has turned into an entirely different person." That resonated with her and she reflected on it a bit.

My client asked for possible metaphors to help her relate better and alter her own reactions to the changes in her mother, so I threw out a few:

It is not your mother. It is an alien that impersonates your mother. It has put on her clothes and looks like her, but when the alien takes over, it is clearly NOT your mother.

It is not your mother. It is a robot. It has been dressed in her clothes but someone programmed it to do and say some awful things. When you look at it, you need to remember it isn't "her."

Your mother's brain is like a sponge. The Alzheimer's fills it up with crap—mud, glue, sticky stuff. It is full of that stuff and doesn't work right.

Your mother is not a grown up. The Alzheimer's has turned her into a grouchy toddler. Like a toddler, she has become demanding, has temper tantrums, displays childlike dependency, says mean things without thinking.

For "therapy homework," she said she would further develop a metaphor that might remind her to react differently when her mother is "not herself." She liked the alien concept, but I thought she might come up with something better on her own.

We had used the nesting dolls in the past so at the end of our session I asked her to "humor me." "In your mind, pick one adult doll and one young child doll."

I suggested,

Show me how you would respond with one of your grandchildren. The child (small one) is tired and grouchy. He is angry and frustrated. He had a long day and did too many things. Now comes the straw that breaks the camel's back. He has a temper tantrum and falls apart. What would you (big one) say to him when he yells at you or starts crying?

My client immediately went into nurture mode. She cuddled the child. "Tell me sweetie, tell me all about it. How can I help? Let's have a cuddle. Poor baby, you had such a hard day."

I observed and said quietly, "That's nice . . . so you wouldn't say, 'I won't let you talk to me like that?'" Her eyes widened a bit and she gave a wry smile.

I added, "Imagine the dolls again side by side, this time it is you and your mother. You still feel like the small child and you want her to still be the big doll."

"Yes," she said, "That's true."

"Switch them," I said.

You are the big doll and your mother is the smaller doll. That's what you have been avoiding, taking charge and being her caretaker. You will need to nurture her, like you do your grandchild. You will need to do that because she will continue to decline.

"That's true too," she said.

We talked about brain changes due to Alzheimer's and how the brain's emotional, limbic, amygdale side remains active as the left brain and cognitive capacity deteriorates. This results in high level confusion, paranoid ideation, poor frustration tolerance and irritability.

"In a way," I said, "It is the ultimate fight-flight reaction. The person senses the loss of self/mind, feels anxiety and fear at the loss of control (threat) and reacts. Anger, you know, is sometimes a fear response."

The client indicated, "You know, once I realized I could dive deep, I stopped trying to swim through storms. I need to remember that with my mother." We talked about this awhile and how she might have to ask her husband to "spell" her when she got confused or upset with her mother.

PROGRESS AND OUTCOMES

In speaking with her at the "tune-up," it was clear that this insightful client has found much joy and gratitude in her rich, full life. Treatment jump-started her, but her leap off a trampoline (her own metaphor) launched her in a new direction. She discovered mindful ways to "reclaim" her identity as a talented educator, loving woman and creative writer.

As we closed out our time together that day, she commented on what a "good fit" it was for her to work with me in therapy. I agreed that her love of writing and stories made it a particularly good fit for the therapeutic alliance. She asked quizzically, "Dr. Pat, have you forgotten that my

189

Case Examples and Applications

dissertation was about training early career teachers to use metaphor in their teaching?" If I had ever known that, I had forgotten, but like the mermaid, I realized it as one of the core threads that connect us. It seems uncanny that we "found" each other given the many therapy providers in that area. Perhaps it was meant to be, if you believe in such things in this universe.

She recently wrote, "You are SO RIGHT that the mermaid story resonated with me at a spiritual level, like it let loose a part of my spirit that was sort of sheltering in place, just waiting for the worst." She signed off "with gratitude and love," and in my eyes, she will always *be* a mermaid, able to seek and find that calm place within when storms come into her life.

QUESTIONS FOR DISCUSSION

1. How did her son's behavior and her mother's dementia threaten her role and security?
2. What are some ways to help clients understand the changes due to Alzheimer's?
3. Why is it difficult for family members to adjust their roles and behaviors when a family member's functioning declines?
4. How did the mermaid metaphor help this client change her point of view?

21

THE WOMAN WHO GOT RID OF A LEECH

A Case of Relationship Choices

CASE INFORMATION AND BACKGROUND

There was a court ordered women's relationship group that met weekly, and the co-therapists brought up topics about cross generational trauma, the cycle of violence, attachment and relationship choices. The women in this group were reluctant participants, and they often raised complaints, started arguments, acted bored or scheduled doctor's visits to get out of group.

PROBLEMS (AND REACTIONS TO PROBLEMS)

Most of the women in the group had been physically and/or sexually assaulted by current or former partners and all had experienced abuse or neglect growing up. Some had spent time in jail, many had drug or alcohol problems, and most had been homeless at some point in time. As a group, they had questionable taste in partners and did not know how to set limits. They chose "love" over "safety" and low self-efficacy prevented them from becoming self-sufficient. The stories they told, often with some bravado, revealed their troubled roots but they avoided personal disclosure. They were a tough group, and the graduate student therapists worked hard to get them to personally engage in group process.

CONCEPTUALIZATION

The woman who "got rid of a leech" had been sexually and physically abused growing up, at the hands of an older brother. Her mother did not work, nor did she protect her daughter from the abuser, so she was pretty much on her own through her teens and latched on early to a boyfriend, eventually having two children. She was somewhat concrete in her processing, and in her late teens she had developed an alcohol problem, later turning to pain medication. She displayed symptoms of depression in the treatment program to which she was referred, with irritability, low self-esteem, hypervigilance and low trust. She wanted to be self-sufficient, responded to the consistency and structure of the program and was making good progress in her recovery until she relapsed on alcohol and Department for Child and Family Services terminated her parental rights.

191

Case Examples and Applications

INTERVENTIONS

This mother attended group regularly and she began to participate and interact more with the other parents as she got to know and trust them. She was easily triggered by criticism and became very defensive without much provocation, sometimes walking out of group with a, "f-this, I'm out of here!" I understood the difficulty of getting court ordered clients to "buy into" therapy and offered the therapists some therapeutic stories to read with the group, to see if the stories might help the women identify with the story characters and talk about their personal experiences. We saw an interesting change in the group process when the therapists began to read a story at the beginning of each group, one that matched the "theme" for that week. One story, *Velma Crow's Sticky Situation* (Pernicano, 2010a, 2014a), is about a new mother who is unprepared for the responsibility of parenthood due to her somewhat "adolescent" lifestyle. It provides a humorous introduction to unmet attachment needs of babies. The mothers, including the one in this case, laughed as the story was read, but they also shared sheepish looks and head nodding as they identified with the story character. When they finished reading, one mom exclaimed, "I do that. I put my baby in the playpen so I can sleep. I make her play by herself until I wake up." Another mom said, "I left my kids alone in the house to go meet a man. My little boy left the house and was out in the street looking for me. A neighbor called CPS." The women began to discuss the past and what they had done that led to their involvement with CPS.

The client in this case stated, "CPS said I drank too much and neglected my kids." She added, "That bird needs to grow up! I guess I put myself first sometimes instead of my kids. But now that I have a second chance, I'm putting my kids first." It was a moment of vulnerability for her, as she rarely "owned" her decisions as contributing to her current life circumstances and usually blamed others for what had happened.

A second story, *The Balancing Act* (Pernicano, 2010a, 2012, 2014a), is a ludicrous story about a thrill-seeking mother flamingo who exposes her children to high stress and fear. She works for the circus walking on the tightrope and insists on the thrill of doing it without a safety net, in the presence of her children. Most of the women in this treatment group had taken big risks in their lives, with substance use, relationships and parenting lapses, and they had exposed their children to those things. They came into the treatment program defensive about their past behavior and it was important to teach them to communicate about their poor choices without fear of judgment.

As the story ended, several voices piped up: "That's like my mother!" "Who would do that to her children?" "That's mean!" "Those little flamingos should have been home in bed." "She's just thinking of herself." The group members first identified things their own mothers had done that put them at risk or resulted in harm when they were growing up. Then they talked about unnecessary risks they had taken in their own lives, such as engaging in unprotected sex, bringing strangers around their children or leaving children unsupervised.

The therapists wanted to acknowledge how hard it is to raise children without emotional, financial or material resources, especially without a stable partner. The mothers were asked how having children made it difficult to be content and self-sufficient. For one mother, it was "private time" with her partner. Another mother wanted to work and didn't have child care. One mid-20s mother of six children announced that she wanted to sleep in but the 2-year-old would no longer tolerate staying in a playpen all morning, and her newborn cried to be held, so she no longer had time to herself. She was "mad at" the children, so this led into a good discussion of normal child development and how to balance caring for children and caring for self.

There were many stories that got the women talking about their early lives growing up and their lives as parents. The group had become lively and interactive. But one of the most memorable groups was the week they read and discussed *Don't Let the Leeches Suck You Dry* (Pernicano, 2012, 2014a). That story was selected to plant a seed about the unhealthy nature of their relationships and the "right" to set good boundaries and limits. That week's group topic was about forming healthy partnerships, thinking beyond sexual attraction, weighing risks and benefits of getting

192

The Woman Who Got Rid of a Leech

involved with someone, and evaluating the quality of the relationship. We wanted to teach them about relationship choice and the right to be valued and respected by a partner. Several of the women had been involved with partners who used or sold drugs, and one had gone to jail due to her association with her partner. Most had "supported" partners who were not contributing to the household financially or helping with child care. Some of the women lived with abusive partners who were unkind to or disregarded their children. The woman in this case had been with the same underemployed, verbally and physically abusive man for many years, allowing him to move into her home. She had spoken of wanting to be free of him but found herself unable to be alone for any long period of time.

They read the story and as a group laughed at the ridiculous content of the story. A woman was sharing her blood with leeches who lived in a lake. The leeches told her she was keeping them alive and that they would die without her. She would not cut them loose because they "needed" her blood. Behind her back, they talked about her and joked about the free room and three-square-meals a day. In the story, the woman had a friend who challenged her, and the woman said she liked being a helper. She found it meaningful to help and care for others. That was OK, her friend said, but no one is expected to give all her life's blood, and there is supposed to be some *give and get*. When someone sucks your life's blood, it leaves you with no energy (or blood) to care for yourself. Her friend said, "Don't let the leeches suck you dry." At the end of the story there is a "leech checklist" that guided the women in the group how to find out if someone was a leech.

The story ended and discussion went on for over 30 minutes: "I had a leech once, let me tell you about him." "Maybe I was a leech a couple times, too." "My mom had a leech, and he hurt us girls growing up." Everyone could identify with the story and the feeling of being taken advantage of. Each woman had a story to tell.

After the group ended, I saw one mother hang back and she came to my office door and knocked. We talked about her progress in the program, and then she asked, "You wrote that story, didn't you?"

"Yes," I said. "Sounded like you all had a good discussion in today's group."

"It was a good story," she replied. "Can I ask you something?" she queried.

I invited her to join me and sit down. She was dead serious as she asked, "Can you tell me how to get rid of a leech?" She told me about the man who had lived in her house with her and her kids off and on for about ten years. Each time she threatened to cut him loose she gave in and let him stay.

She said with consternation,

> He says all those things in that story. Like the leeches. And thinking about that really bothers me. He doesn't really care about me. I don't hear from him until he wants to come back. He doesn't help with the kids. He hasn't worked in a long time. He uses drugs. And that hurts my sobriety.

I asked, "That's a serious question, and I can't tell you what to do. You have to really want to do it if you decide to get rid of a leech. And you have to weigh the risks and benefits."

"I weighed the risks and benefits," she said, "and I don't see any pluses except that sometimes he works and gives me some money. I don't miss him when he's gone. I let him come back when I feel sorry for him."

"One thing for sure," I said. "When you want to get rid of a leech, you have to swim in a different lake. It's hard to get rid of a leech if you swim in the same lake."

She asked, "Swim in a different lake? Like not be around him? Not let him live with me?"

I replied, "Something like that. And be sure you can take care of yourself and the kids without drinking."

"Yah," she said.

> I let him stay because he says he can't live without me. Just like the leeches said in that story. When he says that, I start thinking he might be homeless without me. But I think he would find a new place—he always does. Like in the story, leeches always seem to find a new blood supply.

As she left my office, I said, "I can't tell you to cut him loose or to stay, but let me know what you decide to do, and thanks so much for sharing."

193

PROGRESS AND OUTCOMES

Two weeks later she came to tell me that the previous weekend, she had asked him to move out and he had left. She announced it to the other women and her treatment providers. She stuck with it, and it seemed that the right story at the right time had nudged her from Contemplation to Action in her Stages of Change.

Soon after this she left the program. Child welfare removed her children without notice and terminated her rights when she relapsed on alcohol. She "told on" herself and asked to go back to treatment, saying, "I only drink at night now when they're sleeping. And I don't leave them alone. I know I need to stop." Child and Family Services took a hard line and said no, telling her they had given her "enough chances" and that the relapse showed them she did not take it seriously enough. The removal of her children at this stage of recovery sent her in a downward spiral. As treatment providers, we know that relapse is part of recovery, and I still question their hasty, arbitrary decision that changed so many lives.

I tell her story to honor her, because she had been bound and determined to make a better life for herself and her children. In the end, she became physically ill from the alcohol use and had to be hospitalized for liver disease. She stayed in touch with program staff and another woman in the program until right before she died, of liver disease and a broken heart.

QUESTIONS FOR DISCUSSION

1. How did a story about leeches move this client toward the next stage of change?
2. As treatment providers, how might we educate child welfare workers about a recovery model? What steps could we take to increase awareness and implementation of the concepts in the Stages of Change model?
3. How did this client's depressive symptoms contribute to her relapse?
4. How does sexual abuse early in life contribute to problems in adult relationships?

APPENDIX

Resources for Trauma-Informed Care

THE UNLEASHED PAIN (PERNICANO, UNPUBLISHED MANUSCRIPT)

This story was used with several of the adolescent and adult cases. It is helpful for clients feeling overwhelmed by emotional or chronic pain, controlled by addiction/compulsion, or reacting to life (grief, loss and physical health change) with learned helplessness or reduced self-efficacy. It shifts thinking when the client becomes negative and believes that he/she "can't" change or that a situation is "hopeless."

The Unleashed Pain

Pat Pernicano

Once upon a time, there was a faraway kingdom called The Kingdom of Pain. It had once been a peaceful kingdom, until an army of pain monsters invaded the kingdom and the lives of those within. In the Kingdom of Pain, your life is filled with pain and servitude from the day you are born until the day you die. Those who grew up there thought that living in pain was "normal." You can understand that. When you grow up with pain, that is all you know.

Pain monster rule was harsh and unforgiving, and the monsters inflicted both emotional and physical pain. In our world we put collars on dogs and walk them on leash. In the Kingdom of Pain, children were fitted with "training" collars at birth, and at a very young age they were put on leash and trained to serve. Pain monsters controlled children with threats, criticism and harsh punishment. Only very basic needs for food and shelter were met. Pain monsters controlled adults by luring them into submission and convincing them that they were helpless. Socializing was not allowed in the Kingdom of Pain, because the selfish pain monsters put their own needs above those of others. As you might imagine, it was a kingdom of fear and loneliness.

A young child who lived in the Kingdom of Pain had always done what she needed to do to survive. She had been well trained by her pain monster to sit, sing, fetch or stay on command. She tried to be a good girl so that the pain monster would not punish her for being ungrateful or disobedient. She sometimes wondered what lay outside the Kingdom—perhaps nothing? She could see some woods beyond the moat that surrounded the tall stone walls of the Kingdom. The only way out was a drawbridge that was raised and lowered for deliveries.

Outsiders were not welcome in the Kingdom of Pain. Those who lived on the outside never suspected what lay within and those who lived inside had long forgotten what it was like to laugh and play, to love and be loved.

Appendix

One day the drawbridge was lowered for a delivery and the little girl, who was off her leash, felt a sudden, strong urge to run—to escape. The girl, without really thinking, bolted across the drawbridge and into the woods beyond. Her pain monster, the one she served, saw her leave and followed in swift pursuit. She had a head start, though, and she ran very fast, zigging and zagging through the forest until she came to a small village. The girl was out of breath from running and hid behind a tree in case the villagers proved to be unfriendly.

She stared in amazement and wondered, "What is this place?" There were no walls, moat or drawbridge. Smiling, friendly people were doing business in a marketplace, and each person had a small pain monster on a leash. The monsters seemed totally manageable—they were sitting or staying on command, and they eagerly gobbled up small treats the people tossed them. The people walked freely about, with no one ordering them around.

The girl hid behind the tree and watched as the people in the village went about their business. Children were laughing and playing, and their parents were kind and attentive. The girl felt a sudden rush of sadness and loss, as she had not experienced life like this. No one had told her such a place existed, and she could not decide whether to enter the village or go back to her home in the Kingdom of Pain. She had no idea how to live in a place with freedom and caring. How would she survive? Who would meet her basic needs? Who would she serve? After all, a life of pain and service was all she had known.

The girl curled up and went to sleep, exhausted from her travels and confused by her choices. Awhile later, she was rudely awakened

"THERE YOU ARE, YOU BAD GIRL!" The loud, mean voice behind her continued. "What made you think you could get away from me? Come now, back on your leash and back to the Kingdom!"

It was the dark and ugly pain monster she served in the Kingdom. The monster had sniffed her out and tracked her to the village. He intended to take her back to the Kingdom of Pain.

A wave of fear came over the girl, but she summoned up courage and ran from the pain monster toward the people in the village.

"Help me!" she cried. "I don't want to go back to the Kingdom of Pain. Please give me sanctuary!"

The people had heard stories of a Kingdom where pain monsters had invaded and taken over the land. They thought it was a myth, but now they realized it was true as they saw the young girl standing before them, wearing a heavy collar. She needed their help.

"You don't have to go back," the people told the girl. "We will protect you and keep you safe. But we need to teach you how to tame and manage your pain monster."

"I don't want to tame or train it!" said the girl. "I want it gone! Can't you just kill it? Or lock it up in a dungeon, never again to see the light of day?"

"No," they said. "We live **with** our pain monsters. They protect us and warn us of danger. They can get a little demanding when they want food or attention, but most times we stay busy and forget they are there. Perhaps it is not a perfect solution, but it works for us. A pain monster is not a problem unless he grows too large or tries to control your life."

And so the people captured the girl's pain monster and caged it until it could be tamed. They put a collar on it and taught it the ways of their village.

For a while, the girl was bitter about all that the pain monster and the Kingdom of Pain had taken from her. After all, she had lost her innocence and had lived in fear for so long. She mistrusted others' kind intentions and often blamed them when she had a bad day. But the villagers were patient with her; this helped her mourn what she had lost and let go of the memories of her painful past.

The girl, with the help of the villagers, trained the pain monster. She learned to ignore its loud, rude demands, and it grew smaller and smaller until she could easily manage it on a leash. The pain monster was no longer the center of the girl's life, and she stayed busy discovering many things about herself and others.

Time passed, and one day, as the girl walked through the marketplace, she felt gratitude for the villagers who had welcomed her, many of whom she had come to care about and many who cared deeply for her.

Of course, she still had very bad memories of her earlier life in the Kingdom of Pain, and this story does not mean to say that it is easy to move on or leave pain behind. In a perfect world, we would find a way to conquer pain and have a world of peace and compassion. But as we all know, this is not a perfect world, and sometimes the best thing you can do is to heal your wounds, and make your own peace where you can, one day at a time. After all, to cross a rushing stream,

Appendix

you only use one stepping stone at a time. No one would be foolish enough to leap across the stream without a firm foothold. Who knows where you might land?

"I can live *with* my pain monster, just as they do in the village," she realized. "I can't kill it or hide it away in a dungeon, but I can accept it, manage it and go on with my life."

The girl took back her life with that realization. There is always a choice. Pain would remain in her life, but she would not let it rule her nor would she return to live in the Kingdom of Pain; it is never too late to change, to move on, and to love and be loved.

The Bottom Line: LIVE fully with your pain.

QUESTIONS FOR DISCUSSION

1. *What is your "pain"? (something that has control over you or holds you back from doing things)*
2. *What could you do to manage or live with the "pain"?*
3. *What do you need to leash? (fatigue, fear, hopelessness, anger, etc.)*

PERNICANO TRAUMA-INFORMED PUBLICATIONS

Family Focused Trauma Intervention: Using Metaphor and Play With Victims of Abuse and Neglect

2010 Jason Aronson publication that includes stories and play interventions for family-oriented trauma intervention. The stories and interventions are hands-on and play/metaphor based for family psychoeducation and family-based trauma-informed care.

Outsmarting the Riptide of Domestic Violence: Metaphor and Mindfulness for Change

This 2012 resource includes stories that address experiences common to victims of intimate partner violence. It lends itself well to group treatment in therapy or shelter care. The chapters are organized within the Transtheoretical Stages of Change Model. The book describes the concept of mindfulness as it related to calming arousal post-trauma and Appendix includes some mindfulness meditations.

Using Trauma-Focused Therapy Stories: Interventions for Therapists, Children and Their Caregivers

This 2014 Routledge publication includes a comprehensive set of Pernicano stories for trauma-informed care as well as trauma guides for clients and caregivers. The stories are organized according to the Trauma-Focused Cognitive Behavioral Therapy (TF-CBT) model, and the guides have psychoeducational and hands-on components related to developmental impact, parent-child interactions and the trauma-stress reaction.

PERNICANO TECHNIQUES

Dry Erase Squiggle Stories

This technique involves back-and-forth drawing and storytelling. The therapist closes the eyes and moves a dry erase marker around on the board, to make a simple "Squiggle." Next, therapist invites client to use markers of his/her choice to turn the Squiggle into a picture (without erasing the Squiggle). When client finishes drawing, therapist asks him/her to tell a short story about the picture. Therapist informs client it is his or her story, not something read in a book or

197

Appendix

seen on TV/movie. Therapist can prompt for a beginning, middle and end, or start the client off with "Once upon a time . . ." The therapist can ask questions to get additional information: "How does the fish feel? Where is he swimming? What does he do after the shark bites him?" The therapist pays close attention to the themes in the story, including feelings, thinking, attitudes and outcome, as these say much about the client's view of self, others and the world. Therapist ascertains who the child identifies with in the story if it is not clear.

Next, the therapist asks the client to make a Squiggle. Therapist (or family member) finishes the picture and tells a story. The therapist's story should incorporate something of the client's theme or parallel the dilemma, and then shift the outcome, thus introducing the possibility of change. In this manner, the therapist models problem-solving for the client.

Cracked Glass Bowl Guide

Following is a guide for using the story *The Cracked Glass Bowl* (Pernicano, 2012, 2014a), a story about trauma and healing. With children, I paraphrase or tell a shorter story. With adults, I read the whole story aloud, client's eyes closed if possible. Before reading, I ask the client to listen *as if you are the green bowl*. I state that the story might help him/her experience sensations, memories and emotions without the barrier of language.

The Reading: The story sets the stage for trauma work, to be carried out in therapist's chosen model, across a number of sessions. The first part of the story describes the traumatic event, depicted as a damaging storm; the aftermath "like a war zone." The next part is the bowl's perception of being changed by the storm that left her *cracked* and fragile. Early on, she resists healing, thinking *"perhaps survival is enough."* Later, the bowl decides to pursue healing and goes with her friend to the glassmaker. This part of the story instills hope; it introduces the client to the concept of *"healing from the inside out"* and being "the same and different." It also introduces the client to the idea that trauma work takes time and is painful. The story suggests that healing does not take place in isolation; a friend and the glassmaker are involved.

After Reading: Some clients feel very emotional as the story ends. Ask the client what he or she experienced during the story, to get his or her immediate reactions (cognitive and emotional). While discussing the story and the cracked glass bowl, a therapist might ask questions to facilitate identification with the bowl:

- Why did the bowl think survival was enough?
- What were the risks and benefits of going to the glassmaker?
- What changed her mind that she decides to get help?
- What does it mean to say, "Heal from the inside out?"
- What does "heat" represent in this story?
- Why does she retain some of her original glass?
- What does it mean to say that the healing takes time?
- For you, who is your blue bowl friend? Who is your glassmaker? What is your heat?
- What would it mean for you to be the same and different?

An older male client listened intently to the story with his eyes closed. Then he slowly opened his eyes and said, "Well, I'm clearly the glass bowl. I thought you were the friend that gave support and then I thought maybe you were the glassmaker. I guess you're both. I'm glad you were with me when I talked about the cracks. It felt good to realize that I can heal like that."

The Drawing: Hand the client a piece of paper with markers or provide the dry erase board. Invite the client to silently draw him/herself as the cracked glass bowl. There may be surface scratches, partial cracks, cracks all the way through, large or small gouges, and large or small chips. Each element of damage represents something that happened to the client in his/her life that left the person feeling *different, cracked, broken* or *damaged*. These can be labeled on the bowl, or a separate list may be done below the drawing. Some clients take their drawings home to finish them.

Discussion: Clarify damages and ask at what ages the damages occurred. Discuss what the client experienced, event by event, in subsequent sessions. Address the hope of healing, i.e., what it would take to seal or melt the cracks, one by one.

Appendix

Trauma-Informed Treatment: After talking about the traumatic experience(s), discuss the changes sought by the client and how he/she will know when the changes take place. The term "new normal" has been used in moral injury protocols with veterans, and this term carries some appeal.

Ask the client to *draw him or her as a new creation*, with colors or shape of his/her choosing. This is usually done as a homework assignment, to allow the client time to reflect and consider ways that the bowl has changed. Discuss how it feels to envision the self as healed from the inside out.

Use the information provided in the set of bowls to collaboratively engage in trauma-informed treatment within the chosen theoretical model.

Up the Mountain (Pernicano, Unpublished) Narrative Script

Pre-Climb Preparation With Drawing

I want you to imagine your own magic mountain—any kind of mountain. It is a safe place. We are going to climb it together. You decide how you get to the top—an escalator, elevator, cable car, by magic, by foot or jet-propelled. You might beam up or make yourself invisible. You might climb like Spiderman or fly like Superman. It is your choice. We will stop at two lookouts on the way up—places we can look down. When you get to the very top we will celebrate your success.

OK, take as much time as you need to draw your mountain, with two lookouts. (Ask how he/she wants to travel to the top if it is not clear in the drawing.)

Now, draw a cage at the bottom of the mountain. It can hold anything that bothers you. Fear or worry. Maybe something bad that pops into your mind or your dreams. Someone that hurt you or a bully that picks on you, some awful memory. The cage will hold whatever you want to leave behind when you climb the mountain.

You can put locks on the cage, as many as you need, and pick guards—people, animals or make-believe creatures. Only you and the guards get the key. Feel free to use something like duct tape or chains to secure what you put inside the cage.

OK, take as much time as you need to draw your cage at the bottom of the mountain. (Remind client to add locks and guards if he/she forgets to do that.) Then ask what/who is inside? How many locks? How many guards? Are the guards inside, outside or both? (Whatever the client adds, ask for a description.)

The Climb

OK, let's start our journey up the mountain. I'm going to ring the bell to start. When I ring the bell, you might want to close your eyes and breathe slowly from your belly like we practiced. Or you can leave your eyes open if you want to.

(RING SINGING BOWL) Here we are at the foot of the mountain—as you look at the cage and what's inside, it might bother you but it's good to know it can't hurt you (pause). Let's take a deep breath (model this and breathe with client) and start the climb. It feels really good to start the climb and leave X behind. What a beautiful mountain! The mountain air is fresh and clean.

As we move up the mountain, you might notice that the cage at the bottom seems smaller. Things look smaller as you move away from them.

Here we are at the first lookout. Let's stop climbing for a minute. It feels good to be in a safe place. Let's look down at the cage from the lookout. Wow. See how small the cage is now? It is nice to have some distance between you and the X. What is down there can't hurt you now. That is then and this is now. You won't need to let it bother you while you're climbing the mountain. Mmmm—smell the fresh air! Hear the nature sounds. See the view from the lookout, a nice view.

Let's climb higher now, to the next lookout, another safe place. Here we are at the lookout. Let's take a deep breath (do this together). Now we can see the real beauty of the mountain. Off in the distance are other mountains. Listen to the sounds of the mountain—birds, the wind in the trees, maybe a train whistle off in the distance. You can smell the mountain smells. You can feel the breeze. Relax and breathe in the fresh air.

199

Appendix

Now, look down and see how high up you are. Everything at the bottom looks small—even the cage—cars look like toy cars—houses look like doll houses—the things in the cage look like tiny ants. So small that you could stomp on them and squash them if you wanted to! Maybe you can even look at the cage without getting upset. Then is then and now is now. You are glad you can climb the mountain and leave those things behind.

Let's climb the rest of the way to the top. Here we are. Success! What a beautiful lookout—a safe, peaceful place. The air at the top is very fresh and clear. Take a deep breath, relaxed and calm. You can see some lakes and other mountains in the distance. You hardly see anything below—it is all a blur. Then is then, and now is now. Now is the time to relax—to let go. Now that you have reached the top you can invite someone else to join you if want to. You can share your success with someone you love and trust.

Remember, you can climb your mountain any time. Leave behind anything that keeps you from being calm and relaxed. A worry . . . a memory . . . stress . . . sadness . . . anger . . . Let it go. If you start to feel worried or stressed, you can close your eyes and go up the mountain. Enjoy the view from the top and let go of the rest.

In a minute I'm going to ring the bell. When you hear the bell stop ringing, you can open your eyes and come back to this room. (RING SINGING BOWL)

After re-orienting the client, ask him/her to describe what he saw, heard and experienced. Suggest he/she practice at home and "go up the mountain" when triggered by anxiety in public places.

OTHER RESOURCES

A Handful of Quiet: Happiness in Four Pebbles *(2012)* by *Thich Nhat Hanh*

This is an excellent book for introductory mindful meditation practice, with a four-stone meditation and other exercises. Although developed for use with children, I find it is appealing to clients of all ages. I keep a bowl of smooth polished stones in my office for distribution to clients. To paraphrase and summarize the four elements in the book (flower, mountain, clear water and space):

As a flower, you experience the potential for growth, the childlike awe that lies within. Like a ready-to-bloom bud, you are fresh and new. You feel eager anticipation when you are aware and open in this manner. The mountain is the strong, steady foundation within. When you are a mountain, you are grounded and supported, unmoved by the wind and rain of your life. As a mountain, you endure and persist, even through difficult times. Calm water is clear, reflecting water. I tell my clients that when a lake is stirred up after a storm, there is much debris in it and it becomes cloudy and dark. We need to let all that "stuff" settle back down until the water is again clear. We remain still and quiet, allowing the debris to go back down to the bottom of the lake. Calm, clear water reflects accurately, like the clear surface of a lake on a sunny day. When you experience this calm clarity, you became an accurate reflecting surface for others and they for you. Space is hardest to describe, as it represents freedom within and between. It is space without boundaries, within and around each of us. It is not "aloneness" or "loneliness" but perhaps the freedom to move, to be flexible, without expectations or judgment. I give you space and you give me space, and this allows us to live non-constricted lives that are open and free. To experience the integration of these aspects of self is restorative and healing.

Ahn's Anger *(2009)* by *Gail Silver (author)* and *Christianne Kromer (illustrator)*

This story introduces the concept of "sitting with" anger rather than reacting in potentially harmful ways. Ahn's anger becomes a playful, engaging companion with whom he spends time until the anger "shrinks" and moves on.

200

Appendix

Moody Cow Meditates *(2009) by Kerry Lee MacLean*

This is an all-time favorite book of mine to introduce children to meditation as a way of better managing anger. Children identify with the cow's "bad day" and understand his growing frustration. The author includes a recipe for making a "shakable globe" to watch while letting the anger calm down. Similar things may be purchased on Amazon, filled with gel and glitter or other material that slowly moves down when the object is turned over or shaken. For children who need additional sensory focus, a sound machine may be used while watching the globe.

Sitting Still Like a Frog: Mindfulness Exercises for Kids and Their Parents *(2013) by Eline Snel*

This book includes simple mindfulness meditation practices to help young children deal with anxiety, improve concentration and handle difficult emotions. It includes a 60-minute audio CD of guided exercises read by Myla Kabat-Zinn and uses a frog metaphor to teach younger clients about meditation and relaxation.

201

The *Meaning* of Color in Client Art

A Picture Is More Than a Picture: The brown color of the flower on the left depicts the child's negative life experiences at that point in time. The size and brightness of the yellow "sun" in the middle and color on leaves/petals reflect self-concept across phases of development.

The Mom of Many Colors: The colors on the hair represent different aspects of the child's mother and the client's emotional response to those. She experiences a "rainbow of emotions" to the woman with one eye covered.

The *Meaning* of Color in Client Art

In this drawing, the child's choice and use of colors reflect her jealousy and distress over the "evil baby" and her desire to have him out of her life.

The Bloodthirsty Bats: Without the reddish smudges of blood in the pond (after her abuse), the meaning of the drawing might be missed. In the 2nd drawing, the colors represent the before/after of her *Cracked Glass Bowl.* The last set of drawings illustrates the change in her moods from early treatment to termination.

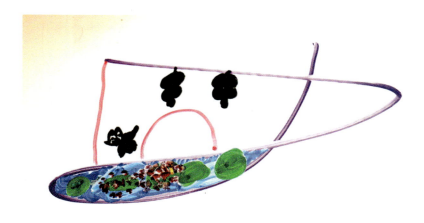

203

The *Meaning* of Color in Client Art

The Boy Whose Sister Who Said Fuck: The black in the smiling mouth shows all the *bad words* ready to be said, and the cloud colors/position suggest that hope is emerging.

The *Meaning* of Color in Client Art

The nose in the center was a waterfall in the first picture, consistent with the colors. The boy then added a circle, open eyes, and mouth, the "waterfall" now a nose. In his 3rd drawing (below), the boy added the closed eyes for his "dead" father, and the picture and meaning were transformed.

The brown and green show the intensity of the "poop" words being flung by this boy's family.

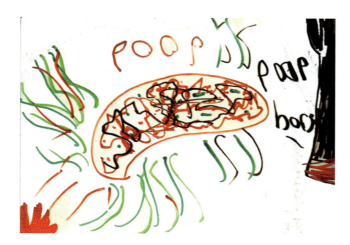

The Wounded Elephant: The intensity of this child's pain is represented by the colored wounds on the elephant.

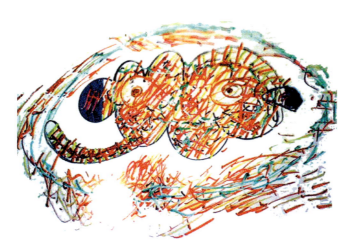

205

The *Meaning* of Color in Client Art

Without the two colors, the reader is unable to capture the relational aspect of the picture, at termination. Therapist and client, purple and blue.

The House with Many Rooms: The use of color shows the contrast between death (female skeleton) and hope (hearts). Therapist is surrounding the child with "kind tings."

The use of color (black/white/red) depicts the girl's "death," fear and self-protection.

The *Meaning* of Color in Client Art

Use of color for self-representation ("One of a Kind" iris among roses).

The use of color in this picture depicts the boy's confusion and intensity of his perceived crisis.

Tell Me Who I Am: This very artistic teen conveys strong emotion and inner struggle in her use of colors and contrast. The colors "shout out" her confusion, depressed mood and gradual change.

The *Meaning* of Color in Client Art

The following drawings, with their vivid colors, show the emergence of hope.

Brother and sister *Up the Mountain* dry erase drawings. The color conveys mood and intensity.

REFERENCES

Blenkiron, P. (2010). *Stories and analogies in cognitive behavior therapy*. West Sussex, UK: Wiley-Blackwell.

Bremner, J. D. (2002). *Does stress damage the brain? Understanding trauma-related disorders from a mind-body perspective*, 1st edition. New York: W. W. Norton.

Bronfenbrenner, U. (1977). Toward an experimental ecology of human development. *American Psychologist, 32*, 513–531.

Burns, G. W. (2001). *101 healing stories: Using metaphors in therapy*. Hoboken, NJ: John Wiley & Sons, Inc.

Burns, G. W. (2005). *101 healing stories for kids and teens: Using metaphors in therapy*. Hoboken, NJ: John Wiley & Sons, Inc.

Burns, G. W. (2007). *Healing with stories: Your casebook collection for using therapeutic metaphors*. Hoboken, NJ: John Wiley & Sons, Inc.

Carlson, R. (1999). Play therapy and the therapeutic use of story. *Canadian Journal of Counseling, 33*(3), 212–226.

Cattanach, A. (1997). *Children's stories in play therapy*. Philadelphia, PA & London: Jessica Kingsley Publishers.

Cattanach, A. (2007). Narrative play therapy. In C. Schaefer & H. Kaduson (Eds.), *Contemporary play therapy: Theory, research, and practice* (pp. 82–99). New York: Guildford Press.

Cattanach, A. (2009). Narrative approaches: Helping children tell their stories. In A. Drewes (Ed.), *Blending play therapy with cognitive behavioral therapy: Evidence-based and other effective treatments and techniques*. Hoboken, NJ: John Wiley & Sons, Inc.

Cozolino, L. (2014). *The neuroscience of psychotherapy: Healing the social brain*, 2nd edition. New York: W. W. Norton.

Cummings, E. M., Davies, P. T. & Campbell, S. B. (2000). *Developmental psychopathology and family process: Theory, research, and clinical implications*. New York, NY: Guilford Press.

Drewes, A. (2009). *Blending play therapy with cognitive behavioral therapy: Evidence based and other effective treatments and techniques*. New York: John Wiley & Sons, Inc.

Drewes, A. (2010). *How to respond to the child's play through metaphor*. Rome, Italy: Italian Association for Play Therapy.

Erickson, B. (2011a). *Constructing therapeutic metaphors and stories (workshop handout)*. Phoenix: Fundamentals of Hypnosis Workshop, 11th International Erickson Congress.

Erickson, B. (2011b). *Telling stories where they belong (workshop handout)*. Phoenix: 11th International Erickson Congress.

Friedman, E. (1990). *The bridge*. In *Friedman's fables*. New York, NY: Guilford Press.

Fritz, R. (Fall, 1998). *Ericksonian therapy*. Retrieved online January 17, 2018 from www.invisiblecows.com.

Gardner, R. (1971). *Therapeutic communication with children: The mutual storytelling technique*. New York, NY: Science House.

Gardner, R. (1980). *Stories about the real world*. New York: Creative Therapeutics.

Gil, E. (1994). *Play in family therapy*. New York, NY: Guilford Press.

Gil, E. (2013). *Family play therapy: Assessment and treatment ideas*. CTAMFT Annual Conference and Meeting. Groton, CT.

Greenwald, R. (2009). *Treating problem behaviors: A trauma-informed approach*. New York: Routledge.

Greenwald, R. (2014). *Slaying the dragon: Overcoming life's challenges and getting to your goals*. Northampton, MA: Trauma Institute & Child Trauma Institute. Retrieved online from www.childtrauma.com.

Greenwald, R. *A fairytale*. Northampton, MA: Trauma Institute & Child Trauma Institute. Retrieved online from www.childtrauma.com.

References

Hahn, T. N. (2012). *A handful of quiet: Happiness in four pebbles.* Berkeley, CA: Plum Blossom.

Jung, C. G. (1964). *Man and his symbols.* New York: Doubleday & Company.

Kopp, R. (1995). *Metaphor therapy: Using client generated metaphors in psychotherapy.* Bristol, PA: Brunner-Mazel.

Kottman, T. (2011). *Play therapy basics and beyond*, 2nd edition. Alexandria, VA: American Counseling Association.

Kottman, T. & Ashby, A. (2002). *Metaphorical stories.* In C. Schaefer & D. Cangelosi (Eds.), *Play therapy techniques.* Northvale, NJ: Jason Aronson.

Langtree, C. B. & Briere, J. N. (2017). *Treating complex trauma in children and their families: An integrative approach.* Thousand Oaks, CA: Sage.

Lawrence, M., Condon, K., Jacobi, K., & Nicholson, E. (2006). Play therapy for girls displaying social aggression. In C. E. Schaefer & H. G. Kaduson (Eds.), *Contemporary play therapy: Theory, research, and practice.* New York, NY: Guilford Press.

MacLean, K. L. (2009). *Moody cow meditates.* Somerville, MA: Wisdom Publications.

Malchiodi, C. (Ed.) (2014). *Creative interventions with traumatized children.* New York, NY: Guilford Press.

Markell, K. & Markell, M. (2008). *The children who lived: Using harry potter and other fictional characters to help grieving children and adolescents.* New York: Routledge.

Meares, R. (2005). *The metaphor of play: Origin and breakdown of personal being.* New York: Routledge.

Mills, J. M. & Crowley, R. J. (2014). *Therapeutic metaphors for children and the child within*, 2nd edition. New York: Routledge.

Mott, J. M., Mondragon, S., Hundt, N. E., Beason-Smith, M., Grady, R. H., & Teng, E. J. (2014). Characteristics of U.S. veterans who begin and complete prolonged exposure and cognitive processing therapy for PTSD. *Journal of Traumatic Stress*, 27, 265–273.

Najavits, L. (2015). *The problem of dropout from "gold standard" PTSD therapies.* Retrieved online March 18, 2018 from www.ncbi.nlm.nih.gov/pmc/articles/PMC4447050/.

Norcross, J. C. (Ed.) (2011). *Psychotherapy relationships that work: Evidence-based responsiveness*, 2nd edition. New York: Oxford University Press.

Norcross, J. C. & Goldfried, M. R. (Eds.) (2005). *Handbook of psychotherapy integration*, 2nd edition. New York: Oxford University Press.

O'Connor, K. J. & Ammen, S. (2013). *Play therapy treatment planning and interventions: The ecosystem model and workbook.* Waltham, MA: Academic Press.

Oldford, L. (2011). The use of harry potter and fairytales in narrative therapy. *Journal of Integrated Studies*, 1(2), 1–10.

Pernicano, P. (2010a). *Family-focused trauma intervention: Using metaphor and play with victim of abuse and neglect.* Lanham, MD: Jason Aronson.

Pernicano, P. (2010b). *Metaphorical stories for child therapy: Of magic and miracles.* Lanham, MD: Jason Aronson.

Pernicano, P. (2012). *Outsmarting the riptide of domestic violence: Metaphor and mindfulness for change.* Lanham, MD: Jason Aronson.

Pernicano, P. (2014a). *Using trauma-focused therapy stories: Interventions for therapists, children and their caregivers.* New York: Routledge.

Pernicano, P. (2014b). Rush to judgment: Beware of the ADHD diagnosis. Reprinted with permission. *Psychotherapy Networker*, 38(3), 53–56, May/June Edition.

Pernicano, P. (2015a). *Using therapy stories and metaphor in child and family treatment.* Retrieved from www.lianalowenstein.com (newsletter).

Pernicano, P. (2015b). Metaphors and stories in play therapy. In K. O'Connor, C. Schaefer & L. Braverman (Eds.), *Handbook of play therapy* (2nd edition, pp. 259–276). New York: John Wiley & Sons, Inc.

Pernicano, P. (2016a). *The hungry heart.* Unpublished manuscript.

Pernicano, P. (2016b). *The unleashed pain.* Unpublished manuscript.

Perry, B. (2006). Applying principles of neurodevelopment to clinical work with maltreated and traumatized children: The neurosequential model of therapeutics. In B. Webb (Ed.), *Working with traumatized youth in child welfare* (pp. 27–52). New York, NY: Guilford Press.

Perry, B. (2009). Examining child maltreatment through a neurodevelopmental lens: Clinical applications of the neurosequential model of therapeutics. *Journal of Loss and Trauma*, 14, 240–255.

Perry, B. & Hambrick, E. (2008). The neurosequential model of therapeutics. *Reclaiming Children and Youth*, 17(3), 40.

Peterson, R. & Fontana, L. (2007). Utilizing metaphoric storytelling in child and youth care work. *eJournal of the International Child and Youth Care Network (CYC-Net)-ISSN 1605–7406*, (101), 1–5.

Rocky Mountain Play Therapy Institute (2018). *Integrative play therapy.* Retrieved online January 17, 2018 from Website Rocky Mountain Play Therapy Institute Website www.RMPTI.com.

Roffman, R. E. (2008, January). Men are grass: Bateson, Erickson, utilization, and metaphor. *American Journal of Clinical Hypnosis*, 50(3), 247–257.

Siegel, D. (2010). *Mindsight: The new science of personal transformation.* New York, NY: Guilford Press.

References

Siegel, D. (2012). *The developing mind*, 2nd edition. New York, NY: Guilford Press.

Silver, G. (2009). *Ahn's anger*. Berkley, CA: Plum Blossom Books.

Smyth, J. & Nobel, J. *Arts & healing: Creative, artistic, and expressive therapies for PTSD*. Retrieved online January 17, 2017 from www.marketingnavigators.com/FAH2/wp-content/uploads/2015/12/PTSD-White_Paper_Smyth_Nobel.pdf (Foundation for Art and Healing).

Snel, E. (2013). *Sitting still like a frog: Mindfulness exercises for kids (and their parents)*. Boston, MA: Shambhala Publications.

Snow, M. S., Ouzts, R., Martin, E. E., & Helm, H. (2005). Creative metaphors of life experiences seen in play therapy. In G. R. Walz & R. K. Yep (Eds.), *VISTAS: Compelling perspectives on counseling* (pp. 63–65). Alexandria, VA: American Counseling Association.

Stuckey, H. & Nobel, J. (2010). The connection between art, healing, and public health: A review of current literature. *American Journal of Public Health*, 100(2), 254–263.

Van der Kolk, T. (2014). *The body keeps the score: Brain, mind, and body in the healing of trauma*. New York: Penguin Books.

Watts, B. V., Shiner, B., Zubkoff, L., Carpenter-Song, E., Ronconi, J. M., & Coldwell, C. M. (2014). Implementation of evidence-based psychotherapies for posttraumatic stress disorder in VA specialty clinics. *Psychiatric Services*, 65, 106–112.

Wedge, M. (2011). Reflections on *Milton Erickson*. Retrieved online January 17, 2018 from www.psychologytoday.com.

Winnicott, D. W. (1953). Symptom tolerance in paediatrics: A case history. In *The collected works of D. W. Winnicott: Volume 4*. Originally presented at proceedings of the Royal Society of Medicine, 1953 .

Woodman, M. & Mellick, J. (1998). *Coming home to myself: Reflections for nurturing a woman's body and soul*. Berkley, CA: Conari Press.

Yasenik, L. & Gardner, K. (2017). *Play therapy dimensions model: A decision-making guide for integrative play therapies*. Philadelphia, PA and London, England: Jessica Kinsley Publishers.

INDEX

Ahn's Anger 86, 200
art: changes in 120; conceptualization 4; interpretation 17, 118; symbolic representation 11, 17, 118
attachment 17, 29–30, 32–34, 39–41, 43–44, 78–79, 99, 102–103, 112, 115, 126–131, 137, 163–164, 166–170, 184, 187–188, 191–192
attention deficit hyperactivity disorder *vs.* PTSD/ trauma 11, 32

Balancing Act, The 192
Bear of a Different Color: case application 87; psychoeducation about trauma 32
Benedict, H. x, xii
Black Cloud, The, treatment of depression 143
Blenkiron, P. 30
Bremner, J. D. 33
Bridge, The treatment application 164–166
Bronfenbrenner, U. 35
Burns, G. W. xi, 30

Carlson, R. 13
Cattanach, A. 29, 30
child development: impact of trauma 34; psychoeducation 192
client centered therapy 9
cognitive behavioral intervention 30, 37, 43, 68, 166, 197
collaborative therapeutic assessment xii
color, meaning in client art 202–210
communication: with families 35; meaning of 11; non-verbal 10; through art 10, 57, 104; verbal 9
complex trauma 39, 98
conceptualization 4, 33, 57
Cozolino, L. 33
Cracked Glass Bowl, The: case applications 38, 65, 69, 108, 142, 175, 181, 203; depicted in art 68, 142, 176; guide 198–199; psychoeducation about trauma 32; universal aspects of story 29
creative modalities in trauma intervention 37–38, 42; with veteran 38
Crenshaw, D. 13

death of child 178
death of parent: case descriptions 12, 27, 51–53, 73–75, 77–79, 85–90, 134, 141; depicted in art 27, 51, 83–84

death of grandparent 120–123
depression: art 27–28; cartoon 144; floating woman 146; signs of 141, 191
dissociation: assessment of 100, 103; case examples 97, 151–154; depicted in stories, play and/or artwork 100–106, 149, 155–159; description 98, 108; *vs.* imaginary friends 103; *vs.* psychosis 151–153; signs of 99, 100, 108, 150–154; symbolic representation 152; triggered 113
dissociative continuum 98
Dive Deep 186
domestic violence, impact of 92, 97, 112–113
Don't Let the Leeches Suck You Dry 175, 192
Dragon's Fire, The 44
dreams: interpretation of 17, 42; symbols 17–18, 40, 42
Drewes, A. xi, 18, 30
dry erase board 43; *see also* squiggles stories

Erickson, B. 18, 30
Erickson, M.: atheoretical stance 13; blocked resources 14; importance of metaphor and storytelling 13; theory of change x, xiii; utilization 13–14
Ericksonian therapy: basic premises 14–15; concepts 4, 14, 15, 41; mining for gold 14; techniques 4, 14–15; transtheoretical 4; use of metaphor xi, 13; *see also* Erickson, M.
evidence based protocols (EBP): limitations 37, 39; *see also* Najavits, L.; Norcross, J. C.

family representation: art 115–116; metaphor 16; puppets 113–115; sand tray 113–115
feelings through art: bees 24; bowl 114; butterfly 136; chaos 26; tornado 81; volcano 20, 114
feelings through stories 135
Feeding the Alligator treatment intervention 96
Friedman, E. 164, 171
Fritz, R. 15

Gabbard 30
Gardner, R. 43
Gill, E. 30
Gold in the Desert 14
good fit: client characteristics 36, 39; evidence based trauma intervention 37

213

Index

Greenwald, R. 30
grief 178

Hahn, T. N. 200
Handful of Quiet 201
head to toe interview 66
Hungry Alligator and the Mean Snake, The: case
    application 94
Hungry Heart, The 129–130

integrative psychotherapy 29–40
interpretation 4, 42

Jung, C.: symbols 17–18, 40; unconscious 17;
    see also symbols

Kopp, R. 30
Kottman, T. 16, 30
Kottman, T. & Ashby, A. 30

Langtree, C. B. & Briere, J. N. 40
language: meaning making 9, 11
Lawrence, M. et. al. 212
Little at a Time, A 29, 135
Lucky the Junkyard Dog: case application 98–99;
    example of trauma narrative 32

MacLean, K. 201
Malchiodi, C. xi, 37
Markell, K. & Markell, K. 30
Meares, R. 30
mermaid metaphor 186–187
Merton, T. xii
metaphor: bridge story 164–166; communication
    30; dog 167; four pebbles meditation 181;
    symbolic meaning 16–17, 57; themes 17–18; toy
    selection 107; Zodiac 149; *see also* sponge, the;
    symbols
Mills, J. M. & Crowley, R. J. 13, 14, 17, 36, 41
mindfulness techniques: case application 79;
    Handful of Quiet 181, 201; Moody Cow
    Meditates 201; singing bowl 79; Sitting Still Like
    a Frog 201
Mom of Many Colors, The: art depiction 117;
    intervention 118
Morris, M. xi
Mott, J. M. et. al. 37
mutual storytelling: case application 44;
    description 43

Najavits, L.: limitations of EBP's 37; VA
    healthcare 37
nesting dolls: case applications 85, 167–168, 189;
    recommended use of 46
neurobiology: impact of trauma 33;
    neurobiological integration 33; pathways 29–30;
    see also Perry, B.; Siegel, D.
Norcross, J. C.: evidence-based responsiveness 39;
    good fit 36, 39; limitations of EBP's 37; stages
    of change 4; therapeutic alliance 5, 36, 39, 41
Norcross, J. C. & Goldfried, M. R. 40

O'Connor, K. J. xi
O'Connor, K. J. & Ammen, S. 35
Oldford, L. 30
outcomes: evidence based 4; limitations of EBP's 37

parenting group 192–193
parent representation: art 117; metaphor 16;
    puppets 113–115; sand tray 113–115
parent substance use: case examples 73, 77, 117;
    impact of 111
Pernicano, K. xi
Pernicano, P. 29, 30, 32, 40, 44, 51, 53, 55, 85,
    95, 98, 102, 120, 129, 175, 186, 192, 195, 197,
    198, 199
Perry, B.: functional impact of abuse 127;
    neurosequential model of therapeutics 33
Perry, B. & Hambrick, E. 33, 34
Peterson, R. & Fontana, L. 11, 29
Poop in the Barnyard case application 85
progress in treatment: behavioral signs of change
    90–91; depicted in art 69–70, 137, 147–148
psychoeducation, using story for 129–131
puppets: case examples 13, 48, 75, 87–88, 94, 99,
    103, 115, 129; categories 42, 45, 113; overview
    45; siblings 94, 107; storytelling 46

relaxation with sound machine 79
risk factors for trauma 34
Roffman, R. E. 14

Safe Place to Call Home, A: case application 102;
    ruling out dissociation 102; story sequel 104
Safety in Numbers 45
safety planning in play 94–99
sand tray: case examples 20, 64–65, 67, 86, 88, 100,
    103–107, 113, 115, 119; character selection 64,
    108; overview 42–46; storytelling 46
Schaefer, C. xi
self-other representation in art: bats and centipede
    69; boat with people 86; butterflies out of
    mouth 147; cartoon strip 144; clown face 145;
    cover art 144; crying giant 88; depressed girl
    28; floating female 146; flowers 1–3, 122–123;
    good-bad 82; grim reaper 23, 100–101; grinning
    monster 88; horse 100–101; mermaid 123–124;
    mom of many colors 117–118; monster 18;
    prism two girls 145; quick-ice 119; rainbow 90;
    rainbow flower 147; rainbow girl kissing 146;
    safe place to call home 104; skeleton 102; snake
    22; space ship 11; wounded elephant 135–136
self-other representation in puppets/objects:
    butterfly 25; clam 113; flowers 100–101;
    kangaroo with alligator 95; ocean police 113;
    wall 168
self-other representation in sand tray: babies with
    castle & monsters 113, 115; bird king of the
    jungle 114; monster 19, 105, 107
self-other representation in stories: Bridge 164–166;
    dragon's fire 40; full of shit 29; kangaroo with
    alligator 95; Velma Crowe 44; Zodiac characters
    153–159
sensitizers and repressors 36–37
sexual trauma case examples 63, 173–177
shift in treatment 4, 58
sibling trauma case 92
Siegel, D. 11, 29, 33, 38, 40, 41
Silver, G. 86, 200
Sitting Still Like a Frog 79, 201
Smyth, J. & Nobel, J. 38, 42
Snel, E. 79, 201
Snow, M. S. et. al. 30

sponge, the 80, 112, 125, 187, 189
squiggles stories: about 42–43, 197–198; case application 44–45, 64, 79, 86, 113, 119, 133, 135–136
stages of change 4
stories: metaphor in 30, 67; neurobiological pathways 19; psychoeducation 129; purpose of 19; *see also* trauma narrative
Stuckey, H. & Nobel, J. 38
Stuck on the River 124
substance abuse, impact 73, 111–112, 118, 178, 180
symbols: art and play 45, 67, 82; case example 108; communication 17; *see also* themes, art
systemic approach 35

themes, art: anger 10; anxiety; chaos/confusion 26; depression/sadness 27–28; hope and wellbeing 25; power and control 18–19; worry or fear 19–21
theoretical orientations 30
therapeutic alliance 4–5, 36–37, 39, 40–41, 132, 189; *see also* Norcross, J. C.
therapeutic toolbag 42
Thich Nhat Hanh pebble meditation 181, 200
Trauma: adult attachment 170; art 1–3, 11, 38, 68–69, 120, 124, 135; cognitive distortion 175; development 34, 126–128; neurobiology 33; spiritual comfort 182; stories 94; symptoms associated with 32, 94, 99, 163

trauma-informed care: developmental context 34–35; integrative care 39; knowledge 32; systemic approach 35; therapist characteristics 32
trauma narrative: art 1–3, 67, 69, 80–81, 83–84, 107–109; play 79, 108; puppets 75, 94; sand tray 66, 86–87; stories 47–48, 67, 69–70, 87–88, 94, 102–103

Unleashed Pain, The 195
Unraveled Tapestry, The xii
up the mountain: art 48–52; case applications 47–53, 105; script 199–200; technique 46–47
utilization *see* Erickson, M.

van der Kolk, B. 16, 31, 41
Velma Crowe's Sticky Situation 44, 192

wall, the 168–169
Watts, B. V. et. al. 37
Wedge, M. 14
Winnicott, D. W. 43
Woodman, M. & Mellick, J. 31, 40

Yasenik, L. and Gardner, K. 40

Zeig, J. 13
zodiac: depicted in art 155, 157–159; portal 152, 158–159; symbolic representation of dissociation 150–156
zone of proximal development 41